Performance Assessment for the Workplace

VOLUME I

Alexandra K. Wigdor and Bert F. Green, Jr.,
Editors

Committee on the Performance of Military Personnel
Commission on Behavioral and Social Sciences and Education
National Research Council

NATIONAL ACADEMY PRESS
Washington, D.C.   1991

NOTICE: The project that is the subject of this report was approved by the Governing Board of the National Research Council, whose members are drawn from the councils of the National Academy of Sciences, the National Academy of Engineering, and the Institute of Medicine. The members of the committee responsible for the report were chosen for their special competences and with regard for appropriate balance.

This report has been reviewed by a group other than the authors according to procedures approved by a Report Review Committee consisting of members of the National Academy of Sciences, the National Academy of Engineering, and the Institute of Medicine.

The National Academy of Sciences is a private, nonprofit, self-perpetuating society of distinguished scholars engaged in scientific and engineering research, dedicated to the furtherance of science and technology and to their use for the general welfare. Upon the authority of the charter granted to it by the Congress in 1863, the Academy has a mandate that requires it to advise the federal government on scientific and technical matters. Dr. Frank Press is president of the National Academy of Sciences.

The National Academy of Engineering was established in 1964, under the charter of the National Academy of Sciences, as a parallel organization of outstanding engineers. It is autonomous in its administration and in the selection of its members, sharing with the National Academy of Sciences the responsibility for advising the federal government. The National Academy of Engineering also sponsors engineering programs aimed at meeting national needs, encourages education and research, and recognizes the superior achievements of engineers. Dr. Robert M. White is president of the National Academy of Engineering.

The Institute of Medicine was established in 1970 by the National Academy of Sciences to secure the services of eminent members of appropriate professions in the examination of policy matters pertaining to the health of the public. The Institute acts under the responsibility given to the National Academy of Sciences by its congressional charter to be an adviser to the federal government and, upon its own initiative, to identify issues of medical care, research, and education. Dr. Stuart Bondurant is acting president of the Institute of Medicine.

The National Research Council was organized by the National Academy of Sciences in 1916 to associate the broad community of science and technology with the Academy's purposes of furthering knowledge and advising the federal government. Functioning in accordance with general policies determined by the Academy, the Council has become the principal operating agency of both the National Academy of Sciences and the National Academy of Engineering in providing services to the government, the public, and the scientific and engineering communities. The Council is administered jointly by both Academies and the Institute of Medicine. Dr. Frank Press and Dr. Robert M. White are chairman and vice chairman, respectively, of the National Research Council.

This project was supported by the Office of the Assistant Secretary of Defense (Force Management and Personnel).

Library of Congress Catalog Card No. 91-67187
International Standard Book Number 0-309-04538-X

Additional copies of this report are available from:
National Academy Press
2101 Constitution Avenue N.W.
Washington, D.C. 20418

S375
Printed in the United States of America

COMMITTEE ON THE PERFORMANCE OF MILITARY PERSONNEL

BERT F. GREEN, JR.(Chair), Department of Psychology, Johns Hopkins University
JERALD G. BACHMAN, Institute for Social Research, University of Michigan
V. JON BENTZ, Elmhurst, Ill.
LLOYD BOND, School of Education, University of North Carolina, Greensboro
RICHARD V.L. COOPER, Ernst & Young, Chicago, Ill.
RICHARD DANZIG, Latham & Watkins, Washington, D.C.
FRANK J. LANDY, Department of Psychology, Pennsylvania State University
ROBERT L. LINN, School of Education, University of Colorado, Boulder
JOHN W. ROBERTS (USAF, ret.), San Antonio, Tex.
DONALD B. RUBIN, Department of Statistics, Harvard University
MADY W. SEGAL, Department of Sociology, University of Maryland
RICHARD J. SHAVELSON, Graduate School of Education, University of California, Santa Barbara
H.P. VAN COTT, Committee on Human Factors, National Research Council
HAROLD WOOL,* Bethesda, Maryland

ALEXANDRA K. WIGDOR, Study Director
CAROLYN J. SAX, Administrative Assistant

---

*Member, 1983-1985

Contents

Preface	vii
Overview	1
1 Psychological Testing and the Challenge of the Criterion	15
2 Policy Goals and Testing	31
3 Improving Job Performance Criteria for Selection Tests	56
4 The Development of Job Performance Measures	73
5 The Testing of Personnel	103
6 Evaluating the Quality of Performance Measures: Reliability	116
7 Evaluating the Quality of Performance Measures: Content Representativeness	128
8 Evaluating the Quality of Performance Measures: Criterion-Related Validity Evidence	141
9 The Management of Human Resources	184
Coda: The JPM Project and Accession Policy	207
References	211
Appendix A Service Bibliographies	225
Appendix B Biographical Sketches	247
Index	251

CONTENTS OF VOLUME II

Implications of Cognitive Psychology for Measuring Job Performance
Robert Glaser, Alan Lesgold, and Sherrie Gott

Work Samples as Measures of Performance
Frederick D. Smith

Measuring Job Competency
Bert F. Green, Jr., and Alexandra K. Wigdor

The Evaluation of Alternative Measures of Job Performance
Linda S. Gottfredson

Range Restriction Adjustments in the Prediction of Military Job Performance
Stephen B. Dunbar and Robert L. Linn

Alternatives to the Validity Coefficient for Reporting the Test-Criterion Relationship
Linda J. Allred

Generalizability of Military Performance Measurements: I. Individual Performance
Richard J. Shavelson

Procedures for Eliciting and Using Judgments of the Value of Observed Behaviors on Military Job Performance Tests
Richard M. Jaeger and Sallie Keller-McNulty

Exploring Strategies for Clustering Military Occupations
Paul R. Sackett

Preface

This is the sixth and final report of the Committee on the Performance of Military Personnel, which was established at the request of the Department of Defense (DoD) in 1983 to provide scientific oversight of the Joint-Service Job Performance Measurement/Enlistment Standards (JPM) Project. That pioneering research effort, now 10 years under way, proposed to develop robust measures of performance in entry-level military jobs so that, for the first time, military enlistment standards could be linked to performance on the job. The JPM Project was launched during a time when the transition to a system of voluntary military service was still a matter of public controversy and the issue of whether the Services could attract enough qualified people into the enlisted ranks a central policy concern. Its fruition is coming after years of great recruiting success, at a time when budgetary stringencies have recast the policy debate to address the cost-effectiveness of high-quality enlisted personnel.

Because of the complexity of the JPM Project research goals, as well as the pressing need to establish the credibility of military selection and classification procedures after technical errors in computing enlistment test scores were discovered in 1980, DoD turned to the National Academy of Sciences to provide independent technical review of the research as it progressed.

Created by act of Congress in 1863 as a private, nonprofit corporation, the National Academy of Sciences enjoys a unique position as an official, yet independent, adviser to the federal government. The Academy accomplishes its work through committees of experts established within the National Research Council. It has demonstrated consistently that it can call on the very best scientific and technical expertise nationwide. The independence and objectivity of NRC committees are carefully protected: the Academy does not reply to competitive requests for proposals; members of study committees serve without monetary compensation and are carefully screened for possible conflicts of interest; and the reports produced by committees are subject to thoroughgoing review before being transmitted to sponsors.

The Committee on the Performance of Military Personnel was selected in accordance with this tradition of excellence and independence. Housed within the Commission on Behavioral and Social Sciences and Education, its membership was drawn from the scientific and policy fields of greatest relevance to the JPM Project: psychometrics, performance measurement, industrial and organizational psychology, research design and statistics, military sociology, economics, human resource management, and military manpower policy. The committee included both scholars and practitioners—those whose scientific sophistication represents the state of the art, as well as those who understand firsthand the exigencies of real-world applications. General John Roberts (USAF, Ret.), former head of Air Training Command, brought to committee deliberations experience at the highest policy levels with military selection, classification, and training issues. John Bentz offered the insights gleaned from 35 years as director of personnel research for a major nationwide retailing company. Biographies of all committee members and staff appear in Appendix B.

The first phase of the JPM Project entailed the development of measures of performance for a sample of military jobs—jobs like jet engine mechanic, avionics communication specialist, infantryman, and medical technician. The goal was to determine how well the Armed Services Vocational Aptitude Battery (ASVAB), the test that is used throughout the military to assess enlistment eligibility, predicts performance on these high-fidelity measures of job performance. The committee's advisory activities in the early years centered on evaluation of the research design and the development of measurement instruments (e.g., hands-on tests, written job knowledge tests, supervisor ratings) and issues in hands-on test administration. Later the focus turned to evaluation of the quality of the measures and analysis of the performance data to understand the relationships among the various new performance measures and to ASVAB scores and other input characteristics. (The second phase of the project, now well under way, is exploring the use of cost/performance trade-off models for setting enlistment standards. A new Committee on Military Enlistment Standards has been established by the National Academy of Sciences to advise on that work.)

In order to enhance its understanding of the job performance measurement research and to place the project in proper context, members of the Committee on the Performance of Military Personnel also learned about military entrance processing, entry-level jobs in the military, technical training,

PREFACE   ix

and the general outlines of how entrance standards are currently set. Committee and staff members made a series of site visits to Army, Navy, Marine Corps, and Air Force bases to see enlisted personnel at work, to talk to their supervisors about the content of entry-level jobs, and to observe the administration of hands-on tests. They experienced at firsthand the operation of military entrance processing stations, visited training facilities, and also made a number of visits to military personnel research laboratories to gather information and discuss the progress of the research.

To facilitate the exchange of ideas, over the years the committee invited JPM Project scientists as well as other experts to explore solutions to specific technical problems in a series of workshops. And, to supplement its own activities, the committee has called on outside experts to prepare background papers on various aspects of the issues involved. A selection of these papers is presented in the companion volume to this report.

This book is a distillation of the experiences and insights and many things learned by the committee over the years since its founding in 1983 and, we hope, conveys at least a modicum of what the Service research scientists learned as well. It represents many years of faithful attention by committee members to the task at hand, frequent delight in the collegial nature of the enterprise, and a lot of sheer hard work. In the course of preparing the report, each of the members took an active role in drafting sections or chapters, providing data, leading discussions, and reading and commenting on successive drafts. Robert Linn bore primary responsibility for drafting the chapter on criterion-related validity. Richard Shavelson made major contributions to several chapters. Frank Landy and Lloyd Bond organized team efforts on the development of performance measures and standardization issues, respectively. John Roberts drafted sections on manpower policy issues.

Our work has benefited over the years from the contributions of many inside and outside the military. We were received with unfailing courtesy and openness at numerous military installations and provided with as much information as we could think to request. We developed a productive working relationship with the Job Performance Measurement Working Group, which coordinates the research effort, under the successive leadership of Col. Charles R. Curran, Lt. Col. Burt Itoga, Lt. Col. Dickie Harris, and Lt. Col. Thomas Ulrich. David J. Armor, former principal deputy to the Assistant Secretary of Defense (Force Management and Personnel) and currently a member of the follow-on Committee on Military Enlistment Standards, stimulated many a good discussion of technical challenges. Our workshops were enlivened by the presentations of many of the military researchers and their contractors, among others Milton H. Maier, Lawrence Hanser, Gerald Laabs, Col. Rodger D. Ballentine, Paul W. Mayberry, John Campbell, Leonard P. Kroeker, and Jerry W. Hedge.

In addition to the authors of papers that appear in the accompanying volume, Brian K. Waters, Janice H. Laurence, and Wayne J. Camara contributed a separately published paper on personnel enlistment and classification procedures in the U.S. military. Stephen B. Dunbar's analysis of JPM data forms the basis of the discussion of group-to-group differences in prediction systems presented in Chapter 8. Gail P. Baxter and James R. Valadez of the University of California at Santa Barbara assisted Richard J. Shavelson with background materials.

Carolyn Sax, the committee's administrative assistant, was indispensable in keeping track of everything from errant committee members to errant commas. We could not have managed half so well without her quiet competence. Thanks are due as well to her extremely able predecessor, Diane Goldman, to research associates Hilda Wing and Anne S. Mavor, and to Christine McShane, who has edited all of the committee's reports and in the process become something of an expert on job performance measurement in the military.

A special note of thanks is due to W.S. Sellman, director for accession policy in the Office of the Assistant Secretary of Defense (Force Management and Personnel), who had the tenacity needed to see the JPM Project through to fruition and a great enough respect for science to subject himself to the ministrations of an independent advisory committee.

Bert F. Green, Jr., Chair
Alexandra K. Wigdor, Study Director
Committee on the Performance of
Military Personnel

Performance Assessment for the Workplace

Overview

Performance assessment has been the subject of a great deal of attention and rhetoric in recent years as part of the movement to reform American education fundamentally. Also called "authentic assessment," this approach eschews written multiple-choice tests in favor of demonstrated performance on tasks in which desired knowledge and skills are used. The emphasis is on giving pupils the opportunity to demonstrate what they can do, rather than how well they can answer questions about a subject.

As the title of this book indicates, performance assessment has also come to the workplace. Ability tests, usually in the multiple-choice format, have been used for generations for employee selection and classification, for certification, and for career guidance. Underlying these practices is a set of assumptions, both economic and scientific, that support the use of tests. The essence of the argument is that a selected work force will be more efficient or productive than one chosen at random, so that it is in the employer's economic self-interest to be selective in hiring. From a broader perspective, the argument is made that improving the person-job match is in the national interest because it results in greater overall productivity and optimum utilization of workers.

Since the advent of industrial psychology in the first half of the century, tests have been a favored tool for screening workers to find out which applicants have the ability to do the work—or enter the apprenticeship program, be certified to work on sophisticated machinery, etc. Psychometrics, the science of mental measurement, strengthened the claims that ability tests can predict which applicants will be the more successful ones by encouraging the use of objective procedures in a controlled setting, with empirical verification of the accuracy of the results.

On the latter point, however—empirical verification of predictive accuracy—justifications for employment tests have been noticeably deficient. Test scores have little meaning in and of themselves. One of the most important psychometric techniques for examining their significance or validity has been through correlation with measures of job performance. If, for example, the people who do well on the job are the same ones who did well on an ability test administered for experimental purposes at the time of hiring, then the employer can have some faith in the predictive power of the test for future hires. The problem is that the measures of success on the job typically used to give meaning to test scores have tended to be measures of convenience—time and attendance records, supervisor ratings, training grades. None of them is a very convincing indicator of how well a worker performs on the job. None of them provides compelling evidence of the significance of test scores.

This is the problem that brought authentic assessment to the workplace and provided the occasion for this book, which describes a large-scale effort to develop hands-on measures of the performance of enlisted military personnel for the purpose of validating selection and classification tests. Although the military as an institution has unique features, it also shares many of the characteristics and concerns of other employers. The research on measuring performance in entry-level military jobs described here should be relevant to employers more generally. Indeed, because so much of the performance measurement methodology is new and, until now, relatively untried, the leaders of education reform will find much to interest them as well.

THE JPM PROJECT

The Joint-Service Job Performance Measurement/Enlistment Standards (JPM) Project is one of the largest coordinated studies of job performance on record. Initiated by the Department of Defense (DoD) in 1980 and scheduled for completion in 1992, the JPM Project represents an investment of many millions of dollars and involved the participation of thousands of people—from the measurement specialists who designed the performance tests to the local base personnel who provided logistical support for the data collection and the more than 15,000 troops who supplied the performance data.

The sheer size of the effort ensures that the JPM Project will provide a wealth of raw material and guidance for the next generation of researchers in the field of human resource management, quite aside from its more immediate goal of improving the selection and classification of military enlisted personnel. The project's many achievements add in important ways to the understanding of personnel selection systems. Even its shortcomings are informative, for they point up the need for additional methodology and highlight the dilemma resulting from conflicting purposes that are inevitable in a project of this magnitude.

The purpose of this volume is to convey to military and civilian human resource planners as well as to the measurement community the advances in theory, technology, and practical knowledge resulting from the military research. It does not present a detailed analysis of the performance data, leaving that to the research teams that carried out the work. We have tried to place the technical discussions concerning the development of performance measures within a larger policy context, providing in Chapter 1 a historical introduction to the criterion problem and sketching in Chapter 2 the many and often competing forces that influence personnel selection in the military. Succeeding chapters describe the design of the project and look more closely at substantive and methodological issues in performance measurement. These issues are for the most part as relevant to the assessment of civilian-sector job performance as to the military and speak to the new interest in performance assessment in school settings as well.

ORIGINS OF THE PROJECT

The JPM Project had its origins in the mid-1970s. In 1973, Congress abolished military conscription, and the military establishment was faced with the prospect of maintaining an active-duty military force on the basis of voluntary enlistment. Intense public debate accompanied the move to an all-volunteer force. Many feared that able volunteers would not sign up in sufficient numbers. Opponents warned that the national security would be weakened. Others were concerned on social and philosophical grounds that the burden of national defense would fall largely to minorities, the poor, and the undereducated—those who would have most difficulty finding work in the civilian economy (Fullinwider, 1983). With the matter of exemptions from the draft made moot by the shift to a volunteer force, military manpower policy came to revolve around issues of recruit quality and the high cost of attracting qualified personnel in the marketplace (Bowman et al., 1986).

Concern about the quality of the all-volunteer force reached a climax in 1980, when DoD informed Congress of an error in scoring the Armed Services Vocational Aptitude Battery (ASVAB), the test used throughout the military since 1976 to determine eligibility for enlistment. A mistake had been made in the formula for scaling scores to established norms, with the result that applicants in the lower ranges of the ability distribution were given inflated ASVAB scores. As a consequence, approximately 250,000 applicants were enlisted between 1976 and 1980 who would not normally have met minimum entrance standards (Office of the Assistant Secretary of Defense—Manpower, Reserve Affairs, and Logistics, 1980a, 1980b).

Not surprisingly, the military oversight committees of Congress had fleeting, though apparently unfounded, suspicions that the misnorming had been engineered in order to help the four Services meet their enlistment quotas. More to the point, both Congress and DoD policy officials wanted to know how the induction of so many people who should have failed to qualify was affecting job performance. Initial attempts to address the question revealed that the relation between ASVAB scores and satisfactory performance in military jobs was more assumed than empirically established (Office of the Assistant Secretary of Defense—Manpower, Reserve Affairs, and Logistics, 1981; Maier and Hiatt, 1984).

In response to the misnorming and to allay its own broader concerns about building an effective enlisted force solely with volunteers, DoD launched two major research projects to investigate the overall question of recruit quality. The first project, conducted in cooperation with the U.S. Department of Labor, administered the ASVAB to a nationally representative sample of young people between the ages of 18 and 23. This *Profile of American Youth* (Office of Assistant Secretary of Defense—Manpower, Reserve Affairs, and Logistics, 1982a) permits comparisons between the vocational aptitude scores of military recruits and the test performance of a representative sample of their peers in the general population as of 1980. No longer do the test scores of today's recruits have to be interpreted with test data from the World War II era.

The *Profile* provided important evidence to quell the worst fears about the quality of the all-volunteer force. The scores of enlistees for fiscal 1981 on the four subtests of the ASVAB that make up the Armed Forces Qualification Test (AFQT) were higher than those of the 1980 sample of American youth. In particular, the proportion of enlistees in the average range was considerably larger, and the proportion of enlisted personnel in the below-average range smaller, than in the general population. Although the results were reassuring, the weakness in the evidence was that *quality* was defined in terms of the aptitudes of recruits, not realized job performance—that is, in terms of inputs, not outputs. The relation between test scores and performance on the job was not established empirically, and thus DoD still could not satisfactorily answer the more difficult questions about the quality of the voluntary military: How much quality is enough to ensure a competent military force? Given the need to compete in the marketplace for able recruits—using the lures of enlistment bonuses, high entry-level pay scales, and educational benefits—how much quality can the country afford?

In 1980, the assistant secretary of defense in charge of manpower and personnel affairs called on the Services to investigate the feasibility of measuring on-the-job performance and, using the measures, to link military enlistment standards to job performance. With the endorsement of the House and the Senate Committee on Armed Services, the Joint-Service Job Performance Measurement/Enlistment Standards Project, DoD's second major research project, got under way. The progress of this massive research effort is charted in an ongoing series of annual reports to Congress from the Office of the Assistant Secretary of Defense.

Now, after more than a decade of research, empirical evidence has replaced assumptions about the efficacy of the ASVAB. The JPM Project has successfully measured the job proficiency of incumbents in a sample of military entry-level jobs. In the process, it has compared several types of measures and different approaches to test development. The performance measures provide a credible criterion against which to validate the ASVAB, and the ASVAB has been demonstrated to be a reasonably valid predictor of performance in entry-level military jobs.

Generalizations from the JPM results will take their place in the literature and lore of industrial and organizational psychology. Because of the superior measures of performance, constructed with a care normally reserved for standardized tests used as predictors, these results provide a solid base for general conclusions formerly based on less satisfactory criteria.

This overview reviews the project briefly, emphasizing those aspects that seem particularly noteworthy, either in illuminating special accomplishments of interest to policy makers or technical experts, or in posing challenges to the technical community.

CONCEPTUAL FRAMEWORK

What is Performance?

The initial goal of the JPM project was to develop measures of job performance that could be used as criteria in evaluating personnel selection procedures. Because so many Service personnel are first-term enlistees, and because the predictive power of entrance characteristics such as ASVAB scores attenuates over time, the project was limited to the study of first-term job performance.

The first necessity was to define job performance. Any concept that seems unitary from afar becomes complex when viewed up close, and job performance is no exception. Should the definition include the full range of the job, or be limited to what the incumbents regularly do? Should motivation or perseverance or willingness to go along with the institutional culture be assessed? For this project, job performance was defined as proficiency, that is, how well an incumbent *can do* the job. The definition explicitly rejected assessment of how well the incumbent *does do* the job. That is, tasks that incumbents are rarely called on to do were to be included, but measures of motivation—the willingness to do well—were not.

A good argument can be made that proficiency is the most appropriate criterion if the intent is to evaluate the placement of recruits, which was indeed the case here. However important such factors as effort, personal discipline, and military bearing may be to the overall functioning of the organization, these factors do not differentiate among jobs. The choice of proficiency as the performance dimension of interest was doubly sensible in this case because the battery used by the Services for selection and classification is not designed to tap the attitudinal or motivational aspects of performance.

The emphasis on proficiency was underlined by the selection of hands-on performance tests as the benchmark measure for the project. Also called work samples, these tests are as faithful to actual job performance as criterion measures can be, short of observing people in their daily work. Giving pride of place to an assessment format that requires workers to *do* job-related tasks was perhaps the most significant decision of the entire development effort. It had, of course, enormous cost implications, for this sort of one-on-one assessment is labor-intensive, very time-consuming, and difficult to develop. Nevertheless, the need to make military selection procedures credible in the face of widespread doubt called for a technology that could anchor them solidly in job performance. No other assessment format is as faithful to actual job performance.

What is a Job?

Having chosen proficiency as the facet of performance to be measured, project planners had next to address the difficult question of proficiency *at what?* As we discuss in Chapter 4, job analysis can focus on either the work to be done in a job or on the personal traits and attributes an incumbent needs to do the job, or both. The former is task-oriented; the latter is person-oriented. For several reasons, trait analysis did not play a major role in the JPM Project. Traditional task analysis complemented the desire to stay as close as possible to concrete job performance. Moreover, the Services have well-established systems for taking inventory of the tasks that comprise each job on a regular basis. In effect, a bare-bones job analysis had already been done for each of the jobs in the JPM Project; it needed only to be refined.

If sheer time and cost considerations made it expedient to use the existing task inventories and soldier's manuals, the absence of any consistent attempt to determine the human attributes that might contribute to the successful accomplishment of tasks had certain costs. A combined task and trait analysis would have provided a richer understanding of the performance requirements of the jobs being studied and may well have improved the generalizability of the JPM results to other military jobs—a matter that has proved difficult.

What is a Task?

The JPM Project is highly unusual in having applied classical test construction methods to the development of criterion measures. To a large extent, the success of this project in measurement terms is due to the thought and care that went into answering the question: What is a task? Not infrequently the existing task statements were at very different levels (either of breadth or of abstraction), and those derived from task inventories were by definition stripped of content richness. The research staff, assisted by subject matter experts, had to identify a coherent set of activities—with a definable beginning and end—that would represent the task. The process of turning tasks into hands-on test items, in light of the goal of measuring "manifest, observable job behaviors," became a matter of decomposing each task into its behavioral subcomponents, or steps, and identifying the associated equipment, manuals, and procedures required to perform the steps.

MEASURING JOB PERFORMANCE

Having chosen the task as the unit of analysis, the Services set about developing a variety of measures to assess the proficiency of incumbents in a sample of some 30 jobs chosen to represent broadly the mechanical, technical, administrative, and soldiering occupations in the military. In addition to hands-on tests, a number of other types of measures were developed as possible surrogates for the real thing. These included interview procedures, simulations, multiple-choice tests of job knowledge, and a variety of ratings intended to elicit performance appraisals from supervisors, peers, and the examinees themselves.

Task selection presented one of the most difficult challenges to the development of measures that could be considered representative of performance on the job. For each job studied, the 300 to 400 tasks remaining after culling redundant, outdated, and other problem tasks had to be reduced to a handful—about 15 for hands-on testing. Tasks were turned into test items by means of careful and thorough understanding of each task and detailed analysis of its component steps. The administration of hands-on and interview procedures, both of which took place under the watchful eye of an examiner, required careful planning and continual vigilance in order to control the quality of the data collection.

The chapters of this report discuss these steps in detail. The committee highlights below some of the most important issues and lessons learned from the Services' efforts.

Relative Versus Absolute Measures

An early and largely implicit decision in the JPM Project was that the proficiency measures would be developed in the style of the usual norm-referenced tests used in prediction. That is, the research paradigm was to rank each job incumbent relative to his peers, rather than determining how well the incumbent could do the job in an absolute sense. This decision fundamentally influenced how the tests were designed and the tasks selected. If the intent is relative measurement, then the test developer avoids tasks that are so easy that everyone will pass or so hard that everyone will fail—the point is to select items of a range of difficulty that will produce a good distribution of scores. This is an appropriate approach if the main goal is correlation with predictor scores. But the resulting test scores do not indicate whether the predicted performance is good enough.

The committee felt strongly that a domain-referenced approach would have been more appropriate to the long-term goal of the JPM Project, which was not simply to validate the ASVAB, but to link enlistment standards to job performance. The argument for this position is laid out in Chapter 9 and in Green and Wigdor (Vol. II). Had this approach been adopted, the tests would have been designed to measure individual performance against a scale of competence or job mastery, and test scores would have indicated how well the incumbent could do the job. Tasks would have been selected to represent levels of mastery, rather than to spread the test takers along a distribution. This challenges the traditional research paradigm, but offers more compelling evidence to policy makers concerned with the question of how much quality is enough. As it is, inferences cannot be made directly from the JPM data about the competence of individuals relative to a job, but only about competence relative to others who perform the job.

Sampling Issues

The JPM Project presented a number of interesting sampling problems. To begin with, there are over 900 different military occupational specialties in the four Services, of which only a small number could be studied. Although the 30 occupations selected—9 in the Army, 6 in the Navy, 8 in the Air Force, and 7 in the Marine Corps (see Chapter 3)—included more than one-third of all current first-tour personnel, the problems of generalizing to the other jobs had to be, and indeed have proved to be, generally vexing (see Chapter 9 and Sackett in Vol. II).

Specifying a sample of personnel to be tested also had its challenges. Ideally, one would want to be able to test all incumbents in a job or, if that proved impossible, a representative sample of the total population. To be avoided at all costs is having a manager provide whoever he or she chooses to make available. In some Services, the central records system was not current enough to permit drawing up a list of those to be tested prior to arrival on location. By and large, however, the Services were able to avoid the worst pitfalls of availability sampling, even if a good deal of creativity was required to overcome logistical problems such as gathering a sample from among widely scattered ships subject to impulsive departures. Chapter 5 provides further detail on these obstacles.

From the point of view of applied measurement, the sampling issues of greatest interest surround the selection of tasks to be tested. If performance test scores are to be a meaningful indicator of performance on the job, then the test must be representative of the job. For policy makers and managers, it is probably enough that a performance measure should "look like" the job. But providing a scientifically supportable basis for extrapolating from performance on a subset of tasks to performance on the job as a whole—whether by judgment-based or empirical means—requires much more than surface similarity.

There are two schools of thought on selecting tasks: one adheres to purposive sampling, by which job experts choose the tasks to be included, while the other calls for random sampling. It was the committee's position that, all things considered, a stratified random sampling approach would put the project on stronger ground scientifically; it is the only approach that allows one to make, with known margins of error, statements that can be generalized to the entire domain of tasks in a job. But purposive sampling was far more prevalent in the JPM Project, as it has been in private-sector test development. The reasons for this are certainly worth consideration. It was feared that using random sampling might create a test that omitted essential job elements. Perhaps even more compelling to the research teams was the belief that only purposive sampling could guarantee an instrument that policy makers would accept because it looks like the job. Chapter 7 presents the arguments of each school of thought on task sampling as well as the committee's suggestions for a possible rapprochement between the two.

Test Administration

The JPM Project is the best reservoir of experience currently available on administering performance-based measures in a way that permits comparisons across test takers, and as such should be of considerable value in the discussions of authentic assessment for education. As Chapter 5 makes clear, any sort of job sample test requires knowledgeable and dispassionate raters to score the performance. Considerable effort in training the raters will pay off. Particular care is needed to get raters to accept their role as passive participants; the tendency of former supervisors is to correct the errors that the test takers make and show them how to do the task correctly. Although this is exemplary behavior for a supervisor—or a schoolteacher—it is inappropriate for a test administrator if one wants to make comparisons.

The logistics of test administration similarly need careful attention with the performance-based methodologies. Early on in the project there were serious problems with moving people through the test stations efficiently and ensuring that each examinee worked independently. By the time the Marine Corps began assessing infantry riflemen, elaborate protocols had become the norm. The test site had seven stations containing tasks to be administered indoors and seven to be administered in the field. Each station was isolated from the others to the extent that the examinees could not see or hear what was occurring at other stations. The number of men to be tested was equal to the number of stations. A balanced randomized block was used to schedule the tasks, and each man had a list of the stations he was to attend, in the order in which he was to attend them. Each station was set up to require no more than 30 minutes to complete the tasks located there, and the time schedule was rigidly adhered to. Not only did the examinees rotate through the test stations, but from day to day the examiners rotated through the stations, so they would not get stale or bored with continually testing the same tasks. Maintaining rater alertness is as important as isolating the examinees.

EVALUATION: THE QUALITY OF THE PERFORMANCE MEASURES

Because hands-on tests have been so little tried in the past, it was not clear that the assessment method would produce measurements of sufficient stability and relevance to be meaningful psychometrically. Moreover, the hands-on format called for creative twists on standard procedure in reliability and validity analysis.

Reliability

When raters are part of a measurement system, the relative contributions of raters and tasks to measurement error should be assessed. Chapter 6 presents the committee's view that the best procedure for doing this involves generalizability theory (Cronbach et al., 1972; Shavelson, Vol. II). Because generalizability theory is an extension of classical test theory in an analysis of variance framework, more elaborate measurement (cf. "experimental") designs can also be studied. Specifically, effects of testing conditions (e.g., administrators, locations, tasks, raters, and the like) can be estimated simultaneously with major sources of error being pinpointed. As reported in Chapter 6, two of the Services used this technique and, surprisingly, found that there was virtually no effect of rater. Raters are commonly found to have a large effect in more subjective settings. Since extensive observations of the rating process did not uncover any large amount of collusion between raters, we infer that the design of the scoring procedures for the hands-on tests was clear and objectively based, with little room for individual subjective variation in judgment. This is an important achievement for the JPM Project; we commend the procedures used to construct the hands-on test scoring forms to others for study and emulation.

By contrast, tasks turned out to be large contributors to measurement error. There is no question that the examinees differed in what they could do on the hands-on test, but how much of that was due to the exigencies of the particular set of 15 or so tasks that made up the test and how much to differences in individual abilities is unknown. The implication is that more tasks are needed to get a clearer picture of the stable performance differences among the Service personnel in the study. This result was not unanticipated. The feasibility of testing enough tasks to achieve stable results in the work-sample mode has been a concern all along. Many committee members were surprised that the hands-on tests turned out to be as reliable as they are.

Validity

The JPM Project provided ample evidence that ASVAB scores are related to job proficiency. Chapter 8 explains the reasoning behind criterion-related validity studies and describes in abundant detail the relationships among the predictor composites and the various criterion measures. A number of interesting trends emerge from the data. For example, the Armed Forces Qualification Test, an ASVAB composite that measures general ability, can predict performance in all of the jobs studied, but better prediction can be achieved in most jobs by using different combinations of test scores from the battery. Another general trend, one that had been anticipated, was the somewhat higher correlation between the entrance tests and the job knowledge performance measure than between the entrance tests and hands-on measures. To some extent this represents a method effect—both the entrance tests and the job knowledge test are multiple-choice paper-and-pencil tests. Finally, it is worth noting that the degree of relationship between the ASVAB and the various criterion measures, while large enough to justify the entrance test's utility in military selection and classification, is modest enough to encourage a search for additional predictors to supplement the ASVAB.

Fairness Analysis

The analysis of how tests function for various population subgroups has been common practice since the 1970s because of concerns over observed group differences in average test scores. Equal employment opportunity laws established a governmental interest in making sure that these score differences are related to real performance differences and not to some artifact of the test.

Subgroup differences were expected and were observed in the JPM data, although the data are thin and should be interpreted with caution. Blacks scored lower than nonminorities on both selection tests and job performance measures. An interesting point for policy purposes, however, is that the magnitude of the average score differences between blacks and nonminorities is much larger on the AFQT (–.85 of a standard deviation) and on the job knowledge performance test (–.78 of a standard deviation), both of which are paper-and-pencil tests, than on the hands-on test (–.36 of a standard deviation). In other words, the two groups look much more similar on the hands-on tests. To the extent that one has confidence in the hands-on criterion as a good measure of performance on the job, these findings, reported in Chapter 8, suggest that scores on the AFQT exaggerate the size of the difference that will ultimately be found in the job performance of the two groups.

THE FINAL STEP: LINKING ENLISTMENT STANDARDS TO JOB PERFORMANCE

Selecting personnel who will turn out to be successful on the job, particularly from a youthful and inexperienced applicant population, is a complicated business. Phase I of the JPM Project has demonstrated that reasonably high-quality measures of job performance can be developed, and that the relationships between these measures and the Armed Services Vocational Aptitude Battery are strong enough to justify its use in setting enlistment standards. But the human resource management problem is not solved by showing that recruits who score well on the ASVAB tend to score well on hands-on performance measures. High-quality personnel cost more to recruit, and the public purse is not bottomless. In order to make reasonable budgetary decisions, Congress needs to be able to balance performance gains attributable to selecting those with better-than-average scores on the ASVAB against the costs of recruiting, training, and retaining high-quality personnel. And to improve their control over performance in the enlisted ranks, DoD and the Services need to be able to make more empirically grounded projections of their personnel quality requirements. The critical policy question is: How much quality is enough?

The second phase of the JPM Project is concentrating on the development of analytical tools that will illuminate for policy makers the effects of alternative enlistment standards on performance and costs. The research is still under way and will have to be reported elsewhere. Chapter 9 of this report lays out the general outlines of the problem of developing cost-performance trade-off models and discusses the strengths and weaknesses of the JPM data for making performance an operative element in such models.

Although the problems are complex and there is still room for improvement at every stage of the research and development, the results of the JPM Project to date indicate that the concept of linking selection standards to objective measures of job performance is basically sound. It appears that it will be feasible for human resource planners and policy makers to incorporate empirical data derived from job performance into the decision process in a systematic way.

The development of cost-performance models for setting enlistment standards has great potential relevance for accession policy. Until now, the standards-setting process has been largely based on an informal process of individual judgments and negotiations among the stakeholders. The manpower management models used by military planners for other purposes have simply assumed an appropriate enlistment standard or have used surrogates at quite some remove from job performance. If the JPM performance data can be successfully incorporated into trade-off models, the models will offer policy officials useful tools for estimating the probable effects on performance and/or costs of various scenarios—say a 10 percent reduction in recruiting budgets, a 20 percent reduction in force, or a downturn in the economy. Although the solutions provided by such models are not intended to and will not supplant the overarching judgment that policy officials must bring to bear, they can challenge conventional assumptions and inject a solid core of empirical evidence into the decision process.

The full implications of the job performance measurement research for military policy makers—and for civilian sector employers—remain to be worked out in coming years. The JPM Project has produced a rich body of data and a wealth of methodological insights and advances. And, as important research efforts so frequently do, it has defined the challenges for the next generation of research on performance assessment.

1

Psychological Testing and the Challenge of the Criterion

INTRODUCTION

The United States is the world's largest user of standardized tests and test products and Americans are, without doubt, among the most tested of people. By one recent estimate, there are 20 million school days of standardized testing per year in elementary and high schools. It is common for major transition points in schooling and in working life to be marked by some sort of standardized test or assessment procedure. Beginning with the assessment of school readiness among preschoolers, the individual faces a long succession of tests designed to do such things as establish grade-level progress; diagnose learning difficulties; track pupils; allocate places in special programs or magnet schools; provide a measure of institutional accountability; ensure that those receiving a high school diploma have achieved minimum levels of competency; screen applicants for admission to college, training programs, the military, or entry-level jobs; and, in many lines of work, certify the achievement of mastery levels for advanced or specialized positions.

Just as school systems have found standardized tests useful tools for organizing and monitoring the education enterprise, so in the world of work tests have assumed important sorting and gatekeeping functions. In traditional societies, hereditary social status largely determines one's occupational niche. The growth of industrial economies with diverse job demands

15

and large population concentrations has tended to substitute individual capability for family, class, and the like as the formal criterion for allocating jobs. Particularly in America, with its great tides of ambitious immigrants and unusually strong attachment to the idea that one can make one's future, sorting on the basis of ability has come in the twentieth century to have widespread appeal.

Testing is the primary means of competitive selection in federal, state, and municipal merit systems, an outgrowth of the reformist beliefs of the Progressive Era that ability and not political cronyism should be the grounds for selection into the civil service. Many private-sector employers look to tests of general or specialized abilities as an important part of human resource management; widespread concern in the business community about the shortcomings of American education has in recent years increased the attraction of testing among employers who hope to maintain their competitive advantage through more effective personnel selection. Labor unions depend on tests like the Department of Labor's General Aptitude Test Battery to screen candidates for apprenticeship programs. The lifting of mandatory retirement laws in recent years under the Age Discrimination Act of 1965 could well mean an increased use of tests to assess employees' continued ability to perform up to standard on the job—a kind of retirement readiness testing.

Testing has, in other words, become a visible and influential force in American life—and to an extent not found in other Western, industrialized societies. The predominant technology, which is about as old as the airplane and as little understood by most people, is the work of psychologists who thought to develop a science of the mind for the solution of social problems.

AMERICAN TESTING TECHNOLOGY

In the words of one early historian of mental testing, American psychology "inherited its physical body from German experimentalism, but got its mind from Darwin" (Boring, 1929:494). By 1900, evolution had quite captured the American imagination and that meant, in psychology, an emphasis on individual differences. The study of individual differences is above all a measurement science; in the early decades of this century, the mental test became its primary measurement tool.

There have been a good number of studies of the intellectual antecedents of standardized ability testing, from the first generation chronicles of Peterson (1925), Pinter (1923), Young (1923), and the aforementioned Boring to recent studies by historians (e.g., Kevles, 1985; Hale, 1980; Fass, 1980; Sokal, 1987), which, with the benefit of distance, provide greater insight into the cultural and intellectual context in which the testing movement grew up. We need not repeat in any detail the influence of Wilhelm Wundt's laboratory techniques for the precise measurement of mental operations such as memory or reaction time; or the development by Galton, Pearson, and finally Spearman of powerful statistical techniques for expressing the distribution of human abilities; or indeed, the crucial work of Alfred Binet and Lewis Terman in translating mental measurement from an experimental into an applied science.

It is essential, however, to appreciate that psychological testing in its American manifestation is a combination of high science and practical purpose, of experimentalism and the correlation coefficient on one hand and human resource management on the other.

The Science of Testing

The psychometric approach to human abilities owes as much to physics as to philosophy. In an interesting brief analysis of Spearman's seminal treatise, *The Abilities of Man* (1927), Irvine and Berry (1988) describe the derivation of the correlational technology of tests and testing from the laws of statics, that is, the study of forces on bodies at rest. They present a diagram drawn from a popular late-Victorian physics school book illustrating the principle that a system is in equilibrium around a fixed point or fulcrum when the sum of the products of force times the distance from the fixed point is zero (reproduced as Figure 1-1 below).

In classical test theory, the fulcrum is the group mean, and individual ability—Spearman actually calls it mental energy—is expressed as a test

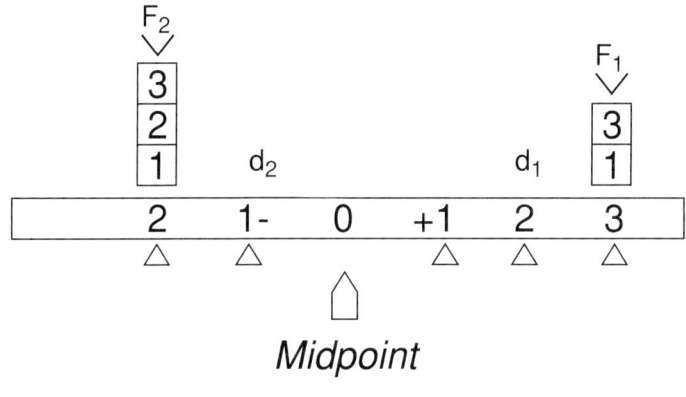

FIGURE 1-1 Moments around a fixed point. SOURCE: Loney (1890). Reprinted in Irvine and Berry (1988).

score's relative distance from the mean. As in physics, the distribution of individuals' abilities are moments around a point, and all the deviations from the mean sum to zero. Moreover, Pearson's product-moment correlation, which is the heart of test validation, is an average value expressing the amount of consistent deviation from the means that the same group of people shows on two measures. As Irvine and Berry conclude, psychological testing in America "takes physics and moments around a point not just as an analog, but as a model for an exact science of the mind" (1988:11).

Despite Spearman's efforts, there was not in the early years, nor has there since emerged a unified theory of intellect or ability that has informed the science of mental measurement. If mental testing is not wholly atheoretical, E.L. Thorndike's quip that "intelligence is the thing that psychologists test when they test intelligence," (reported in Murphy, 1929:354-355) reflects the profession's relative unconcern with what intelligence is in any epistemological sense. The promoters of psychological testing have invested their energies in and rested their claims on test development, on careful measurement under standardized conditions, on developing statistical techniques for the precise quantitative expression of values, and on correlational analysis to establish the validity of the test results. As in many other areas of economic and social research, the persuasive power of numbers has proved to be very great, and society at large rapidly became the laboratory for this science of the mind.

Practical Applications

With the invention of the group-administered multiple-choice test during World War I, the psychology of individual differences found its metier: mass testing, standard procedures to eliminate irrelevant sources of variation, and a response format that lends itself to the quantification of results. Despite its many limitations and periodic public attacks, the multiple-choice test remains the dominant mode of testing to this day, not only because it fitted the empirical mode, but because it provided society with much-needed tools for organizing and ordering its members.

Twentieth-century America has been characterized by increasingly heterogeneous and transient populations. The emergence of modern industrial society in the late nineteenth century, with its hunger for cheap labor, brought massive immigration; the population increased by 68 percent in the 30 years between 1890 and 1920. Schools were deluged with children—Tyack (1974) reported that the high school population grew by 711 percent in these years—and in addition to sheer increase in numbers, educators had to figure out how to deal with children of many different lingual and cultural backgrounds. Industrial production brought with it new demands for regularity in attendance and work habits, care in the use of machinery, and technical skills. Employers, plagued by high rates of labor turnover and industrial accidents, increasingly turned their attention to the more efficient selection and management of personnel (Hale, 1980:Chapter 10). Social dislocation and the movement of peoples did not end with the immigration restrictions imposed in the 1920s. The great internal migrations from East to West and South to North, particularly in the years after World War II, continued the attenuation of tradition, local ties, mutual knowledge, and shared values as social binding agents.

Standardized multiple-choice testing arose and prospered in this context because it appeared to offer an efficient and objective way to classify masses of people on the basis of ability.[1] Group testing via the now ubiquitous multiple-choice item was introduced as a bold experiment in military selection and classification during World War I, and thereby cemented the future of testing as an important instrument of pedagogy, employee selection, and, ultimately, of public policy.

The Army Alpha and Beyond

If World War I and the Army Alpha brought mental testing into the American mainstream, it was Robert M. Yerkes above all others who brought testing to the problem of military screening. As early as 1908, Alfred Binet had urged the testing of conscripts to eliminate defectives; careful scientist that he was, he cautioned that preliminary trials would be necessary to see if the test eliminated those individuals actually found to be inefficient in the Army (Peterson, 1925:292). But Yerkes and his colleagues on the American Psychological Association Committee on Examination of Recruits had a more ambitious vision of the contribution of testing to the war effort. In May of 1917, less than one month after America's entry into the war, he wrote that "we should not work primarily for the exclusion of intellectual defectives, but rather for the classification of men in order that they may be properly placed in the military service" (quoted in Kevles, 1968:567).

This goal is all the more remarkable when one remembers that Yerkes and his colleagues had little precedent to guide them. In 1917, as Goodenough (1949) pointed out, almost nothing was known about measuring the intelligence of the normal adult. Yet, under the auspices of the Psychology Committee of the National Research Council, which the National Academy of Sciences created in 1916 to mobilize the scientific community to serve the war effort, Yerkes, Lewis Terman, and five other psychologists set out to develop an intelligence test that could be used to screen large groups of

---

[1] That testing has also been the conveyer of some of the more distasteful myths of Social Darwinism and has been used to justify cultural and racial bias (Kevles, 1985) is an aspect of the story that should not be forgotten.

men quickly and efficiently. It was Terman and Walter V. Bingham who convinced Yerkes to approve group testing and Terman's student, Arthur Otis, whose work on a group test system provided the inspiration for the multiple-choice format (Von Mayrhauser, 1987; Samelson, 1987). This was the origin of the famous Army Alpha. By late summer the secretary of war had authorized experimental trials, and the results were compelling enough that, on Christmas Eve 1917, universal testing of all enlisted men, draftees, and officers was approved.

In a remarkably short period of time a corps of military psychologists was in place, a school was established at Fort Oglethorpe, Georgia, to train test administrators so that examining procedures would be uniform down to tone of voice and speed of delivery, and, by May of 1918, 200,000 men were being tested per month at 24 Army camps around the country. (The detail of the program can be found in Yerkes, 1921; Kevles, 1968; and Reed, 1987.)

Yerkes and his mental testers were by no means universally accepted by military officials (Kevles quotes General Hugh Johnson's later remarks about the "mental meddlers"). There was a tension between the professional army and the professional psychologists, between experience and expertise that has continued to mark the relationship of military officials and the social scientists who would provide them with "objective tools" to guide decision making. Yet the testing program proved itself useful enough to survive three investigations and, before the end of the war, some 1,750,000 men took the Army Alpha or the Beta, the version for those unable to read English.

Although historians have cast doubt on the extent to which the program contributed to the war effort (Reed, 1987), the testing of one and three-quarter million soldiers during World War I established psychological testing and the intelligence quotient (IQ) in the public consciousness. In a way that could scarcely have been envisioned prior to the war, group multiple-choice tests were looked on as tools for the solution of problems of a practical character. In 1921, the developers of the Army Alpha published a revised version called the National Intelligence Test. Within two years almost 1,400,000 copies were sold, and by 1923 a total of 40 different intelligence tests were available nationally (Freeman, 1926; Fass, 1980). Yerkes and Lewis Terman also joined forces after the war to promote the differentiated school curriculum, based on intelligence tests, and found themselves at the crest of the tide. In a very few years, intelligence tests were adopted in schools all over the country to help sort and track and counsel students in the course of education best suited to their abilities.

The Army test of general intelligence also stimulated the interest of the College Board in the possible use of psychological testing for college admissions in place of written essays covering various subjects. An advisory committee, including Yerkes and Carl C. Brigham, was asked to look into the question and, as a consequence, the Scholastic Aptitude Test—now a cultural icon—was born in 1926 (Angoff, 1971). Employers too showed increased interest in personnel testing, and both general and job-specific aptitude testing became quite common, if not as widespread as standardized multiple-choice testing in the schools. For all of these purposes, testing was widely accepted as a legitimate means of making decisions about the aptitude or abilities of normal people. As a kind of scientific Solomon, the standardized ability test provided a means of reconciling equality of opportunity with the realities of limited educational, employment, and, ultimately, economic opportunities. (There has, of course, been controversy about the technical and social assumptions of testing from the beginning. Walter Lippmann's series of articles in the *New Republic*, published in the early 1920s, remains among the most eloquent statements of misgiving about the grandiosity of the testers' claim to measure important and complex human characteristics with brief written tests and the likelihood that the technology would end up thwarting rather than enhancing equity and social mobility. See, for example, Wigdor and Garner, 1982; Block and Dworkin, 1976; for more recent arguments, Madaus and Kellaghan, 1991; Darling-Hammond, 1991.)

In the following decades, technical aspects of test construction and validation received a great deal of attention as widespread use revealed threats to precision of measurement. Procedures were developed to calibrate the difficulty level of tests so that there was consistency from year to year in, for example, college admissions tests. The need to validate tests, to show that the abilities or skills being measured are relevant to education or employment decisions being made, was recognized early and often, at least by testing professionals. Techniques were developed for assessing the reliability or consistency of measurements, for revealing the factor structure of test batteries, for expressing multivariate relationships.

But for all that aptitude or ability testing has been an American preoccupation since the 1920s, providing "a powerful organizing principle, a way of ordering perceptions, and a means for solving pressing institutional and social problems" (Fass, 1980), comparatively little systematic attention has been devoted over the years to understanding and measuring the kinds of human performance that tests are commonly used to predict. Employers use tests to hire workers, hoping thereby to build a more effective work force. Medical and law schools use entrance tests to determine who will have the opportunity to enter training for those professions. Yet very little is known about the performance of a good doctor or lawyer—or car mechanic for that matter. How, then, can the employer or educator know whether the test scores at hand are meaningful for the decisions being made? By and large, the public has been content to see test scores as a reflection of intelligence or ability and to find in these general concepts a sufficient connection to performance. Applied psychologists quickly came to know that things are more complicated than that when employment tests failed pretty consistently in the 1920s to predict which employees would be the more successful performers. Internal documents of the period show the staff of Walter Bingham's Personnel Research Bureau rather painfully aware of the weakness of the employment tests they were developing for clients (Kraus, 1986). So little success was had in relating IQ test scores to executive and managerial success—indeed, Bingham and Davis reported a negative correlation—that the enterprise was thrown into momentary disarray (Super and Crites, 1962).

THE CRITERION PROBLEM IN VALIDATION RESEARCH

In fact, it has turned out to be far easier to develop sophisticated test instruments and statistical techniques for analyzing the degree of correspondence between the distribution of test scores and the distribution of criterion scores than to find adequate measures of performance to use as criteria in judging the relevance of the tests. Although the criterion problem also exists in educational testing, it has been more frequently raised with regard to employment tests. For the most part, industrial and organizational psychologists and their institutional clients have used measures of convenience such as training grades or supervisor ratings as a surrogate for job performance, concentrating, as Rains Wallace (1965) put it, "on criteria that are predictable rather than appropriate."

The dangers inherent in using inadequate performance measures were brought into focus in Captain John Jenkins' report (1950) on the tests used to select and classify Navy and Army air crews during World War II. The experience of those years merits some retelling, for it shows both the great value of standardized testing procedures for marshaling human resources to the war effort, and sobering limitations as well.

When Germany occupied France in June of 1940, the War Department announced plans to select and train 7,000 pilots and 3,600 bombardiers and navigators. It was well known to military planners that in the period 1926-1935, when eligibility for air cadet training was based on an educational requirement (two years of college) and a stringent physical requirement, some 61 percent had flunked out of flight training (DuBois, 1947). Under threat of war, it was rapidly decided to supplement the physical test with psychological tests for selection and for classification into the three air crew specialties: pilot, navigator, and bombardier. Large numbers of psychologists were brought into the Naval Aviation Program and the Army Air Force (AAF) Classification Program, both to develop new selection and classification tests and to conduct validation research. DuBois reports that, at full strength, more than 1,000 Army aviation psychologists and psychological assistants worked in research and examining units, largely in test development, administration, scoring, records, and reports.

The World War II aviation psychology programs were—and are—considered one of the triumphs of applied psychology. As the war progressed, more and more reliance was placed on psychological testing to make selection and classification decisions. A robust research program supported the test batteries. The AAF classification battery, for example, went through nine revisions between its introduction in early 1942 and 1945 as a result of research findings.

It is important to remember how massive a buildup the military faced. The AAF air crew training program in effect in the fall of 1941 called for the production of 30,000 pilots a year. Given the dismal statistics on completion of training during the interwar years and the pressing need to enlist, train, and produce combat-ready air crews, it is perhaps not surprising that in both Services the criterion against which the selection and classification tests were validated was completion of advanced training. And this was not an insignificant basis for judging the relevance of the tests. Validation of the AAF classification battery included the study of a control group of 1,311 men, constituting a representative sample of the total group of applicants for air crew training, who were sent into pilot training with no requirements as to aptitude or temperament. Figure 1-2, reproduced from DuBois (1947), tells a dramatic story. Slightly more than 70 percent of the control group was eliminated. Of those in the lowest score category on the pilot classification battery (stanine 1),[2] 100 percent were eliminated from the training program. In contrast, only 23.9 percent of those with the highest standard score (stanine 9) failed to complete the training course.

Clearly the pilot classification battery was a powerful predictor of success and failure in pilot training in the Army Air Force. But success in training may well have no bearing on combat proficiency.

Psychologists in the Navy aviation program, under the leadership of Captain John Jenkins, spent a good deal of time thinking about the problem of developing better performance criteria, criteria that would show whether the selection and classification tests were identifying the good combat pilots or just pilots with the characteristics needed to succeed in training (Jenkins, 1946). Fairly well into the war, Jenkins and his group were able to launch one effort to develop a measure of combat effectiveness. To try to establish the elements of success in combat flying, interviews of active combat pilots were begun in the Pacific fleet in 1943; in the fall of 1944, after more than a year of exploratory work and instrument development, full-scale data

---

[2] "Stanine" derives from Standard Nine, a normalized transformation in 9 steps of a weighted raw-score composite of several different tests.

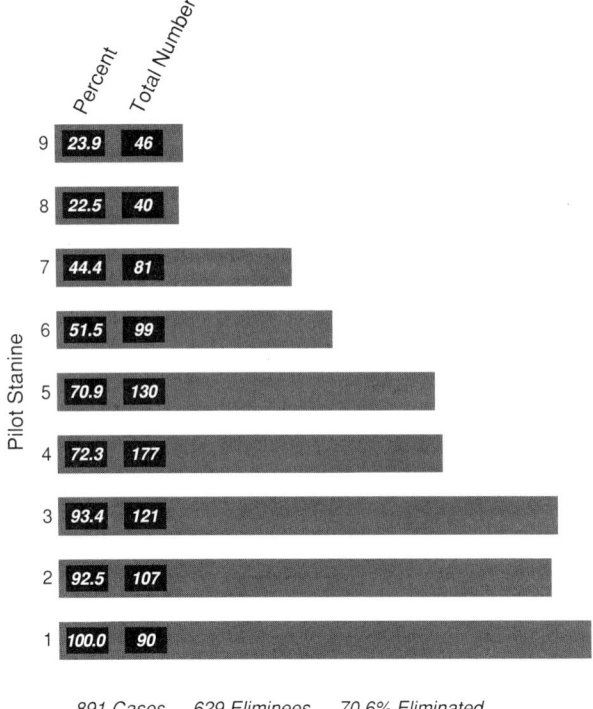

FIGURE 1-2 Elimination rate of experimental group for pilot stanines (elimination for flying deficiency, fear, or own request). SOURCE: DuBois (1947).

collection began. The method chosen to obtain combat criterion data was a nomination procedure, administered to groups of pilots in combat areas, who were asked to make their nominations in writing. Aircraft carrier pilots, for example, were asked to name:

1. Two men, living or dead, known to you, on whom you would be glad to fly wing, if assigned to another air group. (high group)

2. Two men, living or dead, whom you would not wish to have flying wing on you, if assigned to another air group. (low group)

Subjects were also asked to fill out checklists giving reasons for their nominations, the checklists having been developed from free response interviews with over 800 pilots who had completed at least one tour of combat duty.

A total of 2,872 experienced combat pilots in the Pacific theater was involved in the final study, and the names of 4,325 nominees were obtained. Of these, 40 percent were nominated more than once. The analysis of the data, begun by Captain Jenkins and his Combat Criterion Program team, was completed and written up after his death by the National Research Council Committee on Aviation Psychology, chaired by M.S. Viteles.

The sobering conclusion of the report: ". . . it can be said with little equivocation that consideration of the indices of relationship between tests and the combat criterion measures . . . indicates that none of the tests . . . devised to predict success in training, gave evidence of predicting the combat criterion measures to any marked degree"[3] (Jenkins, 1950:256).

Evolution of the Criterion Problem

Summing up the lessons of World War II in his 1946 article entitled "Validity For What?" Jenkins wrote that psychologists had learned that criterion measures are neither given of God, nor just to be found lying around. Test validation is not "a simple technical problem . . . . [T]he criterion itself may provide the psychologist with as great a technical challenge as the procedures incident to the assembly of good predictors" (1946:98).

The years since have shown just how great a challenge. The description and measurement of job performance has been a central theme of postwar psychological and organizational research. There has been fruitful discussion of the nature of job performance and the range of possible performance criteria, with distinctions being made between natural and constructed measures, between concrete and conceptual approaches to performance, or along such dimensions as optimal versus ordinary performance. Some researchers have concentrated their efforts on defining job performance in terms of outcomes, some have examined job behaviors, and others, building on the work of Walter V. Bingham in the 1920s and 1930s, have studied personality traits such as leadership qualities or initiative as correlates of successful performance.

Various types of performance measure have been studied. These include natural measures, such as production or sales records, absenteeism, or accident rates, and constructed measures, including work samples and the ubiquitous rating scale in its many variants. Job analysis has always received a good deal of attention (Gael, 1984, 1988), and the 1970s saw a number of large-scale efforts to develop taxonomies of human performance (see Fleishman and Quaintance, 1984).

Captain Jenkins remarked in 1946 that a review of the literature published between 1920 and 1940 would turn up hundreds of articles on the

---

[3] The report drew the same conclusion about the Army Air Force combat criterion program, which investigated the relationship between test variables and a number of combat criteria in the categories of strike photo studies, administrative action studies, and ratings of combat effectiveness.

construction of predictors, but almost total silence on the subject of the criteria to be predicted. A review of the literature since 1950 would reveal, not hundreds, but thousands of articles on criterion development and validation. Yet in summarizing the previous 30 years of research, Landy and Farr (1983) concluded that accurate measurement of work performance remains elusive and the criterion problem is as vexing as ever.

Performance Appraisal

The research experience with rating instruments is illustrative. Supervisor ratings have been (and remain) the most common criterion measure for the validation of selection tests outside the military, because they are readily available or easily obtainable, because they are an inexpensive source of performance data, and because they are plausible to the client—it makes sense that supervisors would be able to make reasonable judgments about the performance of workers for whom they are responsible. But performance ratings have always been held suspect by measurement experts because they depend on human judgment, with the attendant threats of subjectivity.

Until 1980, the primary focus of research on performance ratings was the rating instrument, its measurement properties, and standardization of raters to reduce error. An enormous amount of professional energy was expended on the quantitative expression of rating error and the control of error variance through improvements in rating technology. There is a vast literature on performance appraisal (see Landy and Farr, 1983; Milkovich and Wigdor, 1990; Bernardin and Beatty, 1984; Bernardin, 1989), which documents the attempts of researchers to quantify the various sources of rating error. Among the most frequently studied are the problems of *halo*, which refers to the tendency of raters to give an employee similar grades on purportedly separate and independent dimensions of job performance; *leniency*, the tendency to give employees higher ratings that their work warrants; *restriction in range*, which describes the tendency of raters to give similar ratings to all employees; and *unreliability*, which is an index of the tendency of raters to make erratic or inconsistent judgments about employee performance.

The ample documentation of these departures from precise and accurate measurement inspired many attempts to find a technological fix—that is, to design rating instruments that would control the problems. A variety of innovations in scale format were experimented with. The early graphic scales presented the rater with a continuum on which to rate a particular trait or behavior of the employee. Some scales presented mere numerical anchors:

Leadership: 1   2   3   4

Others present adjectival descriptions at each anchor point:

Leadership:	1	2	3	4
	poor	satisfactory	exceeds expectations	outstanding

Many scholars attributed the measurement error characteristic of graphic scales to the limited amount of definition and guidance they provided the rater either on the nature of the underlying dimension or on the meaning of the scale points along the continuum.

In response, the behaviorally anchored rating scale (BARS) was developed. The seminal work on BARS was done by Smith and Kendell in 1963, and there have been many further experiments. Although performance is still presented on a continuum in this rating mode, behavioral descriptions are presented at each anchor point to help clarify the meaning of the performance dimensions and to calibrate all raters' definitions of what constitutes good and poor performance. The methods used to develop the behaviorally anchored scales were consciously designed by researchers to form a strong link between the critical behaviors in accomplishing a specific job and the instrument created to measure those behaviors. Hence scale development is based on a careful job analysis and the identification by job experts of examples of effective and ineffective performance.

An even more elaborate attempt to control rater error is seen in the mixed standard scale developed by Blanz and Ghiselli (1972). This format is designed to be proactive in preventing rater bias. The graphic continuum and the definitions of the performance dimensions of interest (e.g., leadership, attention to detail, perseverance) are eliminated from the rating form. Instead, good, average, and poor examples of behavior are developed for each of the dimensions to be assessed and the rating form presents a random ordering of all the behavioral descriptions. The rater's task is to indicate whether an employee's performance is equal to, better than, or worse than the behavioral example presented. The actual performance score for each dimension is calculated by someone other than the rater.

The results of these innovations in rating format have been disappointing. Although the research findings are not entirely consistent, the consensus of professional opinion is that variations in scale type and rating format do not have a consistent, demonstrable effect on halo, leniency, reliability, or other sources of error or bias in performance ratings (Jacobs et al., 1980; Landy and Farr, 1983; Murphy and Constans, 1988; Milkovich and Wigdor, 1990:149). No doubt a great deal was learned, and everyday practice in applied settings has benefited—but improvements in job analysis, scale development, scale format, and rater training, whatever else they accomplished, did not bring dramatic improvements in measurement precision.

As a consequence, many industrial and organizational psychologists turned their attention in the 1980s from the rating instrument to the cognitive processes of the person doing the rating. The motive remains the same as in earlier research, that is, to enhance the accuracy of ratings of employee performance through the elimination, or at least the diminution, of rater bias or error. By understanding how evaluators process performance information and by what heuristic their judgments are stored in memory, the researchers with a cognitive bent hoped to come up with devices for improving those judgments.

One of the early findings of the work on the cognitive processes of raters is that, whether the rating instrument is cast in terms of behaviors or personal traits, evaluators appear to draw on trait-based cognitive models of an employee's performance, and that these general impressions substantially affect the evaluator's memory and judgment of actual work behaviors (Landy and Farr, 1983; Murphy et al., 1982; Ilgen and Feldman, 1983; Murphy and Jako, 1989; Murphy and Cleveland, 1991). The prescriptions for improvement growing out of this line of research concentrate, not on innovations in rating format, but on increasing the physical proximity of the rater to the employees to be rated so there is increased observation of actual work performance; training raters in systematic observation; encouraging the use of aides-mémoire such as performance diaries; and, in the expert systems mode, training in the heuristics used by successful evaluators. But once again, the innovations have failed to show dramatic or consistent improvements in measurement precision.

The most recent developments in the research on performance ratings represent a departure from the psychometric lines of inquiry that have dominated testing and criterion research. A number of industrial psychologists have begun to move away from the traditional view of performance appraisal as a measurement problem. Rather than treating it as a measurement tool, they have begun to look on performance appraisal as a social and communication process (Murphy and Cleveland, 1991; see Milkovich and Wigdor, 1990:145). From this perspective, the other uses of performance appraisal in organizational settings—for improving employee understanding of organizational goals, communicating a sense of fair play in the distribution of rewards and penalties, increasing communication between managers and employees— take center stage. Forty years of research on performance rating technology appear to have led at least some researchers to doubt that the large improvements in accuracy and precision that were at one time anticipated will be forthcoming.

The Importance of the Criterion Issue

The full importance of the criterion issue was only slowly recognized by psychologists, and it is safe to say that the problem is largely unappreciated by employers, educators, test takers, and others who use or are affected by test scores. In part this is because the statistical assumptions that underlie testing technology are complicated; most people are not conversant with correlational analysis or regression analysis and furthermore do not understand the extent to which the statistical procedures provide the meaning in this approach to human abilities. In part, it is because most people think that test scores have some inherent meaning. The nomenclature surrounding testing—ability tests, vocational aptitude tests, intelligence tests—has masked the degree to which meaning is derived, not from a deep understanding of what ability or intelligence is, but from the calculation of external relationships among variables of interest, e.g., the consistency with which the distribution of individuals' test scores around the mean is replicated on a criterion measure. The failure to fully recognize the seriousness of the criterion problem is also due in part to the sheer difficulty in most settings of coming up with an adequate criterion that is measurable and not prohibitively expensive to develop. The performance rating continues to be the most common criterion used in validation research as a matter of expediency.

The truth of the matter is that standardized testing, for all its efficiencies, cannot perform the rational and objective sorting functions that Americans expect it to unless test publishers and institutional users are willing to put as much thought and effort into the criteria used in the validation process as is put into the tests themselves. This is as necessary in educational settings, in which tests are called on to group and screen students, monitor educational progress, and evaluate schools, as it is of the use of tests in business and industry.

In a speech to his colleagues at the 1964 annual meeting of the American Psychological Association, Rains Wallace argued that, at the very least, it behooves industrial psychologists to show that their services do no harm (Wallace, 1965:411):

> The possibility of this macabre event has been soft-pedaled. Somehow, we seem to have convinced our clients, and even ourselves, that the application of our selection techniques is, at worst, neutral in its effect. This is probably the reason that we are allowed and allow ourselves to install selection tests . . . by which prospective employees are rejected for initial employment, even though we have no evidence that those rejected are any different from those who are employed in potential [for] success [in] the job.

The costs of using tests that cannot be shown to be substantially related to *appropriate* and *adequate* performance criteria are twofold. First, of course, is the unfairness to individuals who lose out on job or education opportunities, doubly unfair under a system that advertises itself as an objective means of selecting on the basis of merit. Second are the larger social costs. If the examinations used to decide who shall be admitted to medical school tap only scientific knowledge and not clinical or diagnostic skills, medical research may prosper, but everyday treatment may well be found wanting. If employers put resources into selection procedures that eliminate a large percentage of applicants on dubious grounds, not only have they wasted the costs of the personnel selection program, but they have also lost potentially successful employees. Few have the luxury of an overabundance of qualified workers in their applicant pool. If the policy maker reaches decisions about the health of the education enterprise on the basis of data from tests designed to evaluate basic skills mastery, no matter how suitable the tests for the latter purpose, those decisions are likely to misguided.

The search for new and better measures of job performance has not, of course, been limited to the performance evaluation strategies described above. The major innovation of the 1980s has been the systematic study of the hands-on job-sample test. Applied psychologists have always considered the job sample the most compelling performance measure in the abstract, but they have seldom found it a practical alternative because of the high costs of development and administration. If for no other reason, the military research described in this volume represents a significant contribution to the art and science of ability testing and test validation because it has made a serious, conscientious attempt to construct, administer, and interpret the criterion measure that comes closest to actual job performance, the hands-on job-sample test.

The importance of the military project goes well beyond the attempt to construct a particular type of performance measure that had been too much ignored in the past. There have been few large-scale research projects devoted to the criterion question in the broadest sense. The Joint-Service Job Performance Measurement/Enlistment Standards (JPM) Project, which is the subject of this book, is the exception. Following the example set during two world wars, the military launched an ambitious study of the job performance of first-term enlisted personnel in which the four Services among them constructed and administered some 16 distinct types of measures of job proficiency in a sample of military jobs. As Linda Gottfredson points out in her paper in the companion volume to this report, the JPM Project has brought the tests and measurement field to a new frontier: for the first time, a variety of alternative measures that were designed to serve the same purpose can be evaluated and compared. The experience of the JPM Project—from job analysis to the construction of hands-on and other measures, to the very complicated task of trying to analyze an enormous data base that includes a fairly comprehensive set of input and performance measures—will bring the problem of validating the criterion a long step forward and promises over time to yield a deeper understanding of the meaning and proper interpretation of test scores.

The chapters that follow provide a description of this important initiative, a discussion of the policy needs it is designed to serve, and, in conclusion, a look at the challenges raised for the next generation of performance measurement.

2

Policy Goals and Testing

The Armed Services Vocational Aptitude Battery (ASVAB) is an important tool for human resource management in the military. As is true of tests in the private sector, the ASVAB both influences and is influenced by policy goals and institutional context. This chapter sketches the policy environment in broad outline and then describes how testing operates in that environment.

The operation of the recruitment, selection, and classification system in the military has many distinctive aspects. To begin with, military service is intimately connected with the rights and responsibilities of citizenship. Moreover, the institutional context in which military planners operate is rather more complex than most, and the scale of operations is certainly larger than most. Most important, the military mission is unique: in order to protect the national security, military personnel are entrusted with the means and social permission to use violence, one consequence of which is that the military has much greater legitimate control over the lives of its personnel than do civilian employers.

Nevertheless, many of the basic issues in human resource management are not inherently different for the military planner than for the civilian employer: there is a continuing need to recruit new people, to screen and sort applicants, to avoid selecting too many people who fail or rejecting too many who would have succeeded, to ensure that selection procedures are fair, and to try to get the best workers possible within cost constraints.

Hence the policy issues in personnel management that the military job performance measurement research was designed to address, though of a distinctly military cast, are relevant to employers and applied psychologists more generally.

Current manpower policy is driven by the need to find an appropriate equilibrium between demographic factors and performance requirements, on one hand, and deficit-induced fiscal stringency on the other. To an extent seldom found in other organizations, mental aptitude test scores define the terms of debate. Whether or not to continue with the all-volunteer force will depend in good part on the Services' capacity to attract sufficient numbers of "high-quality" recruits to fill the high-technology jobs at a price the Congress is willing to pay. Likewise, at what level to fund recruiting, enlistment bonuses, and training; how much to emphasize reenlistment rather than recruitment; what percentage of women to admit; and, most directly, how high to set enlistment standards are all discussions that will take place with reference to recruit quality, defined primarily in terms of aptitude test scores.

This chapter is designed to illustrate the fluid nature of military selection criteria. It looks at the impact of legal and regulatory constraints on enlistment standards; the influence of demographic and economic factors on the supply of recruits; the complicated interplay among military quality requirements, manpower supply, and cutoff scores on aptitude tests; and, not least important, the influence of manpower policy goals such as racial and ethnic integration on the recruitment, selection, and classification system.

SELECTION AND TRAINING GOALS

The official statement of military manpower policy calls for the Services to have the plans, programs, and resources to provide trained manpower to meet the demands of global conventional war (U.S. Air Force, 1987). This means that the Services must recruit, train, and maintain a manpower pool adequate to meet the programmed wartime levels. In addition, they must ensure that the training base can be rapidly expanded to sustain and expand the fighting forces. Implicit in this goal statement is the responsibility to look beyond the status quo, to identify changes in the types and kind of personnel needed, and to develop plans and procedures to make those changes.

Effective authority over military manpower policy is shared between the executive and legislative branches of the federal government. The President, in addition to being commander-in-chief of the military, is responsible for organizing, training, and equipping the military forces. These responsibilities are carried out by the secretary of defense as head of the Department of Defense (DoD), which is subdivided into three Service departments—the Army, the Navy (including the Navy and the Marine Corps), and the Air

Force. Each Service department mirrors DoD in having a civilian chief and large combined civilian and military staffs. These staffs provide the executive branch oversight and guidance that influence every phase of military operations: personnel accession and force composition; training programs; research and development; weapons system procurement; and integrated logistics support systems.

Congressional oversight of military manpower policy stems primarily from the power of the purse. As military budgets have grown in the years since World War II, so too has congressional scrutiny. The large standing peacetime Army became institutionalized after the Korean War, and along with this large force (and the dramatic developments in weapons technology that were part of the cold war) came large peacetime budgets. As those budgets grew, congressional staffs, both personal and committee staffs, grew commensurately. Necessary to help the Congress to better understand the scope and impact of military budget requests, expanded staff levels also meant that Congress gradually took on a powerful role in operational decision making. Congress now has great, and sometimes definitive, influence on what to buy and who to buy it from; the specific size of each Service; the ratio of officers to enlisted personnel; entrance requirements for enlisted personnel; and the way DoD should be organized. Annual budget deliberations and periodic authorization hearings have become important settings for the discussion of military manpower policy.

The policy context is further complicated by interservice rivalries—the Services are in competition for recruits and resources—as well as by the wariness the Services all have of the Office of the Secretary of Defense (OSD). For example, the Services compete with each other and against OSD decisions on end strength, officer strength, and hardware procurement. And not least important, in their effort to get the resources needed to recruit and train the necessary people, manpower policy officials within each Service have to compete with those in charge of weapons procurement.

RECRUITING THE FORCE

Each year during the past decade the Services have enlisted approximately 300,000 recruits and trained them for work in hundreds of specialized jobs, from cook to sonar operator to machinegunner to intelligence specialist. Since 1973, the Services have depended on voluntary enlistments to fulfill their personnel needs. Because the majority of enlistees stay in service for only one tour of duty (usually three or four years), the Services experience a large regular turnover of people in entry-level jobs. Consequently, the Services have a large regular need for new personnel.

Recruits are drawn mainly from the population of 18- to 24-year-olds, who might otherwise go to college or take jobs elsewhere. The Services can offer applicants the opportunity to learn technical skills, as well as the less tangible benefits of travel, camaraderie, and service to their country. To maintain an adequate flow of applicants, each Service has a sizable cadre of recruiters and spends large sums on advertising, including highly visible advertising campaigns on television and in national magazines as well as ads in local newspapers (see Dertouzos, 1989, on advertising costs). The size of the recruiting budget is always an important point of negotiation with Congress. In addition, high schools are offered the use of the Armed Services Vocational Aptitude Battery (ASVAB) free of charge for vocational counseling of upper-level students in exchange for permitting Service representatives to speak to the students about the benefits of beginning their working lives in the Army, the Navy, the Air Force, or the Marines Corps. All told, substantial effort goes into military recruiting each year.

In their search for applicants, the four Services must compete with colleges, government, and private industry. Recruiting is a continual challenge in the all-volunteer environment because, like their competitors, the Services do not accept all applicants. A battery of aptitude tests, a physical exam, and a personal history investigation are used to assess the mental, physical, and moral qualifications of the applicants. A substantial number of interested young people are screened out at the local recruiting stations. In recent years, recruiters have been seeking greater numbers of high-aptitude high school graduates. Recruiters will not encourage dropouts or young people who have been involved in illegal activities to apply. The recruiters are rewarded for their "quality" prospects.

Of the 1 million candidates who receive the full regimen of mental, physical, and moral tests each year, more than a quarter are determined to be unqualified for service. Applicants who have not completed high school are currently not accepted unless they have very high aptitude scores because they are far more likely than graduates to leave or to be separated from the military before completing their first tour of duty. Applicants with relatively low aptitude scores are not considered cost-effective investments because they require more intensive training and perform less well (Office of the Assistant Secretary of Defense—Manpower, Reserve Affairs, and Logistics, 1981:8). Some applicants are rejected for medical reasons or because of prior illegal activities. Of those who are found qualified to enter military service, a good number—in 1989 it was 21 percent—eventually choose not to enlist.

A candidate who qualifies for entry and who wants to enlist must still qualify for a particular job. Each military occupational specialty has its own special aptitude requirements that have been established on the basis of past experience to reject those who are poor risks to complete technical training without discouraging the better prospects. This is not a simple matter, because to some extent the various jobs within a Service must vie with each other for the available recruits. Each of the many jobs needs a regular flow of new personnel into training slots and then job vacancies, and the available talent must be allocated in a balanced way so that in every career field the next generation of leadership is under development. Moreover, the applicants' desires must be addressed; since applicants have the option of not enlisting, they must be "sold" a job.

The task of selling a job to an applicant falls to a group of counselors, called Service classifiers, at one of the 68 Military Entrance Processing Stations (MEPS) currently in operation across the country. Service classifiers try to place applicants in jobs in which the Service can make the best use of them; they try to offer a selection of jobs that is consonant with the Service's needs and the applicants' skills and interests. The classifier wants to place the candidate in the most demanding job for which he or she is qualified and to avoid jobs that would exceed the candidate's capabilities. To fill unpopular jobs, some Services offer a cash bonus to induce qualified applicants to select these specialties.

Service classifiers are aided by computer programs that follow complex algorithms for allocating people to jobs. The heart of each Service's computerized allocation system is a nationwide data base linking all 68 MEPS into one interactive information bank that registers, for each occupational specialty, the number of slots or billets earmarked for that specialty, the rate at which the slots are being filled in the current recruiting period, the places available in the relevant technical training school, the aptitude scores required for the job, and other information relevant to placement decisions. The allocation algorithms are driven to some extent by the applicant's predicted performance on various jobs, based on scores on the ASVAB, the DoD-wide enlistment test. The algorithms are also driven by the current importance of the jobs to the Service and by the current demand of the jobs for recruits, based on the *fill rate* of the job compared with other competing jobs and the availability of school seats for training. Issues of minority and gender balance are also considered. The computer produces a ranked list of possibilities, typically in batches of five; the Service classifiers move on to the second batch only if they cannot interest the applicant in one of the top five jobs. A job is never listed if the applicant's aptitude scores are below the minimum standards for the job.

Some jobs have minimum standards well above the standards for entry into the Service, but each Service has some jobs with entrance standards roughly equivalent to Service entry. Nevertheless, it is possible that on rare occasions, an applicant will meet the qualifications for Service entry but will not meet the minimum standard for any specific job. It is more likely that the applicant won't be qualified for the job that he or she wants, but Service classifiers are well prepared for such cases and can usually offer a job in the same or a related job family that has lower test score requirements.

Occasionally an applicant will be overqualified for his or her first choice, and again it is up to the Service classifier to raise the applicant's aspiration level.

There are several indirect participants in the enlistment process. Foremost among these are the trainers. There is a technical school associated with nearly every job or cluster of jobs, where novices are trained to do the work. The leaders of the schools are proponents or spokespersons for the associated jobs. In addition to keeping curricula up to date, proponents help to manage personnel accessions. They influence the flow of applicants to their occupational specialties by adjusting the schedule of training sessions and specifying the numbers of people to be trained for each job in each session. With the help of proponents and other manpower managers, classifiers may arrange for applicants to delay entry into the Service in order to have a school seat awaiting them in the job of their choice when they enter. Proponents are also the major advocates for the entrance standards that are set for the jobs under their leadership.

Demographic Trends in the Youth Population

With the passage of the post–World War II baby boom generation into middle age, the cohort of 18- to 24-year-old males from which the military draws the vast majority of its recruits is on a significant downward slope. This downward trend, combined with the change to voluntary military service in 1973, presented military planners in the 1970s and 1980s with the prospect of an increasing shortage of qualified men. The issue was of great concern until the recent easing of the confrontational posture of the United States and the Soviet Union. The consequent reductions in force size planned for the 1990s have reduced its salience; still, it provides an interesting illustration of the interplay of military and congressional policy interests, and particularly of the intricate relationship between questions of recruit quality and recruiting costs.

One obvious solution to the shortage of eligible men was to look to the other half of the population. The change in women's roles in civilian society since the 1960s, particularly their increased labor force participation, made an effective argument for the increased use of women in the military. From the 1970s, there was a gradual shift in policy, accompanied by the hesitancies and pockets of resistance one would expect given the tradition of male domination of the military, not only to increase the number of women in the enlisted and officer ranks, but also to assign them to a wider variety of (noncombat) jobs. Congress has had a role in the policy shift, as have high-level military planners, line managers, and the job counselors whose task it is to find enough qualified people to fill the training slots in all kinds of jobs.

A recent example is illustrative of the concern with recruit quality and recruiting costs that has led to greater use of women in the enlisted ranks. In 1988, the House Armed Services Committee, concerned by a projected decline of 25.3 percent in the number of men in the youth population by 1991, directed the Services to review their procedures for determining their total capacity for women. The committee's assumption was that a smaller cohort of available men would mean that more women would be needed to serve if recruiting goals in the volunteer force were to be met. Each of the Services conducted a study of the recruiting environment and subsequently expanded assignment opportunities for women and eased the enlistment ceilings somewhat (Office of the Assistant Secretary of Defense—Force Management and Personnel, 1988).

The reorientation of policy on the utilization of women in the military in the last two decades was in some sense validated during the recent war in the Persian Gulf, when sizable numbers of women staffed artillery positions, piloted helicopters and cargo planes, worked as mechanics, and served in a variety of combat support functions. But ambivalences remain, within the military and in the larger society, about the use of women and about its effect on the military mission. Certainly the Services did not view the increased use of women as a total solution to the recruiting problems foreseen in 1988—if for no other reason than that women were by law (Air Force and Navy) or policy (Army) prohibited from serving in combat positions.

The Army response to the congressional committee's concern about the increasingly competitive recruiting environment due to the declining youth population was to emphasize the importance of cash enlistment bonuses, educational incentives and Army College Fund Programs, and competitive compensation in order to attract and retain high-quality enlistees. All of these tactics have cost implications. The Air Force, widely viewed as the Service with the greatest potential to increase the number of women because fewer enlisted positions are subject to combat exclusions, concluded that the male youth decline would not drive its recruiting success or failure.

The Navy, however, quite accurately foresaw that its attainment of recruiting goals would be very difficult under the existing marketing conditions, with keen competition for a shrinking recruitable population and constrained recruiting resources, particularly for advertising. Among other things, the 9,000 billets opened up to women as a result of the Navy review of its policies would require additional effort to attract them to the nontraditional, sea-intensive jobs (Office of the Assistant Secretary of Defense—Force Management and Personnel, 1988).

Military recruiting for the 1990s poses a rather different set of issues. In line with congressional instruction, the Department of Defense intends to reduce substantially the size of the military. The plan is to reach an active-duty force of 1,630,000 in fiscal 1995, which represents a reduction of 25 percent from a peak of 2,174,000 in fiscal 1987. The reserve force will be reduced by 21 percent (Jehn, 1991). At the same time, the effects of recession and the budget deficit that are affecting government spending more generally will also require severe cuts in the defense budget, and more specifically in recruiting resources.

Downsizing of the force, reduced budgets for advertising and recruiting, base closings, possible involuntary separations—all these conditions affect the recruiting environment and thus create uncertainties for military human resource planners. Even if the demographic trends no longer loom as large, the task of recruiting high-quality personnel, male and female, promises to remain challenging.

Recruiting Policy and Fairness Issues

One of the important goals in military manpower policy has been to build the Services to reflect the ethnic and racial diversity of American society (MacGregor, 1981; Eitelberg, 1986). As mentioned above, one of the factors built into the computerized allocation systems is minority recruiting goals; the jobs that the computer brings up for the Service classifier and the applicant to consider will take account of the applicant's racial or ethnic status and the so-called minority fill rate in the otherwise available jobs. For example, jobs to which few minorities have been assigned during the current recruiting period will be offered to minority applicants before other jobs, all other things being equal. The Services also have proactive recruiting programs to advertise the benefits of military service in minority communities.

And indeed, for the last several decades, the military has been an important route to upward mobility for American minority-group members (MacGregor, 1981; Moskos and Butler, 1987; Jaynes and Williams, 1989; but see Laurence et al., 1989, for evidence that low-aptitude recruits do not reap civilian-sector benefits from military service). Although wartime needs for manpower at times brought large numbers of blacks into military service—blacks made up almost 11 percent of the Army in World War I (MacGregor, 1981:7)—traditional policies of segregation and outright exclusion began to break down only in World War II, due in part to the sheer inefficiency of maintaining separate black units. There was also a change at the top policy levels. Whereas the policy of exclusion was revived after the conclusion of the World War I, so that by 1940 only about 1.5 percent of Army and Navy personnel were black, the increasing influence of civil rights leaders prevented any such retrenchment after World War II. In 1948, President Truman issued Executive Order 9981 decreeing equality of treatment and opportunity for all in the armed forces "without regard to race, color, religion or national origin." In 1954 the secretary of defense announced that the last segregated unit in the armed forces had been abolished (MacGregor, 1981:473) and over the next quarter-century the Department of Defense gradually embraced a policy of integration, both in the sense of providing equal opportunity and of achieving racial balance.

Participation rates do not begin to tell the full story of the integration of the military—integration on the job, in schools, in housing and in recreational facilities, well before such changes were effected in civilian society—yet they are illustrative. In 1955, during the Korean conflict, blacks constituted about 9 percent of enlisted personnel and 2 percent of officers. By the 1980s, these figures had increased dramatically. For example, by 1986 almost 30 percent of Army personnel were black, and although the largest numerical increases occurred in the lower grades and ranks, there have been very large increases over the last 30 years in the proportions of noncommissioned officers who are black. Table 2-1, reproduced from an earlier National Research Council report, shows the increases in black par-

TABLE 2-1 Black Participation in the U.S. Army as a Percentage of Officers and Enlisted Personnel, 1962-1986

Rank	1962	1972	1980	1986
Officers				
General	—	0.7	5.4	7.0
Colonel	0.1	1.6	4.5	5.0
Lt. Colonel	0.9	5.1	4.9	4.4
Major	2.5	5.1	4.4	6.8
Captain	5.2	3.7	7.5	12.7
1st Lieutenant	4.3	2.9	10.2	14.4
2nd Lieutenant	2.3	2.5	10.4	11.4
Total	3.2	3.9	7.2	10.4
Enlisted Personnel				
Sergeant Major	2.9	7.0	20.5	30.9
Master Sergeant	5.5	14.0	25.3	24.4
Sergeant 1st Class	7.8	19.6	24.7	25.5
Staff Sergeant	12.7	23.9	23.9	35.7
Sergeant	15.7	16.6	31.2	36.0
Specialist 4	13.0	13.5	37.2	29.9
Private 1st Class	10.8	15.9	39.0	23.6
Private	13.3	17.9	37.0	22.2
Recruit	11.4	18.3	27.0	22.8
Total	12.3	17.0	32.5	29.6

SOURCE: Moskos and Butler (1987:27).

ticipation in the Army enlisted ranks and officer corps at four points between 1962 and 1986.

Figure 2-1 presents the trend in the percentage of black enlisted personnel for all four Services since the institution of the all-volunteer force in 1973. The pattern of change is generally in an upward direction, although there has been little or no change in the proportion of enlisted blacks in the Air Force since 1982 or in the Marine Corps since 1986. The success of the military's equal opportunity policies and the general attractiveness of the military as an employer to blacks and other racial minorities is indicated by comparisons with the civilian labor force. According to the most recent figures available from the Department of Defense, the proportion of blacks and other racial minorities in the enlisted ranks was roughly twice their respective representation in the civilian labor force (see Table 2-2). This is a far cry from the days when blacks had to "fight for the right to fight." So thoroughgoing was the change in policy, in fact, that the Vietnam War brought charges that blacks were doing more than their fair share of the fighting, a worry that also accompanied the creation of the all-volunteer

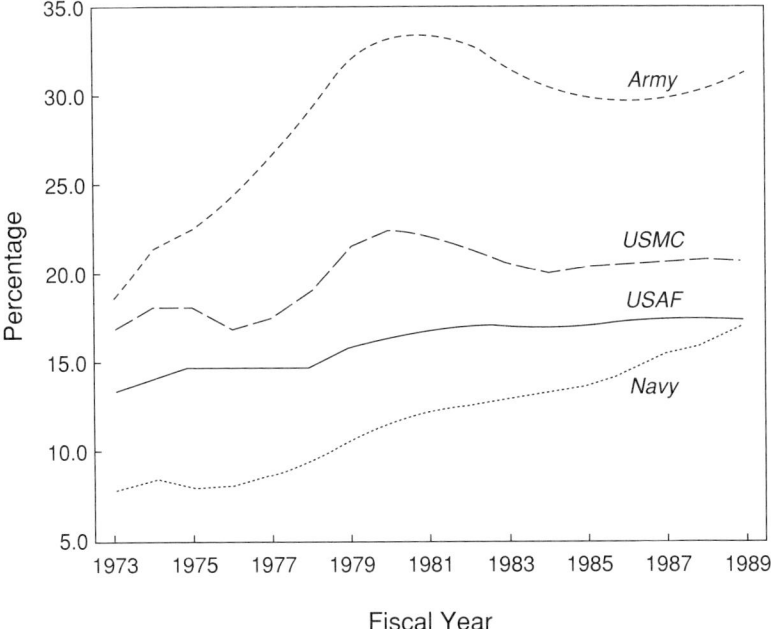

FIGURE 2-1 Blacks as a percentage of active-duty enlisted members, by Service, fiscal 1973-1989. SOURCE: Office of the Assistant Secretary of Defense—Force Management and Personnel (1990).

TABLE 2-2 Race of Active-Duty Enlisted Personnel, by Service, and Civilian Labor Force 18-44 Years Old, Fiscal 1989 (Percentage)

Race	Army	Navy	Marine Corps	Air Force	DoD	Civilians 18-44 Years Old
White	62	77	72	78	71	85
Black	31	17	21	17	23	12
Other	7	6	7	4	6	3
Total	100	100	100	100	100	100

Columns may not add to totals due to rounding.

SOURCE: Office of the Assistant Secretary of Defense—Force Management and Personnel (1990).

force, and emerged again during the Persian Gulf War, in which, according to news reports, black soldiers made up 28 percent of the ground forces.

If military accession policy has shown real progress with regard to the participation of American minorities, classification policy goals have been more difficult to achieve. The distribution of minorities and women across the spectrum of military career fields has tended to be skewed away from the highly technical jobs. Table 2-3, taken from a 1990 DoD report on the representation of subpopulations in the military, lists the major military occupational areas and shows the proportions of enlisted personnel in each. The report describes three of the occupational areas as generally employing low-level skills: the infantry and related specialties, craftsmen, and service and supply handlers. Medical and dental specialists, functional support and administration, and electricians/mechanical equipment repairers, which together make up about 44 percent of the enlisted force, are considered to include largely mid-level jobs. The high-skill, high-tech jobs fall mostly in the areas of electronic equipment repair and communications and intelligence and other allied specialties.

From a career field perspective, the low- and semiskilled occupational areas have tended to be composed of proportionately high concentrations of minority and female personnel. Until the Truman executive order mandated equal opportunity, blacks were, with a few notable exceptions such as the Tuskegee Fighter Squadron, assigned mainly to unskilled occupations in service and supply. In the 1950s and 1960s, blacks moved up the skill ladder into infantry and administrative support jobs. For their part, women have traditionally served as nurses and clerk/secretaries, both considered semiskilled occupations. As the DoD report from which this discussion is largely drawn documents, 88 percent of female enlisted personnel were

TABLE 2-3 Occupational Areas of Active Duty Enlisted Personnel (percentage in each area), Fiscal 1973 and 1989

Occupational Area	Women Fiscal 1973	Women Fiscal 1989	Blacks Fiscal 1973	Blacks Fiscal 1989	Total Enlisted Personnel Fiscal 1989
Infantry, Gun Crews, and Seamanship Specialists	**	4	27	19	18
Electronic Equipment Repairers	1	6	4	6	11
Communications and Intelligence Specialists	6	12	4	11	10
Medical and Dental Specialists	24	15	5	7	6
Other Allied Specialists	3	2	1	2	3
Functional Support and Administration	64	38	23	24	16
Electrical/Mechanical Equipment Repairers	1	9	15	16	22
Craftsmen	**	2	4	3	4
Service and Supply Handlers	**	11	17	12	10
Total	100	100	100	100	100

NOTE: Data exclude personnel classified as "nonoccupational" or "occupation unknown." Columns may not add to totals due to rounding.

** Less that half of 1 percent.

SOURCE: Office of the Assistant Secretary of Defense—Force Management and Personnel (1990).

concentrated in these two career fields in 1973. Table 2-3 also shows marked changes DoD-wide in the occupational distribution of women and blacks since 1973. Although slightly more than half of enlisted women were still assigned to the two traditional female occupations in the military in 1989, the percentage of women in the high-skill career fields (electronic equipment repair, communications and intelligence, and other allied specialties) approached that of men. The proportion of blacks in the high-skill jobs also grew substantially, from 9 to 19 percent, although the proportion of whites is also quite a bit higher at 26 percent.

Although the 1989 figures appear encouraging, the distribution of minorities and women across military career fields has been and will no doubt continue to be a sensitive policy issue for military human resource managers to deal with. The pooling of minorities and women in traditional low- and semiskilled jobs, which until recently also meant a heavy presence of minority men in infantry specialties, has had troubling implications both for the Services' commitment to fairness and for the Services' capacity to meet their recruiting goals in an increasingly technological military environment. Military service has long been recognized as an avenue to education, social, and financial opportunities for citizens from modest circumstances. But the military is a pyramidal organization, very broad at the base and ascending sharply to a point. Not many recruits will have the opportunity to make a career of it; a large majority will serve only one term. Many of those who have been trained in technical fields such as electronic communications or jet engine mechanic will be able to translate their military experience into a rewarding civilian career, and for them the military can provide a bridge to a better way of life. This is far less true of the low-skill jobs and most of the combat jobs, which have no direct relevance to civilian life.

These considerations led some policy analysts in the 1970s and 1980s to argue that, as long as minorities are concentrated in the low-level and combat jobs, the opportunities offered by military service may be outweighed by the risks; from this perspective, the likelihood that blacks and Hispanics would suffer a "disproportionate" share of the combat fatalities in the initial stages of conflict is troubling (e.g., Binkin, 1982). Other analysts argued that blacks reenlist at a higher rate than other social groups, are well represented in the career force, and, in that sense, reap the benefits of military service. Nevertheless, the participation rates of blacks and whites in infantry occupations as of 1989 indicate that military policy makers were sensitive to the threat of disproportionate combat fatalities and have managed to equalize the risks, if not yet the benefits, of military service.

The problem for military planners, of course, is to figure out what can be done to smooth out the distribution of minority populations across the career field spectrum while still fulfilling the primary organizational mission of being able to rapidly provide the trained manpower necessary to meet the demands of conventional war. This leads directly to the issue of enlistment standards and the use of ASVAB test scores to select and allocate recruits among competing military jobs. The scores obtained on mechanical, electronic, administrative, and general aptitude composites determine which jobs the individual is qualified to enter.

Historically, minority recruits as a group have not performed as well as whites on military selection and classification tests and other standardized multiple-choice tests. An obvious consequence is that lower-scoring social groups will be screened out in greater proportions than their higher-scoring peer groups, all things being equal; of those who meet the operational enlistment standards, a larger proportion of recruits from the lower-scoring minority groups will be allocated to those jobs with less stringent entry requirements.

The number of strategies that military planners might adopt to address the problem is fairly limited, and each has cost implications. The Services could lower the minimum scores required for classification into more technically oriented career fields in order to broaden the eligibility base for those jobs. If the scores are predictive of training success and later performance on the job, the corollary expectation is that lowering standards would require a longer period of training to bring the recruits with lower skill aptitudes to the same level of competence as those who met the higher standard. There would also be the possibility of higher error rates on the job, which could prove very costly.

Other options include more aggressive recruiting of minority members capable of meeting current standards, looking for other predictors to supplement the ASVAB and broaden the decision base of current placement procedures, and improving the counseling of minority and female applicants to increase the proclivity of those who are qualified to accept assignment to high-skill jobs. The latter strategy is particularly relevant to female applicants who tend to gravitate to administrative and clerical jobs of their own accord. All but the counseling option have cost implications and, in times of austere budgets and shrinking training dollars, become difficult to implement.

The Changing Technological Environment

One of the greatest challenges facing military planners in charge of manpower and personnel is to build a force that can respond to the technological innovation that has unequivocally altered modern warfare and the national defense in the last two decades. Mini-computers, word processors, advanced telecommunications, and other sophisticated technologies have altered the way duties are performed from the headquarters to the front-line troops. Tanks, aircraft, and ships of all kinds are affected by the high-tech boom. For example, a typical tactical fighter squadron now requires up to 25 different skills and as many as 300 maintenance people for deployment. Analysts point out that it took more than 40 years to go from vacuum tubes to transistors, and but a fraction of that time to move from transistors to microelectronics. It is likely that the pace of technological innovation will continue to accelerate, bringing a steady accretion of new systems on top of the old: the Air Force could well be operating aircraft like the B-2 Stealth bomber as well as the B-52, a 1950s vintage bomber, in the next century. Such a wide range of technology presents a challenge to the military personnel charged with maintaining the systems.

Efforts to plan for the new high-tech requirements can be viewed from two perspectives: one is an engineering perspective, which focuses on designing weapons systems with the human operator in mind. The other perspective on the challenges of technology comes from the "people systems" side: all systems require that people be recruited, trained, and managed to operate and maintain them. A common approach from the engineering side, called technician transparency, is to build systems such that tasks are "deskilled." Then technicians with a minimum of training can perform well via simplified troubleshooting techniques incorporated into the system—for example, replacing an entire module in an engine rather than repairing or replacing a smaller component part.

But engineering design cannot provide all the answers. Even in a black box or fail safe system, troubleshooting tasks can become complex. And overall, the effect of advanced technology has been to increase the skill requirements of military jobs substantially. Similar changes are occurring in private industry. For example, General Motors predicts that 50 percent of its work force in the year 2000 will be categorized as skilled trades, compared with 16 percent in 1980.

These changes are reflected in military training. In the Air Training Command, for example, there are presently over 7,900 technical training courses offered, of which 38 percent must be contracted out because of the advanced technology involved. In addition to formal training, all of the Services provide extensive on-the-job training—the Air Force estimates that at any given time over half of all airmen are being trained on the job.

THE ROLE OF TESTING

To human resource managers in the military, aptitude tests are an attractive gauge of applicant potential for a variety of reasons: the lack of other indicators in its relatively young and inexperienced target population, the large number of jobs that need to be filled, and the need, in wartime, to bring large numbers of men and women in and up to battle readiness in as little time as possible. No matter what the method of assessing job applicants, in any selection system that is more sophisticated than hiring all comers at the gate, the aim is to balance performance effectiveness and cost-effectiveness or efficiency. Building an effective work force depends on selecting workers who can do—or can be trained to do—the job and rejecting those who cannot; at the same time, efficient use of recruiting resources requires that the selection process not turn away workers who could have succeeded. This implies the use of some sort of standard or cutoff score above which candidates are accepted and below which they are not. The location of the cutoff score is in part a function of job requirements and the distribution of abilities needed to meet them for all jobs; it is also sensitive to supply and demand relationships in the job market (and, often, social policy considerations). When the supply of applicants is large relative to the employer's needs, selection standards can be stringent; but if the employer must hire, say, five out of every eight applicants, then pressure mounts to lower the entrance requirements—or to funnel more resources into recruitment in order to enlarge the applicant pool.

The Evolution of Mental Aptitude Screening in the Military

The history of testing in the military is a story of constant fluctuations in enlistment standards in response to changes in the recruiting environment. As recounted in Chapter 1, the use of psychological tests in the classification and assignment of military personnel can be traced, historically, to the Alpha and Beta tests administered to recruits and draftees at Army training camps during World War I. It was not until World War II, however, that such tests were also used to screen potential entrants into military service. The Services applied four screens to those designated as eligible for induction by the Selective Service: aptitude testing, psychiatric evaluation, physical examination, and an administrative check of moral character. The specific aptitude criteria varied with the course of the war. During the early phase of wartime mobilization, the standard for induction was defined as "the capacity of reading and writing the English language as prescribed for the fourth grade in grammar school." Beginning in June 1943, the Army General Classification Test (AGCT), previously administered to all enlisted personnel after entry into service for purposes of classification, was used to screen out people with limited ability to absorb basic military training in a reasonable period of time. The minimum requirement was set at "a capacity above the lower three-fifths of Grade V," the lowest of five categories on the AGCT (Eitelberg et al., 1984:Appendix A:9). This test was a simple multiple-choice test that included three types of items: vocabulary, arithmetic reasoning, and spatial relations. (For a detailed treatment of military screening, see Eitelberg et al., 1984.)

In the face of intense wartime pressures to broaden the manpower pool available for induction, the passing score on this test was set at a very low level, corresponding roughly to a percentile score of about 5.5. Following the end of World War II, mental aptitude screening was retained under separate tests administered by each Service. However, the passing scores were substantially increased, reflecting the reduced manpower needs of peacetime, as well as the higher aptitude requirements considered appropriate for a career-oriented regular military force.

In 1948, the military draft was briefly reinstituted to meet the Army's increased manpower requirements during the Berlin crisis. The Selective Service Act of 1948 prescribed for the first time a statutory "mental standard" for induction, i.e., a standard score of 70 (equivalent to a percentile score of 13) on the AGCT. This precedent was retained when inductions were resumed on a large scale in late 1950, during the Korean War buildup. The Armed Forces Qualification Test (AFQT) had meanwhile been developed by a joint-Service working group, to serve as a common screening test for both draftees and first-time male Service enlistees. Patterned closely on the AGCT, its primary function continued to be to serve as a general measure of trainability. Following enlistment or induction, each Service administered its own more comprehensive aptitude test battery for purposes of classification and assignment.

In 1951, in the face of a possible depletion of the Selective Service manpower pool, the Congress—in enacting an amended draft law (the Universal Military Training and Service Act of 1951)—adopted a number of measures to stretch the available draft manpower pool, including a reduction of the cutoff score on the AFQT from a percentile score of 13 to 10. At the same time, under a "Qualitative Distribution" directive from the secretary of defense, an identical AFQT mental standard was administratively prescribed for male first-time Service enlistments into all four Services. In addition, each Service was required to accept a prescribed minimum percentage of all of its new enlisted entrants from the lowest acceptable score grouping, Mental Group IV, which covered percentile scores from 10 through 30. This policy was designed to avoid having the Air Force and the Navy (which then relied solely on enlistments) skim the cream of the available manpower pool, resulting in a disproportionate concentration of the low-scoring group in the Army's inductee pool. Under this directive, the AFQT thus became a tool for broad qualitative allocation of manpower among the Services, in addition to its primary use as a screening measure.

Following termination of the Korean War in 1953, active-duty military strengths were reduced from a peak of more than 3 1/2 million in 1952 to less than 2 1/2 million by 1960. Although the draft was retained throughout this period, draft calls were sharply reduced, from more than 1/2 million in fiscal 1953 to only 60,000 by fiscal 1961. In the face of these trends, and of accumulating evidence concerning difficulties in training and utilization of personnel with low test scores, Service pressures mounted for relief from the statutory and administrative constraints on the mental standards for enlistment. Beginning in 1955, the Department of Defense authorized higher standards for regular enlistees than for draftees and progressively reduced the Group IV enlistment quotas. In 1958, the draft law was again modified to permit increases in the inductee minimum mental standards as well.

During the succeeding years, minimum mental standards were effectively raised by all Services through a number of procedures. The first was a simple increase in the operational passing scores on the AFQT, to as high as 31 in some Services. A further refinement was a requirement that individuals who scored in the Mental Group IV range and who attained a minimum passing score (e.g., AFQT 21) were also required to qualify on supplemental aptitude test batteries previously administered only following entry into service. In addition, higher mental test scores were prescribed for non–high school graduates than for applicants with high school diplomas, based on considerable research evidence that the former were much poorer risks, in terms of disciplinary problems and other difficulties leading to premature discharge from service.

This upward drift in mental standards was reversed, however, following the large-scale commitment of U.S. troops in Vietnam, beginning in 1965. Draft calls again rose sharply, averaging more than 300,000 per year in the second half of the decade. These calls, and accompanying increases in draft-induced enlistments, were met from a relatively large manpower pool, consisting of young men born in the initial years of the post–World War II baby boom. As a result, manpower supply stringencies never became as critical a consideration in shaping manpower procurement policy as during the Korean War period. Nevertheless, considerations of fairness (as then perceived) and related social policy concerns dictated that mental standards be substantially reduced.

One of the social policy considerations was the perception by top administration officials, including Secretary of Defense McNamara, that a period of military service and training would be beneficial to many underprivileged youth in development of needed skills, which would help them in subsequent civilian job careers. These considerations (as well as expressed skepticism regarding the validity of the mental aptitude tests as predictors of military job performance—rather than training), resulted in initiation by Secretary McNamara, in October 1966, of a program identified as Project 100,000. The program provided for a carefully controlled reduction of the prevailing standards of induction and enlistment, so that 100,000 men would be accepted annually who would not have previously qualified for service. High school graduates who scored as low as AFQT 10 and non–high school graduates as low as AFQT 21 were accepted without further testing. Only non–high school graduates scoring between AFQT 10 and 20 were subject to supplemental testing. The system of mental group quotas that had been discontinued in the late 1950s was also reinstituted, with an objective of procuring over 22 percent of total first-time Service enlisted entrants from the Mental Group IV category during the period fiscal 1967-1970. Project 100,000 continued through 1971, when it was terminated by congressional action.

In reaction to the extreme unpopularity of the war in Vietnam, the draft was abolished in 1973. The administration's commitment to meet future peacetime military personnel needs through volunteer programs was accompanied by a fundamental shift in DoD policies affecting enlistment standards. In the new all-volunteer force (AVF) environment, the policy adopted was to decentralize the authority to establish and revise mental screening standards. In setting their minimum qualification standards, each of the Services experimented with a combination of test scores and educational standards. It soon became common practice for the Services to fine-tune their standards to changing recruiting conditions, with operational cutoff scores being modified on a month-to-month basis, in combination with changing quotas for high school and non–high school graduates. As a consequence, the de facto enlistment standards during favorable recruiting periods—and the 1980s were very favorable indeed—have tended to be much higher than the official minimum standards.

Another significant policy response to the all-volunteer force has been the increased importance of enlistment programs under which qualified applicants are guaranteed specific occupational training and job assignment. Although it varies by Service, a majority of today's volunteers sign an enlistment contract that specifies their job choice.

In the early years of the all-volunteer force, mandatory use of the AFQT for screening enlisted personnel was discontinued, and each Service was authorized to choose its own enlistment screening criteria. However, in 1976, the ASVAB was officially adopted as a combined enlistment and classification test for all four Services.

The Armed Services Vocational Aptitude Battery

The ASVAB was developed as part of the DoD Student Testing Program in the late 1960s. It was originally intended for use in high schools to stimulate interest in military career opportunities and to provide guidance to students, counselors, and military recruiters in making academic and career decisions. And it continues to play that role. A form of the ASVAB is administered to more than 1.3 million students annually in approximately 14,000 high schools, in addition to its use in screening about 1 million young people who express an interest in military service and classifying those who actually enlist.

The ASVAB consists of 10 separately timed subtests that are combined in various ways to form the Armed Forces Qualification Test for enlistment screening and Service-defined area aptitude composites for job assignment. The ten subtests are:

1. Paragraph Comprehension (PC)
2. Arithmetic Reasoning (AR)
3. Word Knowledge (WK)
4. Mathematical Knowledge (MK)
5. General Science (GS)
6. Numerical Operations (NO)
7. Coding Speed (CS)
8. Auto and Shop Information (AS)
9. Mechanical Comprehension (MC)
10. Electronics Information (EI)

The first four subtests—PC, AR, WK, and MK—make up the current AFQT. As was traditionally the case, this composite is considered a general measure of trainability. The Service-specific composites used to determine eligibility for military technical training schools and subsequent job assignment are presented in Table 2-4. The number of composites that were in use as of 1987 ranged from 4 in the Marine Corps to 10 in the Navy. All of the Services have composites labeled mechanical; clerical or administrative; electronics; and general but, except for electronics, the subtests differ somewhat for similarly named composites (Waters et. al., 1987). The entire battery of tests that makes up the ASVAB has about 334 multiple-choice items and requires three hours to administer.

Until the last decade, the aptitude levels of military recruits were established with reference to a norming sample representing all men serving in the armed forces during 1944 (Uhlaner and Bolanovich, 1952). In 1980, DoD, in cooperation with the Department of Labor, undertook a study called the *Profile of American Youth* (Office of the Assistant Secretary of Defense—Manpower, Reserve Affairs, and Logistics, 1982a) to assess the vocational aptitudes of a nationally representative sample of young people and to develop current norms for the ASVAB. Subsequent forms of the ASVAB have been calibrated to this 1980 youth population, making it the only vocational aptitude battery with nationally representative norms.

The ASVAB norms are based on a sample of 9,173 people between the ages of 18 and 23 who were part of the National Longitudinal Survey of Youth Labor Force Behavior. The sample included 4,550 men and 4,623 women and contained youth from rural as well as urban areas and from all major census regions. Certain groups—blacks, Hispanics, and economically disadvantaged whites—were oversampled to allow more precise analysis

TABLE 2-4 Current ASVAB Composites Used for Classification by the Services

Army	Navy	Marine Corps	Air Force	Component Subtests
—	General Technical	—	General	AR + WK +PC
—	—	General Technical	—	AR + WK + PC + MC
Electronics	Electronics	Electronics Repair	Electronics	AR + GS + MK + EI
Clerical	—	—	—	AR + MK + WK + PC
—	Clerical	—	Administrative	NO + WK + PC + CS
—	—	Clerical	—	MK + WK + PC + CS
Motor Maintenance	—	—	—	NO + AS + MC + EI
—	Mechanical	—	—	AS + WK + PC + MC
—	—	Mechanical Maintenance	—	AR + AS + MC + EI
—	—	—	Mechanical	GS + 2AS + MC
Combat	—	—	—	AR + CS + AS + MC
Field Artillery	—	—	—	AR + CS + MK + MC
Operators/ Food	—	—	—	NO + WK + PC + MC + AS
Surveillance/ Communications	—	—	—	AR + AS + MC + WK + PC
—	Basic Electricity/ Electronics	—	—	AR + GS + 2MK
Skilled Technical	—	—	—	GS + WK + PC + MC + MK
—	Engineering	—	—	AS + MK

Continued on next page

TABLE 2-4 *Continued*

Army	Navy	Marine Corps	Air Force	Component Subtests
General Maintenance	—	—	—	GS + AS + MK + EI
—	Machinery Repairmen	—	—	AR + AS + MC
—	Submarine	—	—	AR + WK + PC + MC
—	Communications Technician	—	—	AR + WK + PC + CS + NO
—	Hospitalman	—	—	GS + WK + PC + MK

SOURCE: Waters et al. (1987).

of groups of particular salience for manpower policy (Office of the Assistant Secretary of Defense—Manpower, Reserve Affairs, and Logistics, 1982a).

This contemporary normative data is useful to policy makers in interpreting the test scores of recruits. In 1981, for example, the cohort entering military service scored somewhat higher on the AFQT composite than did the norming sample representative of the general youth population.

ENLISTMENT STANDARDS AND QUALITY GOALS

The Contemporary System

As presently structured, the operation of the military recruitment, selection, and classification system takes place within the parameters defined by enlistment standards and quality goals. Enlistment standards provide the basic filtering or gatekeeping function for military entry. The standards include minimum scores on mental and physical tests, as well as a background check for arrest record, drug use, and so on. The mental qualifications of applicants are determined by scores on the AFQT subtests of the ASVAB and by high school graduation status. The single most important determinant of eligibility in the enlisted ranks is an applicant's score on the AFQT.

For policy purposes, the AFQT score scale is divided into five categories (formerly called Mental Groups), as shown in Table 2-5. Service quality goals are determined annually with reference to these categories and pre-

TABLE 2-5 AFQT Score Scale

AFQT Category	Percentile Score	Population Distribution[a]
I	93-99	8
II	65-92	28
III	31-64	34
IV	10-30	21
V	1-9	9

NOTE: Category III is frequently subdivided into IIIA (50-64) and IIIB (31-49).

[a]1980 reference population

sented in a report to Congress in preparation for appropriations hearings. Recruits with scores in Categories I through IIIA—that is, at the 50th percentile and above, are considered to be "high quality."

The current enlistment standards and quality goals imposed by Congress for the entire armed forces are as follows. The legislated minimum enlistment standard for high school graduates is an AFQT score of 10; in other words, those with scores in Category V are not eligible for military service. They represent about 9 percent of the youth population. Since some military occupational specialties are much more difficult than others, and the more difficult jobs will be beyond the capabilities of lower-scoring recruits, it is necessary to enlist people in the upper score ranges. Current legislation requires that no more than 20 percent of enlistees be drawn from Category IV (score range 10-30). This forces at least 80 percent of the distribution of enlistees to fall within Categories I through III. During the past decade this goal has been met; indeed, the distribution of talent among service recruits roughly approximates the available talent in the 18- to 23-year-old cohort, although the Services draw slightly more from Category III, slightly less from Category IV, and, of course, none from Category V (Waters et al., 1987).

For their part, the Services would prefer to recruit the most talented people possible. Each Service has set formal enlistment standards that are well above the legislated minimum, and the recruiting climate for most of the 1980s permitted operational standards that far exceeded the formal ones.

At the Service level, technical school proponents are important players in the policy process. Proponents naturally want the most highly qualified applicants that they can get for their specialties. Highly qualified recruits are easily and quickly trained and are likely to complete the course successfully. Poorly qualified recruits are more likely to require more intensive training or to fail the course. These differences in trainability are likely to translate into similar differences in performance on the job. Moreover, marginally qualified recruits are less versatile; they can be placed in fewer of the positions within an occupational specialty.

Proponents want the minimum aptitude standards for their specialties to be set so that a high percentage (usually 90 percent) of recruits will successfully complete technical training (Eitelberg, 1988). But the pass rate is not the only check on quality. Reporting mechanisms exist between the field and the school so that the proponents are informed if new batches of recruits are not performing up to standard as they move through the first term of enlistment, or if each cohort does not include enough people who can take on the more complex responsibilities of the job. Recruiters report how successful they have been in meeting recruiting quality goals. The entire process of monitoring, reporting, and negotiation is overseen by Service headquarters accession policy staff, who make the final decisions about formal enlistment standards.

The actual operational standards for each job are adjusted, within the limits set by the formal entrance requirements, in response to market forces. In an especially good recruiting year, entrance requirements can be tightened. In 1984, for example, 90 percent of new Army recruits were in AFQT Categories I through III, compared with 69 percent in 1981. In the same two years, the Marine Corps recruited 95 and 80 percent high school graduates, respectively. In addition to market forces, the quality of recruits assigned to a given job depends to some extent on the competitive interplay of jobs in the job allocation system and to some extent on the candidates' preferences.

How Much Quality is Enough?

If the natural impulse of the proponent is to seek to get the most highly qualified recruits possible, it is also true that there is a considerable cost in setting high standards and ambitious quality goals. Intensive recruiting effort is needed in order to get enough recruits who score in Categories I to IIIA, the accepted definition of high quality.

In a sense, Congress functions as a board of directors for the Department of Defense; its control over recruiting budgets and other spending for military personnel gives it an important voice in manpower policy. The Services seek recruiting budgets that will extend their ability to attract the best available youth. Congress, in the role of management, seeks prudent use of resources and wishes to appropriate only enough funds to guarantee an adequate flow of acceptable candidates.

In order to justify their budget requests to Congress, the Services report their recent recruiting experience and their quality goals for the upcoming year in terms of numbers of recruits needed in various AFQT categories. Service-wide goals are presumably amalgams of the separate quality goals for each job, which depend in turn on the minimum standards and the aptitude distribution desired.

Whether their quality goals are realistic and necessary, as the Services maintain, or too high, as Congress often claims, has been difficult to ascertain. One of the major weaknesses of DoD's position is that quality requirements have been related to the aptitude of recruits rather than to realized on-the-job performance. That is, the discussion has been cast in terms of scores on the AFQT—Service X needs this level of funding in order to attract so many recruits in Categories I through IIIA—without being able to show empirically what this ability distribution means in terms of performance gains. The AFQT categories do not denote levels of job mastery and, indeed, the link from recruit quality to job performance has been largely unknown.

In the economic climate of the 1980s, the old "more is better" way of doing business was no longer credible. As the decade progressed, Congress became increasingly insistent in asking: How much quality is enough? DoD launched the Joint-Service Job Performance Measurement/Enlistment Standards Project to provide the data base and the methodologies necessary to provide more explicit, scientifically defensible answers to that question.

3

Improving Job Performance Criteria for Selection Tests

Every employer is faced with the need to balance the costs of selecting high-ability personnel against the anticipated performance gains. Yet all too often, selection policy is made in the absence of reliable information about the performance gains that can reasonably be expected when people are selected on the basis of test scores (or other indicators of ability), not to mention the paucity of knowledge about whether such performance gains have a payoff commensurate with the costs. The Job Performance Measurement/Enlistment Standards (JPM) Project was prompted by the need of the military policy community for a better grasp of the complicated linkages between entry characteristics, job performance, and costs.

The design of the JPM Project is best appreciated against the historical backdrop of public debate about the future prospects of the all-volunteer force. As we recounted in the Overview, the uncertainties introduced by the misnorming of the Armed Services Vocational Aptitude Battery (ASVAB) and the general dismay in Congress and the Department of Defense when it became clear that the resulting inflation of scores meant that, not 20 percent, but closer to 50 percent of those enlisted between 1976 and 1980 were in Category IV (percentile score range 10 to 30) created a good deal of doubt about the ASVAB, not to say skepticism about voluntary military service.

To combat this doubt about the DoD-wide selection test and its value in building a competent military force was going to require a concrete demonstration of that value. From its inception, the central premise of the JPM Project was that a good behavioral criterion measure was the necessary condition for demonstrating the predictive value of the ASVAB.

THE CONCEPTUAL FRAMEWORK

Phase I: Developing Performance Measures

The first—and in the early years, the most pressing—goal of the JPM Project was a retrospective examination of the ASVAB to determine if its value for predicting job performance was sufficient to support its continued use.

Given that the purpose of employment testing is to identify those who will be capable of successfully meeting the demands of the job or jobs in question, the testing enterprise should begin with a conceptual and operational definition of success. Grade-point average is an unusually pertinent measure of success for validating tests used to screen applicants for admission to colleges, universities, and professional schools. No equally satisfying measure is readily available in most employment situations, however.

Traditionally, the use of military entrance tests to determine enlistment eligibility has been justified with the criterion of success in technical training school. Training school outcomes are recorded in each enlistee's administrative file and, at least until the widespread introduction of pass/fail grading and self-paced instructional systems, they provided a reasonable measure of the relative success of trainees that could be related to scores on selection tests. Minimum entrance standards were typically set so that at least 90 percent of recruits could pass the regular training course (Eitelberg, 1988).

But, as Jenkins (1946, 1950) taught an earlier generation, performance in technical training is not the same as performance on the job. Although technical training is organized fairly narrowly by job specialty (e.g., jet engine mechanic, avionics specialist, machinist's mate), it provides only a partial introduction to a job—witness the amount of on-the-job training required for many military occupations. Moreover, the instructional emphasis in technical training is largely job knowledge, which does not translate directly into actual performance. And finally, success in technical training requires academic skills that may not be of great importance in the workplace. To the extent that training departs from actual job requirements, either in what it omits or in the additional skills or characteristics it demands, its value for validating selection and classification procedures is lessened.

In the context of the debate about voluntary military service and congressional reactions to the misnorming episode, the training criterion no longer offered a credible defense of the ASVAB as an effective instrument for selecting a competent military force. Hence, DoD's overriding concern became the development of criterion measures that were as faithful as possible to actual job performance.

The JPM Project is highly unusual in having applied classical test construction methods to the development of criterion measures. It is perhaps unique in having chosen the hands-on, job-sample test as the premier, or benchmark, measure. That decision could bring about a substantial change in the way empirical validation studies are conducted in the future.

Jobs Viewed as a Collection of Tasks

The project's commitment to building a measurement system that closely replicates what people do on the job ordained a preference in the research design for the concrete and observable over the abstract. This orientation influenced both the definition of what constitutes a job and what aspects of performance would be assessed.

The JPM Project defines a job as "a formally specified set of interrelated tasks performed by individuals in carrying out duty assignments" (internal memorandum, October 10, 1983). Each task in turn can be broken down into a series of steps to be executed, so that job performance consists of a prescribed set of observable acts or behaviors. This definition of a job corresponds with what the Army and Marine Corps call a military occupational specialty (MOS), and the other two Services, an Air Force specialty (AFS) and a Navy rating. It is important to note the words *formally specified* and *prescribed* in the definition above; a job in the military is what policy makers say it is. In the 1970s, the Air Force developed occupational surveys that have become the model for all the Services. Each Service now conducts periodic surveys of job incumbents, using a task-inventory approach, to define the content of each occupational specialty in terms of job tasks and to determine specific job requirements. Detailed specifications of job requirements are vetted by officials in each Service and then become a matter of doctrine.

In adopting the existing and highly articulated system of defining jobs in terms of their constituent tasks, the JPM Project availed itself of a rich body of data on the task content of particular jobs. These data are contained in the *Soldier's Manuals* (Army), the *Individual Training Standards* (Marine Corps), and the computerized task inventories (based on the Air Force Comprehensive Occupational Data Analysis Program, or CODAP, system), from which they are drawn. At the same time, conceptualizing a job as a set of tasks is a highly particularistic approach because the exact content of a task or the sequence of its component steps might vary, say, from one type of jet engine to another. The project designers recognized from the beginning that the very concreteness of tasks and steps raised the possibility that performance measurements might not be comparable across apparently similar jobs or even across subspecialties within a job.

Assessment of Job Proficiency

The JPM Project defines job performance as "those behaviors manifested while carrying out job tasks." Since the primary aim of the project is to provide performance-based empirical support for enlistment and classification decisions, individual (as opposed to group or unit) performance was made the object of measurement. To delimit further the universe of interest, a distinction was drawn between the *can-do* and *will-do* aspects of job performance, which translate roughly into *proficiency* and *motivation*. Job proficiency was chosen as the central criterion because the AFQT tests are measures of cognitive skills and have little or no relation to motivational factors.

In line with these decisions, the project has concentrated on the evaluation of the individual performance of enlisted personnel who are in their first tour of duty and who have had at least six months experience on the job. The primary indicator of job performance is individual proficiency on a set of tasks specific to a job—tasks that elicit "manifest, observable job behaviors" that can be scored dichotomously (go/no go, pass/fail) as a prescribed series of steps (internal memorandum, October 10, 1983).

The JPM Criterion Construct

In the field of personnel research, the use of work samples to predict job success is becoming increasingly popular. A *work sample* is an actual part of a job, chosen for its representativeness and importance to success on that job, that is transformed into a standardized test element of some sort so that the performance of all examinees can be scored on a common metric. Thus, for the job of secretary, a work-sample test might include a word processing task, a filing task, and a form completion task. For the job of police sergeant, it might involve detailing officers to particular sectors, checking completed police reports for accuracy, and resolving a dispute between two officers about the use of a two-way radio. The notion is that if one can identify an aspect of job performance that is crucial to success in that job, one cannot help but have a valid predictor. The validity is built into the predictor. Historically, the use of work samples has been assumed to satisfy the demands of the content-oriented validation model or design (Campbell et al., 1987; Landy, 1989). The strength of this approach is that it ensures that the construct of job performance is fairly represented in the predictor. If the work-sample units are chosen with care to represent the important aspects of the job, the validity should be axiomatic.

The JPM Project took this work-sample logic as a point of departure and then added a dramatic twist. Instead of developing work-sample measures for the predictor side of the equation, the project embarked on an ambitious attempt to develop work samples for the criterion side of the equation. The heterogeneity of jobs and work environments in the Services militates against the widespread use of work-sample tests for selection and classification, as does the fact that most recruits are without prior training or job experience. The Services, for example, do not enlist electricians or mechanics, by and large; they train people to become such. With over 600 jobs across the four Services and the need to screen approximately 1 million young people annually during the 1980s to select some 300,000 recruits to fill those jobs, there was substantial interest in the continued use of the ASVAB, perhaps revised or expanded, for selection and classification.

Given the desire to strengthen the credibility of the ASVAB, it followed that the best possible criterion should be chosen for inclusion in a validation study in order to give the ASVAB a reasonable opportunity to reveal its predictive value. For the same reasons that work samples are chosen as predictors, they are prime candidates for the criterion side of the equation. They bring with them an aura of self-evident validity because they consist of hands-on performance of actual job tasks or portions of tasks (change a tire, dismantle a claymore mine). They are as faithful to actual job performance as criterion measures can be, short of observing people in their daily work, and they also allow for standardization (albeit with difficulty, as Chapter 5 illustrates).

As the most direct indicator of the underlying construct of job performance, the hands-on performance test was given primacy in the project in terms of resource expenditures. It was also accorded scientific primacy. Project designers agreed that the hands-on test would be the benchmark measure, the standard against which other, less faithful representations of job performance would be judged.

Benchmarks and Surrogates

The hands-on test is an assessment procedure honored more in the breach than in the observance. Despite the inherent attractiveness of assessing actual performance in a controlled setting, the enormous developmental expense and the logistical difficulties in administering hands-on tests have meant that the methodology has been largely unrealized until now. The performance rating, despite its many and well-documented frailties, continues to be, by far, the most common criterion measure used to validate employment tests (Landy and Farr, 1983).

The expense and sheer difficulty of collecting hands-on data convinced the project designers of the need to develop a range of performance measures, one or a combination of which might turn out in the long run to be a viable substitute for the hands-on measures. All four Services were to develop hands-on measures for several jobs, and each Service agreed to take the lead in developing a particular type of surrogate measure for its jobs as well. For example, the Army developed paper-and-pencil job knowledge tests covering both the tasks to be tested hands on and additional tasks; the Air Force developed interview procedures; and the Navy developed simulations of its hands-on tasks. Most of the surrogate measures also reflect a task-based definition of jobs as the point of departure, but they differ from the hands-on tests in the fidelity with which they represent job performance.

Phase II: Linking Enlistment Standards to Job Performance

Assuming success with Phase I—the development of accurate, valid, and reliable measures of job performance, the second objective of the project was to link job performance to enlistment standards. The meaning of that linkage has evolved during the life of the project, however. Initially, to allay concerns about the quality of military recruits, the project designers focused on using the performance data in validation studies of the ASVAB. The validation effort would determine whether individual differences in ASVAB scores were correlated with individual differences in performance scores. The index of validity would indicate how closely the ranking of a group of people on job performance replicated their ranking on the predictor.

Strengthening the empirical basis of military selection by itself, however, would not resolve the policy concerns that prompted the project. As the current economic climate makes obvious, the quality of the enlisted force becomes at some point a question of resources, of weighing performance against costs. To contribute to this decision, the project would have to provide information that enables policy officials to make rational inferences from test scores to overall job competence. From this vantage point, the crucial question with regard to enlistment standards is not so much whether the ASVAB is a valid selection instrument, but how high the standards need to be to ensure that service personnel can do their assigned jobs competently. The hope was that the job performance data gathered in Phase I of the project would permit development in Phase II of models for setting quality standards that would enable DoD to estimate the minimum cost required to achieve alternative levels of performance and to evaluate the policy trade-offs.

The critical concept here is the relation of the *mental enlistment standard* (a combination of minimum test score and high school graduation status) to the distribution of expected job performance. If the Services were in a position to select from just the very high scorers on the AFQT—say, categories I and II, and if the correlation between the AFQT scores and job performance was reasonably strong, then one could expect that many, if not most, of those selected would turn out to be highly competent performers. But this would be neither socially acceptable nor economically feasible. In reality, a far wider range of scores must be included in the selection pool, and military planners cannot expect a preponderance of outstanding performers. They must anticipate a mix of performance based on selection from several predictor categories (I through IV). Each aptitude category adds an additional layer to the mix. Policy makers need to know what the effect will be on the accomplishment of each Service's mission if changes are made in enlistment standards—if the mix of recruits from each predictor category (I through IV) is altered in some particular manner. The extent to which such sophisticated projections can be made depends, to a great extent, on how closely enlistment standards (e.g., ASVAB scores) can be tied to on-the-job performance. The effort to develop the linkage between enlistment standards, performance across military jobs, and a variety of recruiting, training and other costs got under way in 1990. The dimensions of the problem are discussed in Chapter 9.

THE RESEARCH PLAN

The long-term goal of military planners is to have a DoD-wide program for collecting job performance data that can be related to recruit capabilities. With the hands-on test as its anchor in reality, the JPM Project sought to develop a comprehensive set of performance measures for a sample of military jobs so that it would be possible to evaluate the relative merits of the various types of measures. It was also hoped that the project would be able to identify one or a combination of measures that would be less expensive and easier to administer for an ongoing program of performance measurement than the hands-on test. The initial hands-on test data were also intended to be robust enough psychometrically to provide the data pool for testing the Phase II standard-setting models.

Selection of Occupations for Study

The project's emphasis on concrete, observable job behavior necessarily implied a focus on specific jobs and the development of proficiency measures that would reflect the performance requirements of a particular job. The Services used the following seven criteria, enumerated in the Second Annual Report to Congress on Joint-Service Efforts to Link Standards for Enlistment to On-the-Job Performance (Office of the Assistant Secretary of Defense—Manpower, Reserve Affairs, and Logistics, 1983), to select the occupational specialties for study:

IMPROVING JOB PERFORMANCE CRITERIA 63

1. The military specialties selected should be of critical importance.
2. There should be enough people assigned to the job to ensure adequate sample size.
3. The population of job incumbents should be sufficiently concentrated to allow data collection at a small number of military bases.
4. Important tasks of the job should be measurable.
5. Problems in the specialty (e.g., attrition) should be known and well documented.
6. The job should include enough minorities and (where applicable) women to permit evaluation of the impact the measurement procedures would have on these groups.
7. The set of jobs selected should be a reasonable cross-section of the major aptitude areas measured by the ASVAB (electronic, mechanical, administrative, and general aptitudes).

There was some overlap in the jobs selected for the project by the four Services, but each Service also selected a number of occupational specialties that best represented its special mission—for example, infantryman for the Marine Corps and air traffic controller for the Air Force. The jobs for which each Service agreed to develop performance measures are identified below.

Army

The Army selected the following nine military occupational specialties for study:

Infantryman
Cannon crewman
Tank crewman
Radio teletype operator
Medical specialist
Light wheel vehicle/power generation mechanic
Motor transport operator
Administrative specialist
Military police

As part of a larger study of job performance, called Project A, the Army developed criterion measures for an additional 10 occupations, but the critical hands-on measures were developed only for the 9 jobs listed above.

Navy

The Navy is developing hands-on performance measures for six ratings (jobs):

Machinist's mate
Radioman
Electronics technician
Electrician's mate
Fire control technician
Gas turbine technician, mechanical

In addition, for a special Joint-Service technology transfer demonstration, the Navy is adapting a package of performance measures developed by the Air Force to the corresponding Navy and Marine Corps job of aviation machinist's mate (jet engine). And in another demonstration of technology transfer, the Navy is recasting the test items developed for the machinist's mate and aviation machinist's mate ratings for a related Navy rating, gas turbine technician (mechanical).

Air Force

The following eight specialties were selected for the Air Force component of the project:

Jet engine mechanic (M)
Aerospace ground equipment mechanic (M)
Personnel specialist (A)
Information systems radio operator (A)
Air traffic control operator (G)
Aircrew life support specialist (G)
Precision measurement laboratory equipment specialist (E)
Avionic communications specialist (E)

The specialties are evenly divided among the four ASVAB aptitude area composites: In descending order, the first two specialties listed are predicted by the mechanical (M) composite; the third and fourth, by the administrative (A) composite; the fifth and sixth specialties by a general (G) composite and the final two by the electronic (E) composites.

Marine Corps

The Marine Corps focused on testing multiple specialties within occupational fields (functionally similar collections of specialties). Occupational fields were selected to be representative of the four Marine Corps aptitude composites. The infantry occupational field was tested to represent the general technical aptitude composite. Performance measures were developed for five infantry specialties:

Rifleman
Machinegunner
Mortarman
Assaultman
Infantry unit leader (a second-tour position)

In the spring of 1989, the Marines began the study of eight specialties in the motor transport and aircraft maintenance occupational fields (representing the mechanical maintenance aptitude composite). Data collection for the following specialties was completed in 1990:

Motor transport occupational field:
    Organizational automotive mechanic
    Intermediate automotive mechanic
    Vehicle recovery mechanic
    Motor transport maintenance chief (a second-tour position)

Aircraft maintenance occupational field:
    Helicopter mechanic, CH-46
    Helicopter mechanic, CH-53A/D
    Helicopter mechanic, U/AH-1
    Helicopter mechanic, CH-53E

Future plans call for similar data collection efforts of multiple specialties for the data communications maintenance and avionics occupational fields (representing the electronics repair aptitude composite) and the personnel administration and supply administration occupational fields (representing the clerical/administrative aptitude composite).

Types of Criterion Measures Developed

Hands-On Tests

Hands-on tests were developed for 28 occupational specialties. Each hands-on test consisted of a sample of about 15 tasks and took from 4 to 8 hours to administer. Task performance was evaluated by having the examinee actually do a particular instance of a real task or a very close replica of it. Each behavioral step in the performance of the task was scored either pass or fail by a trained observer. The number of steps in each task ranged from about 10 to 150.

The hands-on work-sample test involved observation of a job incumbent performing a sample of important, difficult, and/or frequently performed tasks in a controlled setting and with the appropriate equipment or tools.

For example, the testing of naval machinist's mates took place aboard ship in the engine room. One task required the sailor to perform casualty control procedures that would be put into action if an alarm signaled loss of pressure in the main engine lube oil pump. Examinees were graded as they went through the prescribed responses to the emergency—checking for proper operation of stand-by pumps, checking the appropriate gauges, meters, and valves to locate the source of the problem, taking corrective action if appropriate, and reporting the casualty to the appropriate supervisor. For any steps that were not observable, such as visual checks of a gauge or valve, examinees were instructed to touch the relevant piece of equipment and tell the test administrator what action was taken and what the examinee had determined (Chapter 5 includes additional details on how testing was conducted).

In many complicated jobs involving machinery, technical manuals specifying repair or maintenance procedures are used in day-to-day operations. Jet engine mechanics, for example, are required to work according to the manual. The potential for damage to expensive equipment or loss of life is simply too great to rely on memory. Part of the hands-on test in such jobs was the selection of the appropriate technical manual and identification of the relevant procedures for accomplishing the task at hand.

Certain kinds of tasks, particularly tasks that are primarily intellectual in character, do not lend themselves easily to hands-on tests. Ways were found, albeit with some loss of fidelity, to do so. One of the tasks for Marine Corps infantrymen, for example, assessed the subject's ability to move a platoon through enemy territory and respond to various impediments, such as artillery emplacements or passing convoys. In order to elicit the first-termer's understanding of small-unit tactical maneuvers, the Marine Corps used a TACWAR board, a large, three-dimensional model of a stretch of terrain. Such models are typically used in training or in preparation for military action. In this instance, the test administrator presented a scenario and the subject responded by moving chips representing an infantry platoon.

Walk-Through Performance Tests

The Air Force developed walk-through performance tests, a novel type of test that combines hands-on measures with interview procedures. Examinees actually perform some tasks; for others, they describe how they would do the task. The interview component was developed as a means of assessing those tasks for which hands-on tests would be too time-consuming or expensive or would entail too great a risk of injury or damage to equipment.

Like the straight hands-on procedure described above, the walk-through performance test is administered in a worklike setting, with the relevant equipment at hand. The interview tasks are administered as a structured questionnaire, and the examinee demonstrates proficiency on the task by way of oral responses and gestural demonstrations of how the steps in the task would be carried out. This is a more interactive procedure than the hands-on test, and the behaviors assessed are both less concrete and less observable.

Simulations

The Navy took the lead in developing performance tests that are detailed simulations of a real task. Two levels of fidelity to actual performance were attempted. The first, and more faithful, measure was administered through computer-based interactive video disks; for example, dials representing pressure gauges in a ship's engine room would respond with higher or lower pressure readings according to the actions of the examinee. The second simulation was a paper-and-pencil analogue that made liberal use of illustrations and pictures of actual equipment.

Job Knowledge Tests

The project also made use of the traditional multiple-choice test instrument to measure task proficiency in specific military jobs. The Army and the Marine Corps developed job knowledge tests for each job they studied, and the Air Force for half of the specialties. Some individual test items corresponded to a certain task or to a specific step within a task, and others related to more global aspects of the job that could not be assessed in the hands-on mode. Whatever the level of specificity, the items tended to ask about or portray perceptions, decisions, and actions that corresponded closely to behavioral operations. All of the tasks the two Services assessed in the hands-on mode were also covered in this format to permit comparisons of the two assessment procedures. For the sake of more extensive coverage of the job domain, additional tasks were included as well.

Ratings

Performance evaluations or ratings are the most common technique for assessing job performance, and as such, they were included among the surrogate performance measures studied in the project. The Army, the Navy, and the Air Force developed rating forms of one type or another to elicit the judgments of supervisors, peers (those who worked side-by-side with the subject), and the examinee. These included ratings of task-level and more global performance related to a specific job, task-level performance common to many jobs (in the military, even a cook or a musician must know how to use a weapon or protect against biological or chemical agents), dimensional ratings, and ratings of general performance and effectiveness (e.g., military bearing and leadership).

Two types of rating scales were experimented with, one calling for an absolute rating and the other for an indication of the standing of the subject relative to others. To make the rating process more concrete, the absolute rating scales were accompanied by behavioral illustrations of each anchor point.

Types of Predictors Assessed

In addition to studying the relation between various criterion measures and the ASVAB, the Services looked at a variety of other predictors as possible supplements to the ASVAB. These tests were intended to assess cognitive processing abilities not well addressed by the ASVAB, such as perceptual speed and spatial skills. The Army and the Navy developed computerized batteries of cognitive, perceptual, and psychomotor skills. The Army also developed predictors of *will-do* performance, based on biographical and interest inventories.

Development of Performance Measures

The specific procedures used to develop hands-on and other performance measures differed from Service to Service, but the project's emphasis on fidelity to actual job performance is evident in the common approach to defining the criterion domain. All the Services began the process of specifying the performance domain for a job by consulting task-inventory data (e.g., the Air Force CODAP system) and manuals (e.g., the Marine Corps *Individual Training Standards*) that provide detailed information about the tasks within an occupational specialty. These sources provided the substance for job analyses and, in some cases, the percentage of incumbents performing each task, the frequency of task performance, and the relative amount of time spent on each task. In addition to detailed information on the tasks or job responsibilities for each job, the Marine Corps had lists of the specific skills or knowledge required by the tasks, so that its table of specifications for each job was composed of both task and behavioral requirements. This table then became the blueprint for constructing the performance tests.

All the Services used subject matter experts to help identify and select tasks and to review test content. The experts were usually noncommissioned officers who knew the job at firsthand and had supervised the work of entry-level job incumbents. All the Services also used purposive or judgment-based methods of sampling from the universe of possible tasks to select those to be turned into hands-on, interview, and written test items. The Navy agreed to conduct a side experiment to study the feasibility of selecting tasks using stratified random sampling techniques, but the Services generally (and from the point of view of advancing the field, unfortunately) shied away from random sampling techniques for fear the resulting performance tests would seem arbitrary to the military community (sampling issues are discussed in Chapters 4 and 7).

The process of turning tasks into hands-on test items involved breaking down each task into its subcomponents, or steps, and identifying the associated equipment, manuals, and procedures required to perform the steps. The steps were then translated into scorable units the test administrator could check off as either *go* or *no go* as the examinee performed the task. Not infrequently, tasks were too long to be included in full and the test development staff had to select a coherent segment for the test. Chapter 4 provides more detail on how the hands-on tests were developed.

A closer look at how one Service developed its hands-on tests might be useful. The Army team designed particularly elaborate task-selection procedures (see Figure 3-1). The process began with an examination of the *Soldier's Manual* for each occupational specialty. These manuals, which contain task lists and task descriptions that represent Army doctrine on the content of the job, determine the content of technical training. Supplementary task descriptions were drawn from the Army Occupational Survey Program (AOSP), a job-task inventory system based on questionnaires circulated to job incumbents. About 800 tasks were designated for each job under study.

The central development activity consisted of refining and narrowing the task domain until only a sample of tasks remained to represent the job. A panel of three subject matter experts reviewed the initial list of tasks put together by the scientific staff and deleted any tasks not usually performed by first-term personnel or no longer current because of changes in doctrine or equipment. This culling reduced the number of tasks by about half. The scientific staff further reduced the number of tasks under consideration by removing tasks that were performed infrequently or in restricted-duty positions. The remaining 150 tasks per job were considered candidates for selection and were subject to further analysis. A total of 15 subject matter experts from the appropriate proponent school[1] were asked to rank the 150 tasks for a particular job on the basis of their importance in a European theater combat situation; they were also asked to group the tasks into 8 to 12 clusters based on similarity of procedures or principles. As a basis for

---

[1] Proponent schools provide technical training for each military occupational specialty. They are called *proponent* because they determine the *doctrine* for the specialty, i.e., the content of the job and how the job is to be used in carrying out the overall mission of the Army.

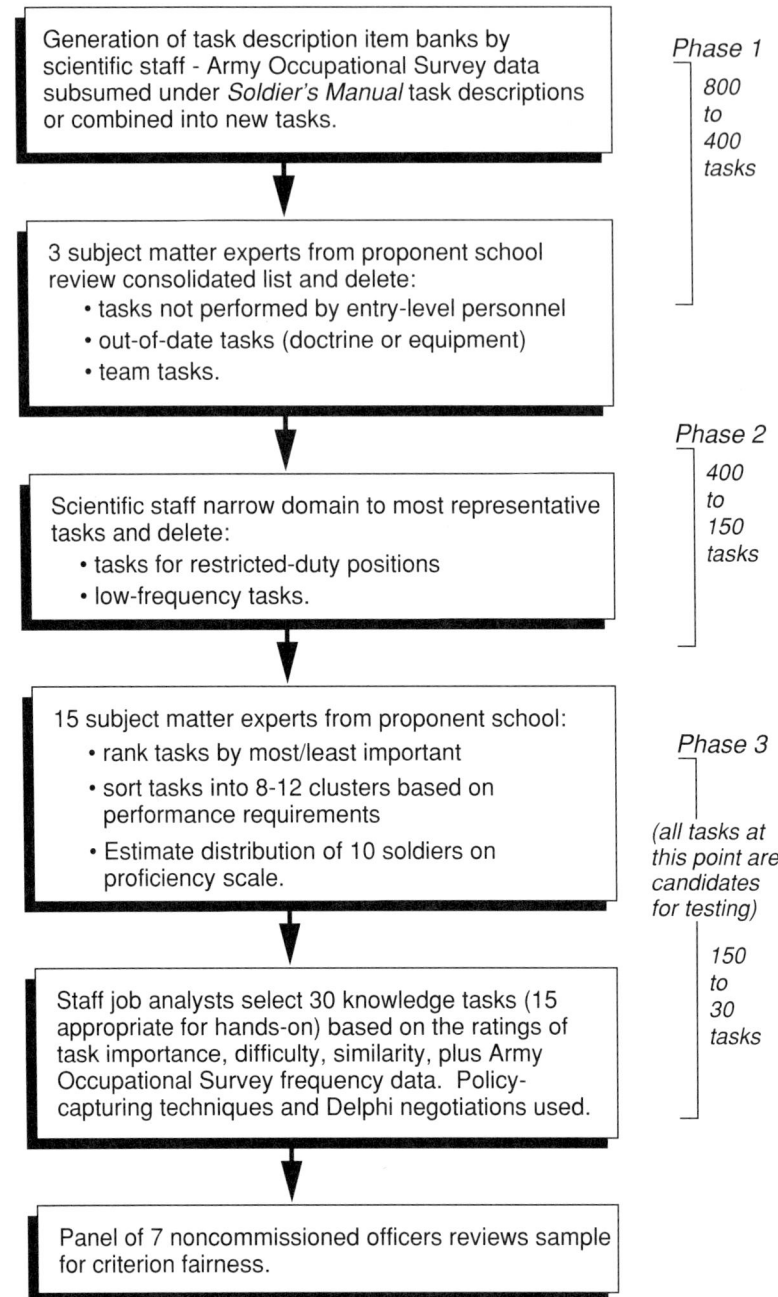

FIGURE 3-1 Army task selection procedures.

ascribing a level of difficulty to each task, they were also asked to estimate how many in a typical group of 10 soldiers could do the task and with what frequency (the five possible answers ranged from "all of the time" to "never").

Informed by these expert judgments as to the importance, similarity, and difficulty of the tasks, project scientists selected 30 tasks to represent each job, 15 of which were to be suitable for hands-on testing. All 30 tasks were to be incorporated into the written job knowledge tests. The group was not given strict decision rules to follow, but policy-capturing techniques were used to introduce consistency into each scientist's selections, and the scientists were brought to consensus on the final list of 30 tasks through a process of Delphi negotiations. A review panel of seven noncommissioned officers, including minorities and women, reviewed this set of tasks for fairness. (In the second wave of test development, project scientists worked with military experts to make the final task selection and the fairness review become part of the overall task selection process.) The prototype performance measures were then field tested, after which they were sent to the commander of the appropriate proponent school for approval.

SIZE OF THE RESEARCH EFFORT

This overview of the JPM Project concludes with a brief discussion of the human and monetary resources that were expended on developing the criterion measures and collecting data. Listed below are the dollar amounts expended for the project between fiscal 1983 and 1989, with budget projections through fiscal 1991:

1983	$3.2 million
1984	3.8 million
1985	4.8 million
1986	4.2 million
1987	3.7 million
1988	4.4 million
1989	3.8 million
1990	(4.1) million
1991	(4.3) million

The four Services and the Office of the Secretary of Defense (OSD) reported expenditures through September 1989 totaling almost $28 million, about half of which was devoted to the Army's research. By the time the Marine Corps and Navy finish their data collection in 1992, it is anticipated that an additional $8 million will have been spent by all Services and OSD.

It is not possible to estimate the human resources devoted to the JPM Project with any precision. The largest class of participants, of course, was the examinees. In addition to 1,369 soldiers who participated in field tests of the criterion measures, the Army gathered the full complement of criterion data from 5,200 soldiers in 9 occupational specialties at 14 sites in the United States and Europe. Another 4,000 subjects provided data on a more limited set of measures (excluding the hands-on tests).[2] In its initial data collection, the Marine Corps tested over 2,500 subjects in 5 specialties in the infantry occupational field at Camps Lejeune and Pendleton. Of the 1,200 riflemen tested, 200 were retested with alternate forms of the performance tests to determine the reliability of the measures. A second set of performance measures was administered to approximately 1,800 helicopter and ground automotive mechanics in 1990. Test development is in progress for several electronics specialties (e.g., ground radio repairman and avionics technician) with data collection scheduled for 1992. And plans are under way to develop measures for administrative jobs (e.g., personnel clerk and supply clerk). The third and fourth rounds of testing are expected to add 1,600 and 2,000 subjects, respectively, to the Marine Corps data base. For the eight Air Force specialties investigated, 1,493 airmen took the hands-on and interview procedures at 70 bases. Performance rating forms were also completed by each examinee and by his or her supervisor. Over 3,400 additional rating forms were completed by peers of the examinees. Faced with even more complicated logistics, the Navy tested 184 first-term machinist's mates assigned to either the engine room or the generator room aboard 25 1052-class frigates. The radioman sample consisted of 257 first-term personnel, 185 of them male and 75 female. Of these, 131 were ship based and 126 (including most of the women) were land based.

These are but partial numbers, since the Navy and Marine Corps are still involved in data collection. In addition to the service personnel who were test subjects, many hundreds of research scientists, test administrators, and base personnel who provided logistical support played a part in the JPM Project. The level of effort is not likely to be duplicated by any other institution, or indeed by the military in the foreseeable future.

---

[2] In addition, the Army conducted a longitudinal validation during which 49,397 soldiers were tested on predictor measures (1986-1987), 34,305 on end-of-training tests (1986-1987), and 11,268 on first-tour performance measures (1988-1989).

4

The Development of Job Performance Measures

Most studies that attempt to link applicant characteristics to job success assume a perfectly reliable and valid job performance criterion (e.g., supervisory ratings) and seek predictors of that criterion (e.g., ability tests, educational attainment). The JPM Project made no such assumption. Rather, it focused on the construction of criterion measures that capture job performance in order to validate already available predictors and to justify selective entrance standards. The central goal was to design and develop a measure of job performance with high fidelity to the actions performed on the job for a sample of military jobs. This measure was expected to "look like" the job to job incumbents, supervisors, and policy makers; to represent the important aspects of the job; and to exclude extraneous requirements that might inflate or depress the true relation between the ASVAB and the criterion—military job performance.

It was an ambitious undertaking, with lessons to be learned at every step of the way. Because so few precursors existed in the published literature, the Service research teams had to work out the nuts and bolts of constructing hands-on performance measures of sufficient psychometric robustness for the intended use. In this chapter, we draw on the methods used by the Services to illustrate the difficulties inherent in any serious attempt at performance measurement in employment or educational settings.

JOB PERFORMANCE AS A CONSTRUCT

The measurement of job performance might appear to be relatively straightforward, particularly for military jobs, which have specified training requirements and on-the-job responsibilities. The apparent simplicity, however, is misleading. Job performance is not something that can be readily pointed to or simply counted. Except for the most highly routinized jobs, in which the measurement of a person's performance is almost a by-product of doing the job, what we call job performance for operational purposes is an abstraction from objective reality—its functional definition is a product of constructions or concepts developed for particular purposes, such as personnel selection and classification, training, performance-based compensation decisions, or test validation.

There are a number of obvious and not-so-obvious hazards that confront the analyst who would construct a definition of job performance for any given occupation. Even if it were possible to follow a sample of job incumbents for several weeks, videotaping each worker's every action, and then testing the consequences of each action (e.g., did the valve leak; did the wires used to secure screws come loose after X hours of jet engine vibration), the observations would not automatically suggest a useful concept of the job nor necessarily produce an adequate measurement of job performance. Some critical job tasks may be performed only very occasionally and might easily elude the observer. Or they may occur only in crisis situations and thus defy easy interpretation. Some critical job tasks may be difficult to observe directly—complex troubleshooting tasks, for example, are performed largely within the mind. Furthermore, the outcomes of an individual's task performance may depend on a wide variety of environmental factors, such as the state of repair of the equipment used, the actions of coworkers, or, as every sales representative and military recruiter knows, the state of the economy. Even if one had a wealth of observational data, however, this would not resolve the difficult conceptual issues regarding what aspects of job performance to measure, how each aspect should be measured, or how the measures should be combined.

In other words, a job is not a fact of nature to be stumbled upon and classified. In order to speak about a job, it is necessary to construct a conception of the job. In order to assess job performance, it is necessary to translate that conception into measurable bits. And in order to evaluate the quality of job performance measurements, it is necessary to demonstrate the validity of construct interpretations—that is, to defend the appropriateness of the construct for the purpose at hand and to show that an incumbent's performance on the measure is representative of performance on the job.

The purpose of this chapter is to describe the steps involved in the development of job performance measures, and in particular the hands-on job sample measures that characterize the JPM Project. We describe methods used by the Services to: (a) define the universe of job tasks and their performances, (b) reduce that universe to a manageable number and kind of tasks, and (c) create performance measures based on task samples.

STEPS IN DEVELOPING JOB PERFORMANCE MEASURES

The design and development of a job performance measure begins with the specification of job content and ends with the development of test items from a reduced set of tasks/actions to be included in the performance measure (Guion, 1979; Laabs and Baker, 1989). More specifically, design and development of job performance measures follow a process of progressive refinement of the job construct, involving:

(1) *Definition of the Job Content Universe*. This initial examination of a job involves the enumeration and description of all tasks that comprise the job, as well as the corresponding acts (behaviors) needed to carry them out (Guion, 1977).

(2) *Definition of the Job Content Domain*. The job content universe is all inclusive. It is likely to contain redundant or overlapping tasks, tasks rapidly being made obsolete by technological change or job restructuring, and tasks performed in only a few locations. At this stage, the total universe is distilled to a smaller set of tasks that comprise the "essential" job.

(3) *Specification of the Domain of Testable Tasks*. Further refinement of the domain of interest is made for reasons relating to testing. Financial constraints, for example, might call for the elimination of tasks requiring the use of expensive equipment and for which no simulators are available. Safety considerations might preclude some tasks.

(4) *Development of Performance Measures*. At this point, a sample of job-tasks that are amenable to testing are translated into test items.

This sequence provides a framework for describing and evaluating the approaches and variations in approaches taken by the Services in developing performance assessments.

THE JOB CONTENT UNIVERSE

A job may be described by a set of tasks and the behavior needed to perform them, including the knowledge and skills underlying that behavior. These tasks and behaviors in the job content universe are enumerated through a job analysis.

Four approaches have been used to analyze jobs. One method, *task analysis*, was the central component of the JPM job analyses. The specifics of the task analysis varied from one Service to another because of differences in task definition, in the level of detail at which tasks were described, and in the extent to which only observable or both observable and cognitive behavior was accounted for. The second method, *trait analysis*, identifies the human abilities necessary to successfully complete the tasks on the job. The third method, *task-by-trait* analysis, embodies both of these (Guion, 1975; Wigdor and Green, 1986). The fourth approach, *cognitive task analysis*, goes beyond specifying abstract traits to identify the cognitive components involved in successfully performing a task in a conceptual and procedural system. We describe these methods and how the Services use them in the sections that follow.

Task Analysis

A task is commonly defined as a well-circumscribed unit of goal-directed job activity with a discernable beginning and end. It is generally performed within a short period of time, but it may be interrupted and it may share time with other tasks. Some tasks may be performed by individuals, others by a team.

The beginning of a task is signaled by a cue or stimulus that tells a person to perform the task. These cues may be embedded in training material or a written procedure, specified by a supervisor, triggered by the completion of a preceding task, or called for by some displayed item of information such as a warning light. The task is completed when the goal is reached.

Task analysis is carried out by analysts who may observe the job, perform some of the tasks, interview job incumbents and supervisors, collect job performance information from incumbents and supervisors by questionnaire, or do some combination of these (Landy, 1989). The most common method is to observe the job and collect data by taking notes or filling out a checklist or questionnaire regarding tasks that appear important. A second method is to collect information in interviews or with questionnaires from large numbers of incumbents and supervisors.

The analysis results in a written record comprised of descriptive statements enumerating the behaviors exhibited in the performance of the job tasks. These descriptive statements may take the form of a simple sentence consisting of a *person* who performs a job (e.g., rifleman), an *action verb* (e.g., lifts, aims, pulls), and an *object* (e.g., the weapon, the trigger). The analysis also identifies the starting conditions, the actions required to reach the task goal, the goal itself, and each person by job title or name involved in performing the task (e.g., supervisor, operator, technician).

These statements are often translated into tabular form. Each task is entered in a row divided into successive subject-verb-object columns. Additional columns may be used to enter enabling attributes and conditions and other information related to tasks, such as task importance as judged by subject matter experts. Sometimes tasks are subdivided into steps, each step describing the detailed actions necessary to achieve the task's goal.

The Marine Corps' use of task analysis illustrates one approach taken in the JPM Project. The Marine Corps found its task analysis ready-made in training doctrine (Mayberry, 1987). Its individual training standards (ITS) defined the tasks that were required of each Marine in a job and the level of competence to which the tasks were to be performed. The ITS also defines the pay grade level associated with the job. More specifically, the ITS divides a job (e.g., basic infantry) into mini jobs called duty areas (e.g., grenade launcher), which, in turn, are divided into tasks (e.g., inspect grenade launcher; maintain launcher; zero grenade launcher; engage targets; engage targets with limited visibility). The process of performing a task, for example, engage target, is specified by a set of subtasks, as are the performance standards. The ITS, then, provides the definitive statement of the tasks that comprise each and every Marine Corps job (Figure 4-1).

Task: Engage target with grenade launcher.
Administrative instructions: This ITS is identical to the actual task. Targets may be constructed using locally available material. All students at Infantry Training School will perform this ITS. The ITS must be performed quarterly by grenadiers in conjunction with zeroing the weapon.
Training objective:
  Behavior: Engage target with grenade launcher.
  Conditions: The Marine being evaluated is provided: M203 grenade launcher and seven rounds of 40mm HE DP or practice ammunition on a live-fire range.
  Standard: Obtain hits on three of the following four targets:

• From a kneeling position, place a round through a window (.75 meters wide by 1 meter high) at a range of 90-100 meters.
• From a fighting position, hit the front of a bunker at a range of 135-150 meters.
• From a prone position, hit within 5 meters of targets in an open emplacement at a range of 275-300 meters.
• From a prone position, hit within 5 meters of targets in the open at a range of 325-350 meters.

  Training steps:
  • Set rear sight.
  • Establish position.
  • Aim.
  • Fire round, sense the impact of the grenade, and make sight adjustment.
  • Take immediate action, if necessary.

FIGURE 4-1 Individual training standards for one task of the M203 grenade launcher duty area. SOURCE: Mayberry (1987:16).

The ITS, however, provides only limited information about the behaviors required to carry out a job. To complete the task analysis, the Marine Corps researchers identified the major activities relevant to each of the subtasks. The five tasks in the duty area called grenade launcher, for example, were broken down into 12 subtasks, which among them included 19 behavioral elements (Figure 4-2). These behavioral elements (*verbs* in a task description) were themselves further defined by the steps required to carry them out (Figure 4-3). Taken together, then, the tasks and subtasks defined by the ITS and their behavioral elements and steps defined by a detailed task analysis constituted the job content universe for each of the Marine Corps jobs.

While no other Service has *Individual Training Standards*, they all have elaborate task inventory systems. The Air Force, for example, used its Comprehensive Occupational Data Analysis Program, CODAP (Christal, 1974) to define a job content universe for developing performance measures. CODAP is a collection of data management programs that assemble, quantify, organize, and summarize information obtained from job analyses. Task inventories for each Air Force specialty have been compiled (and regularly updated) since the 1970s by job analysts who observed people at work, actually performed parts of the job themselves, and interviewed job incumbents and supervisors. From this collection of information, a questionnaire was developed for each job specialty to collect specific background and task performance information from job incumbents and supervisors.

The questionnaire for jet engine mechanics, for example, consists of no fewer than 587 questions; the first 28 address background information, and the remaining 559 address task performance information (Table 4-1). The questionnaire data are entered into CODAP periodically; information can be obtained on which tasks are performed in what amount of time by whom (incumbent, supervisor), at which work station, and on what aircraft. In this way, the job of jet engine mechanic is described exhaustively.

Trait Analysis and Task-by-Trait Analysis

Trait analysis is predicated on the notion that a great deal could be learned about a job by knowing what personal attributes—abilities, traits, and skills—enable an incumbent to successfully perform that job. In early applications of trait analysis, expert judgments about underlying abilities were translated into tests used in employee selection. Shortly after the end of World War II, trait analysis was abandoned in favor of the less direct, yet seemingly more empirical, criterion-related validity analysis. Criterion-related validity analysis attempted to predict job performance by "blind empiricism": analysts sought a set of ability tests that significantly discriminated between the performance of job experts and job novices. This approach led to a proliferation of new tests but did little to increase understanding of the underlying behavioral foundation of job performance.

THE DEVELOPMENT OF JOB PERFORMANCE MEASURES

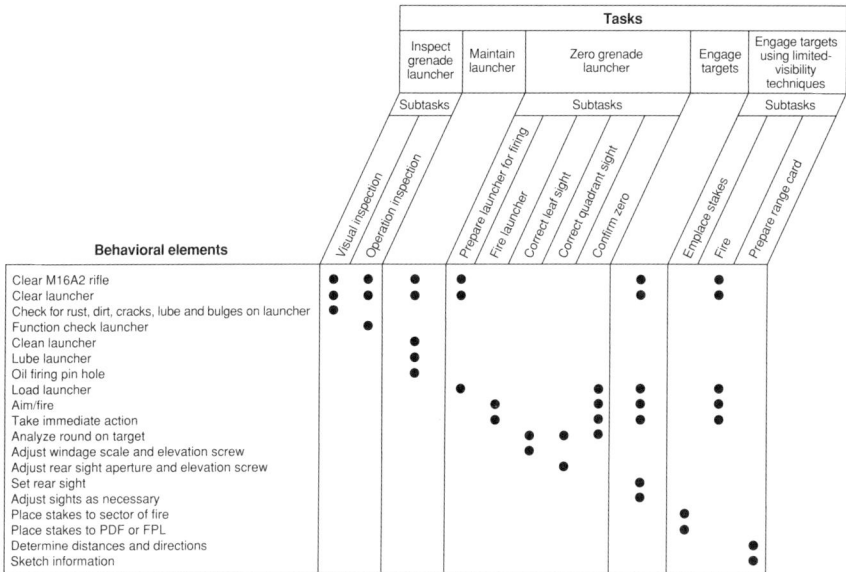

FIGURE 4-2 Behavioral element by task matrix for M203 grenade launcher duty area. SOURCE: Mayberry (1987:18).

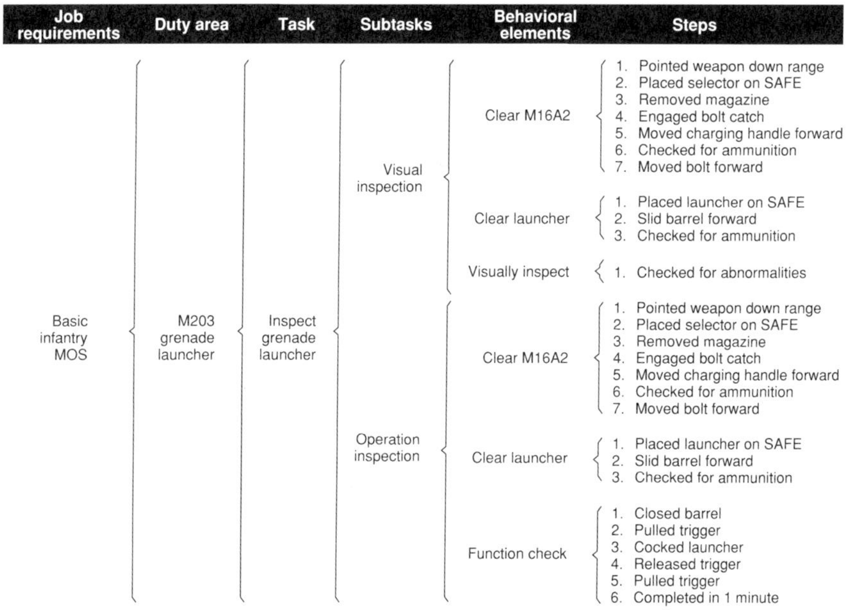

FIGURE 4-3 Hierarchical delineation for one task of M203 grenade launcher duty area. SOURCE: Mayberry (1987:12).

TABLE 4-1 Jet Engine Mechanic Job Inventory: Selected Items

Background Information
9. How do you find your job (Extremely dull ... Extremely interesting)?
21. Indicate the function which best describes where you work in your present job. Choose only one response (Accessory Repair, Afterburner Shop, ..., Balance Shop, ..., Flow Room)
26. Indicate any test equipment or special tools you use in your present job (I do not, ..., Bearing Cleaners, ..., Carbon Seal Testers, ..., Freon Testers, ..., Variable Vane Pumps, ..., "Yellow Box" Testers)

Task Information: Check Tasks Performed and Fill in Time Spent When Requested

A. Organizing and Planning
   1. Assign personnel to duty positions
  21. Plan work assignments

B. Directing and Implementing
  26. Advise maintenance officers on engine maintenance activities
  55. Supervise Apprentice Turboprop Propulsion Mechanics
  62. Write correspondence

C. Inspecting and Evaluating
  63. Analyze workload requirements
  70. Evaluate maintenance management information and control systems

D. Training
   86. Administer tests
  100. Evaluate OJT trainees

E. Preparing and Maintaining Forms, Records, and Reports
  109. Cut stencils
  116. Maintain engine master roster listings

F. Performing Quality Control Functions
  145. Inspect areas for foreign object damage matter
  149. Observe in-process maintenance

G. Performing Flightline Engine Maintenance Functions
  158. Adjust gearbox oil pressure
  163. Compute engine thrust or efficiency on trim pads
  186. Remove or install engines in aircraft

H. Performing In-Shop Engine Maintenance Functions
  203. Inspect engine oil seals
  229. Prepare engines for shipment
  247. Remove or install turbine rotors

I. Performing Balance Shop Functions
  249. Assemble compressor units
  255. Measure blade tip radii

SOURCE: U.S. Air Force (1980).

Today, pure trait analysis is rarely used. Rather, trait analysis is used in combination with task analysis in one of two ways: (a) generic task-by-trait analysis and (b) local task-by-trait analysis.

Generic Task-by-Trait Analysis

The generic approach assumes that any task can be decomposed into a parsimonious set of human abilities. Each task is analyzed by job analysts or subject matter experts who attempt to link task performance with underlying traits or abilities. A job, then, would be described by the smallest set of human abilities that underlie the performance of its constituent tasks. Conceptually, generic attribute analysis results in a profile of necessary and desirable attributes needed to perform the job successfully. An early example is Lipmann's (1916) psychograph, the first formal and widely used job analysis instrument. It contained 148 questions related to human traits necessary for success in any of 121 occupations. Thus, for example, the job of quiller (a job in a cotton mill that dealt with keeping yarn supplied and knitting machines running smoothly) was thought to require a particular pattern of mental abilities (Figure 4-4). Those abilities were posited after observation of the job by a trained observer, who then rated the job on each of the 148 traits using a 5-point scale of importance from "negligible" to "utmost" importance (Viteles, 1932).

In recent years, Fleishman's research has carried on the task-by-trait line of analysis. Called the ability requirements approach, the Fleishman taxonomy has been developed in both laboratory and field settings and has been revised and refined over 30 years (Fleishman, 1975; Fleishman and Quaintance, 1984). The objective of the work has been to define a parsimonious set of ability factors in psychomotor, physical, cognitive and perceptual domains, then to develop a rating scale methodology by means of which the ability requirements of tasks could be described as a basis for classifying these tasks. The Fleishman taxonomy currently consists of some 52 abilities; Table 4-2 shows a selection of general abilities, each accompanied by three definitional anchors representing levels of that ability. Subject matter experts and job analysts can compare the ability requirements of the job they are studying to the definitional anchors.

In practice, task analysis usually precedes trait analysis. Critical tasks or broader task groups are identified so that the job analyst can then apply trait analysis either to all tasks or only a subset of the most important of them. The human abilities are then collapsed across tasks to obtain a final, parsimonious profile of the abilities required by the job. Thus, when completed, the analysis provides a picture of the job from both the task and trait perspectives.

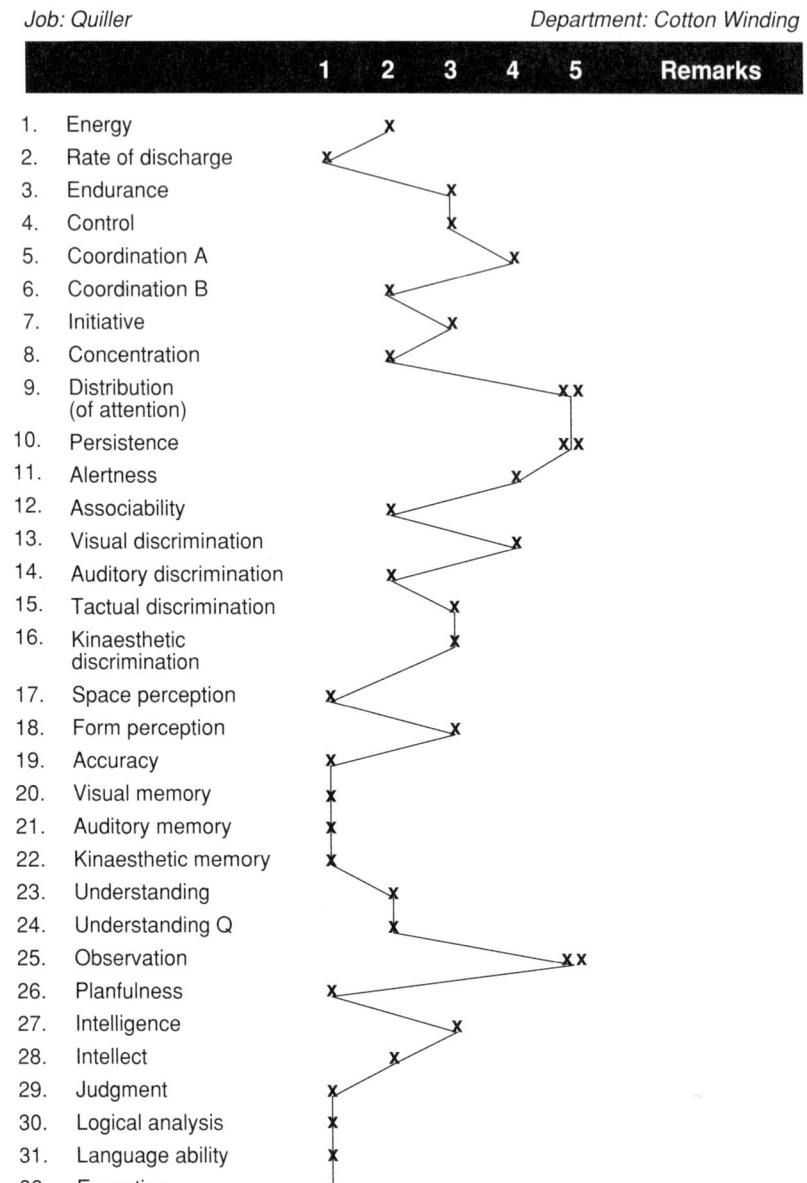

FIGURE 4-4 An early example of job analysis. SOURCE: Viteles (1932:153).

TABLE 4-2 Ability Requirement Scales: Tasks Representing Different Ability Categories

1. Written Comprehension
    Understand an instruction book on repairing a missile guidance system.
    Understand an apartment lease.
    Read a road map.

2. Problem Sensitivity
    Recognize an illness at an early stage of a disease when there are only a few symptoms.
    Recognize from the mood of prisoners that a riot is likely to occur.
    Recognize that an unplugged lamp won't work.

3. Speed of Closure
    Interpret the patterns on the weather radar to decide if the weather is changing.
    Find five camouflaged birds in a picture.
    While listening to the radio, recognize and start to hum an old song after hearing only the first few lines.

4. Visualization
    Anticipate your opponent's as well as your own future moves in a chess game.
    Know how to cut and fold a piece of paper to make a cube.
    Imagine how to put paper in the typewriter so the letterhead comes out at the top.

5. Reaction Time
    Hit back the ball which has been slammed at you in a ping-pong game.
    Duck to miss being hit by a snowball thrown from across the street.
    Start to apply brakes on your car 1 second after the light turns red.

6. Finger Dexterity
    Play a classical flamenco piece on the guitar.
    Untie a knot in a long-awaited package.
    Put coins in a parking meter.

7. Time Sharing
    As air traffic controller, monitor a radar scope to keep track of all inbound and outbound planes during a period of heavy, congested traffic.
    Monitor several teletypes at the same time in a newsroom.
    Watch street signs and road while driving 30 miles per hour.

8. Stamina
    Bicycle 20 miles to work.
    Mow a small yard.
    Walk around the block.

9. Depth Perception
    Thread a needle.
    Operate a construction crane.
    Judge which of two distant buildings is closer.

10. Sound Localization
    Locate someone calling your name in the midst of crowd.
    Find a ringing telephone in an unfamiliar apartment.
    Take legal dictation.

SOURCE: Fleishman and Quaintance (1984:Appendix C).

Local Task-by-Trait Analysis

Rather than using a predetermined set of human abilities such as the Fleishman taxonomy, job analysts may develop a list or taxonomy for the particular job at hand. Such an analysis might be created through discussions with subject matter experts or by combining attributes from other ability lists that seem to bear on the current analysis. Examples of local trait-by-task analysis can be found in the JPM Project. In their analysis of jobs, the Army research team developed a list of attributes considered important to job performance (Figure 4-5). This list is actually a combination of attribute labels from several distinct taxonomies, including Fleishman's. In part, the Army's list reflects the broader nature of the Army's research, which was committed to exploring alternative predictors of service success and, as a result, had an interest in predictor as well as criterion development. In addition, the list reflects the Army's interest not only in the attributes that related to the can-do aspect of performance (i.e., possession of requisite knowledge, skills, and abilities) but also in the will-do aspect (i.e., possession of attitudinal, affective, motivational, and habitual personal attributes).

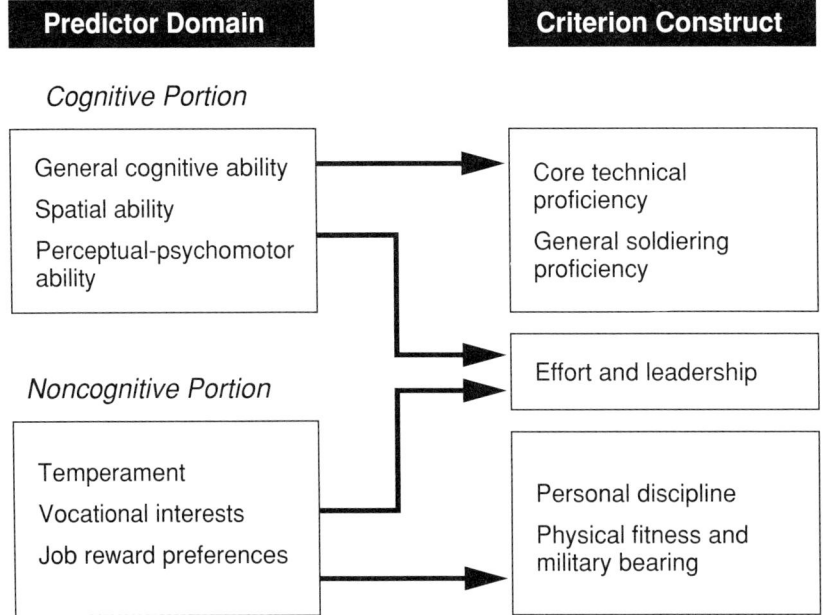

FIGURE 4-5 Local taxonomy for attribute analyses.

Cognitive Task Analysis

An emerging technology, too new to be employed in the JPM Project, is a modern version of task-by-trait analysis called cognitive task analysis (Glaser et al., Vol. II; Lesgold et al., 1990). Like task analysis, cognitive task analysis segments jobs into tasks; like trait analysis, it examines the human abilities underlying performance. Where it differs from the traditional task-by-trait analysis is that the giant leap from observed behavior to psychological traits/abilities underlying job performance is replaced by a careful analysis and empirical testing of the procedural and contextual knowledge used by an individual in performing job tasks.

Cognitive task analysis concentrates on both observable performance and on the individual's mental representation of the task. Specifically, it leads to a description of the knowledge an individual possesses about a task and the rules the individual uses in applying that knowledge to performing the task. For purposes of analysis, knowledge is divided into two general categories: procedural knowledge—the content of the individual's technical skills—and contextual/background knowledge used in applying skills to task performance.

Procedural knowledge is composed of the individual's mental representation of (1) the goals and subgoals of the task, (2) the procedures for performing the task, and (3) the rules followed in selecting and applying procedures to the achievement of task goals and subgoals. Contextual/background knowledge is defined, in part, by the depth of the individual's understanding of the content of the task—whether the individual has an explicit or implicit representation of the task's goal structure, whether the individual knows the basic principles and theories—and the sophistication of mental models and metaphors that have been developed to guide task performance.

Research by Glaser et al. and Lesgold et al. suggests significant differences in the ways novices and experts represent a task. These differences are characterized by variations in depth of knowledge, familiarity with task goals and content area principles, and level of goal orientation in problem solving. According to Glaser et al. (Vol. II:7):

> In particular, we know that the knowledge of experts is highly procedural. Facts, routines, and job concepts are bound by rules for their application, and to conditions under which this knowledge is useful. . . . The functional knowledge of experts is related strongly to their knowledge of the goal structure of a problem. Experts and novices may be equally competent at recalling small specific items of domain-related information, but proficient people are much better at relating these events in cause-and-effect sequences that reflect the goal structures of task performance and problem solution.

The primary purposes of distinguishing between the mental representations of experts and novices are: (1) to define effective performance, (2) to design training programs targeted to instilling in novices the knowledge representations of experts, and (3) to develop computer-based expert systems that will function effectively as advisers to both novices and experts. With advances in technology, a greater proportion of job tasks are relying on higher cognitive processes rather than on rote learning of procedures—that is, lower-level jobs are being replaced by automation. These changes suggest that assessing the cognitive processes of an individual is becoming a more important part of specifying what is meant by effective task performance. As a result, cognitive task analysis is likely to play a significant role in future research on job analysis.

Current procedures for performing cognitive task analysis are time-consuming and expensive. Subject matter experts cannot do cognitive task analyses of their own mental processing because much of their expertise is automatic. For the most part, the analysis process is conducted by "knowledge engineers," and their standard method is to have the expert critique the performance of a novice—iterative critiques lead to a refined understanding on the part of the knowledge engineer. A need for the future is to develop a clear set of rules and practices for cognitive task analysis—at the present time it is more of an art than a science.

Glaser et al. (Vol. II) undertook a cognitive task analysis of expert and novice electronics technicians performing an avionics troubleshooting task. One of their goals was to create a task analysis that directly reflected experts' views of which cognitive activities were critical to effective troubleshooting. Luckily they found one subject matter expert who had extensive experience in observing novice performance. He was able to point out (p. 16):

> It was not a big chore to specify all of the steps that an expert would take as well as all of the steps that any novice was at all likely to take in solving even very complex troubleshooting problems. That is, even when the task was to find the source of a failure in a test station that contained perhaps 40 feet . . . of printed circuit boards, cables, and connectors, various specific aspects of the job situation constrained the task sufficiently that the effective problem space could be mapped out.

In the end, between 55 and 60 key decision points could be identified in the troubleshooting task. The research team constructed 45 questions that could be asked of the job incumbent as he or she performed the task. The responses to these questions were used to map out the conceptual and procedural knowledge used to complete the task (Figure 4-6). In this way, the incumbent's plan for finding the fault in the circuit was made explicit. The

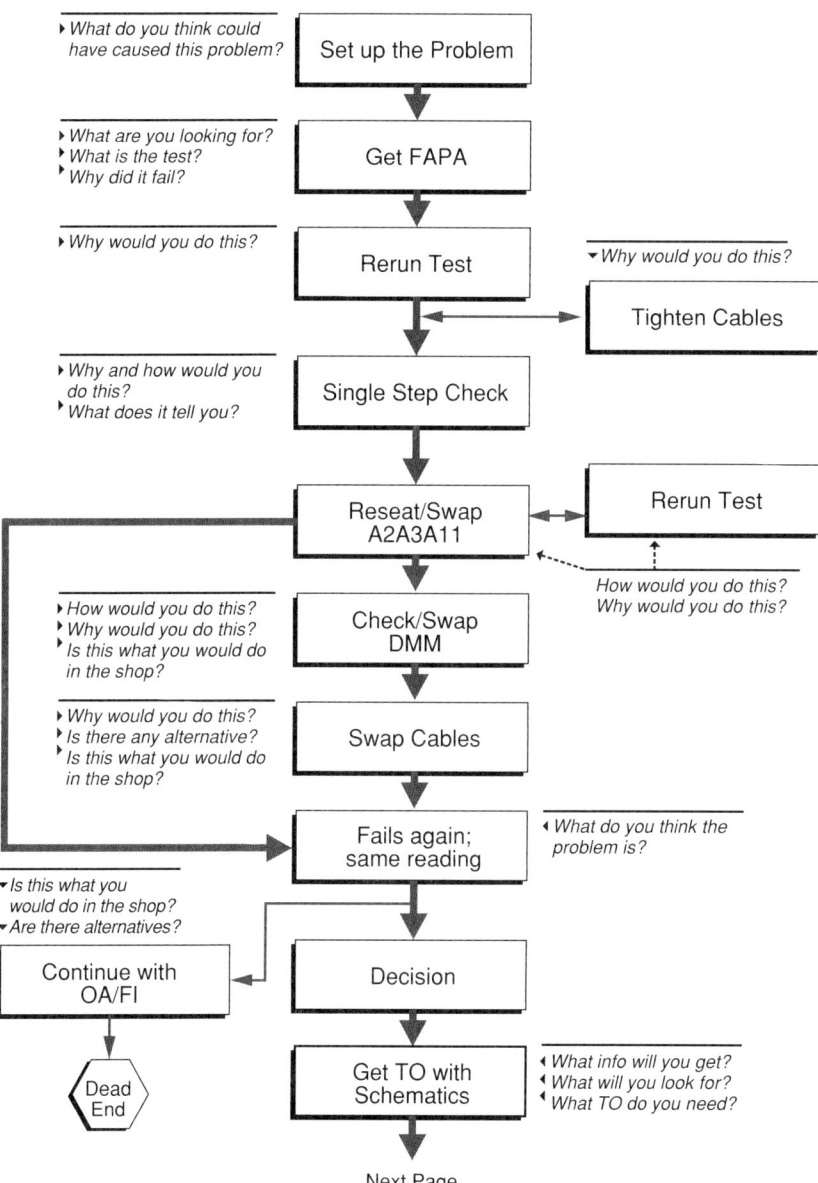

FIGURE 4-6 Problem space map to guide probed protocol gathering. SOURCE: Glaser et al. (Vol. II).

results provide a strong basis for evaluating the job performance of an incumbent as well as diagnosing the need for specific types of training.

Characteristics of Job Tasks and Traits

A job analysis is not yet complete when the universe of tasks and traits has been enumerated. Not all tasks, for example, contribute in the same way to the job. Some require more training time than others, some are performed more frequently than others, some are more important to job success than others, and some engender more errors than others. Consequently, in characterizing a job and constructing a measure of performance on that job, it is necessary to go beyond task and behavior descriptions and evaluate tasks according to such characteristics as frequency, difficulty, and importance. Such information further describes the job and also permits the weighting of tasks in selecting them for inclusion in a job performance measure. In this section, we consider some of the alternative dimensions on which tasks or traits might be evaluated and the consequences of using each.

Importance

Certainly, one would be interested in distinguishing tasks along some continuum of importance or criticality. The importance might refer to the position of a single task in a larger domain of tasks that make up the job, or it might refer to the contribution of a particular knowledge, skill, or ability (i.e., trait) in a larger domain of personal attributes that define the full set of resources that a worker might bring to a task (or job). For example, a firefighting task involving fire suppression is more important than one involving the cleaning of equipment. Similarly, for the job of firefighter, the attribute known as stamina or cardiovascular endurance is more important than the attribute known as finger dexterity. In the military setting, a task involving the repair of an electronic circuit controlling fuel flow to a jet engine would probably be more important than a task related to cleaning repair equipment after every use.

Frequency

In addition to importance, one might be interested in whether the task is performed frequently relative to other tasks or if the attribute is used frequently relative to other attributes. In the case of the firefighter position described above, equipment maintenance tasks are performed more frequently than fire suppression tasks. Similarly, the attribute of verbal comprehension is more frequently required in activities than is deductive reasoning.

Similarly, the jet engine mechanic may replace washers and O-rings much more frequently than circuit boards.

Difficulty

Independent of importance and frequency, one might investigate the relative difficulty involved in completing a task or applying a knowledge, skill, or ability. Another way of addressing the same issue might be to examine the level at which the task must be performed or the extent to which the attribute must be developed to be useful in the job. To remain with the firefighter example, it seems clear that suppressing a chemical fire is more challenging than suppressing a brush fire. With respect to personal attributes, it seems true that problem sensitivity must be developed to a considerably greater extent than eye-hand coordination. For the jet engine mechanic, troubleshooting and diagnostics may be considerably more difficult than routine maintenance.

Modifiability

Often, a worker will receive training after being hired. Thus, when considering attributes required for success, one is often interested in the extent to which a task is required immediately after placement on a job rather than after some period of on-the-job training. Similarly, the job analyst might be interested in knowing if an attribute is likely to be modifiable through training or if the skill in question will be part of a training program. Those attributes least modifiable might be more central to the job analysis than those easily changed, particularly when those attributes are also central to job success.

Variability

From both the task and attribute perspective, it is often useful to identify those tasks or attributes for which the differences among incumbents are likely to be the greatest. This is important, for example, if the purpose is to make selection decisions (but not if the purpose is to assess job mastery). Tasks or attributes for which there is little variability are of limited value from the perspective of personnel selection. This follows from the psychometric foundation for prediction: the greater the variance in predictor and criterion, the higher the potential empirical relationship between the two. Conversely, if either the criterion or predictor variable is constant (or nearly so), there will be no (or little) chance of demonstrating a relationship between the two and there will be little utility in using the predictor to make selection decisions.

Other Characteristics

It is possible to think of other characteristics that might play a role in job analysis, but they would be less common and might relate more to the situation than the job analysis procedures generally. As an example, in some situations one might introduce the notion of *contribution to profitability* if the environment was a highly competitive one with narrow profit margins. Similarly, in an environment in which personal danger and safety were at issue, one might consider the extent to which a task was dangerous or the extent to which the possession of a particular attribute might reduce risk to a worker or colleague or consumer—a *safety* dimension. One might also consider the extent to which a task or attribute is an aspect of many jobs rather than only one or a few jobs. This might be called a *commonality* dimension. Finally, one might consider the effect that a radical change in environment might have on a task or an attribute. Consider the differences between a precomputer and postcomputer workplace. As another example, consider the sophisticated firing mechanisms in modern tanks that permit one to fire the cannon while the tank is in motion. This was a radical departure from previous weapon systems that required the tank to come to a stop (and assume a position of maximum vulnerability in the process) before firing the cannon. Aside from providing the air-conditioned comfort enjoyed by computers and tank crewman alike, the combat environment in the new tanks places a premium on rapid response to computer-generated targeting information.

This kind of consideration is of particular importance in the context of the JPM Project. A central point of discussion has been wartime versus peacetime conditions. The question that might be asked with respect to job tasks or personal attributes is the extent to which they become more or less important in conditions of open conflict. In the private sector, an equivalent concern might be a midyear budget reduction for an industrial unit or the threat of a corporate takeover. The question of tasks and attributes that become more or less important under hostile conditions was a central issue in the planning for the JPM Project, since the purpose of the armed forces is to be prepared to fight a war, not simply to maintain equipment during peacetime conditions.

The JPM Definition of the Job Content Universe

The JPM Project did not break new ground in identifying and analyzing tasks that comprise a job content universe. Instead, project scientists carried out a traditional job analysis. For several reasons, trait analysis did not play a major role in the project. First, the Air Force CODAP system and its variants provided the Services with an available knowledge base for task-based job analysis. Sheer time and cost considerations made it expedient to use the existing system and data. In addition, the credibility or face validity of the criterion measures to be developed was inordinately important. The misnorming incident described earlier led some legislators and military policy makers to question the value of the ASVAB. Hence a central premise in the JPM Project was that a good behavioral criterion measure was the necessary condition for demonstrating the predictive value of the ASVAB. Project planners wanted to stay as close as possible to concrete job performance in order to allay the apprehensions of policy makers. Although any project faces financial and contextual constraints, the failure to pursue a task-by-trait analysis has some unfortunate consequences. It is important to keep in mind the value of the task-by-trait approach for predictor development, for construct validation, and for theory building. In general, the most informative job analysis will embrace both facets of performance: the tasks inherent in jobs and the enabling human traits or attributes that produce successful performance of those tasks.

DEFINING THE DOMAIN OF INTEREST

The job content universe is likely to contain more tasks than can or should be incorporated into a job performance measure. For example, the universe may contain tasks that duplicate one another, or are judged by subject matter experts to be trivial or so dangerous that using them in a job performance measure cannot be justified, or are so expensive that if an error is made, the cost far exceeds the information value (e.g., damaging a jet engine). The art and science of job performance measurement consist in good part in the finesse with which the essential job (whose definition may well depend on the measurement goals) is distilled from the total universe of possible tasks.

There are many possible approaches to specifying the domain of interest. The Marine Corps, for example, reduced the content universe to the domain of testable tasks by identifying behavioral elements shared in common by different tasks. The rationale was that "sampling of test content with regard only to tasks may be somewhat misleading because one cannot explicitly identify the specific behaviors that are being measured or assure that all behaviors relevant to the performance of the job are even being tested" (Mayberry, 1987:17). To identify behavioral elements, a detailed task analysis was carried out, and job experts constructed behavioral elements—"generic verb-noun statements denoting identifiable units of performance that underlie the performance of the ITS (Individual Training Standards) tasks" (p. 17). Thus, across the tasks comprising the grenade launcher duty area, a parsimonious set of behavioral elements was identified. The domain of interest for the grenade launcher was then defined by five tasks and a set of behavioral elements common to one or more of the tasks (see Figure 4-2).

The Air Force took a different approach. For each job studied there was occupational survey data available organized as a list of tasks, each with information on the percentage of incumbents performing the task, relative time spent on the task, time required to learn the task, and the importance of training to mastery of the task.

The list of tasks was reduced using complex decision rules. For the job of jet engine mechanic the rules were as follows:

(1) Select tasks that are included in the Plan of Instruction (training curriculum) or that are performed by at least 30 percent of first-term incumbents.

(2) Group tasks into clusters that will facilitate ease of development of hands-on measures.

(3) Weigh clusters in terms of relative importance.

(4) Determine percentage of tasks within a cluster to be selected for further consideration.

(5) Select tasks on the basis of learning or performance difficulty.

The Navy's approach to task selection depended heavily on the use of experts to reduce the initial task universe. As an example, for the Navy rating of radioman, the job analysis began with a list of 500 tasks that defined the job content universe. This list was generated by examining prior job analyses, reviewing training material, interviewing first-term incumbents and their supervisors, and observing on-the-job performance. Only tasks performed exclusively by first-term radiomen were included in the initial list.

At this point, a series of individuals and groups examined and modified the list, as follows:

(1) Two senior staff members of the training facility for radiomen deleted (a) tasks not performed by first-term radiomen, (b) those performed Navy-wide and not specifically by radiomen, (c) military tasks (such as standing for inspection), and (d) administrative tasks (such as maintaining a bulletin board; Laabs and Baker, 1989).

(2) This reduced list of tasks was then examined by 17 radioman supervisors, who combined subtasks into larger complete tasks and separated broad, general tasks into more specific tasks. In addition, they reworded tasks so that all tasks were written at the same level of specificity. This refinement reduced the list from 500 to 124 task statements.

When steps 1 and 2 were completed, a questionnaire using the 124 statements was developed and sent to 500 first-term radiomen and 500 supervisors. The radiomen rated statements on the basis of frequency of performance and complexity. The supervisors rated the statements on the basis of importance for mission success and the percentage of time the task was performed incorrectly (an index of difficulty). The process by which a final sample of 22 tasks was selected for the radioman hands-on test is described in Chapter 7 (see also Laabs and Baker, 1989).

Approaches to Task Sampling

As indicated above, various decision rules were employed by the Services to reduce and refine the universe of tasks in a job to a subset of candidates for hands-on criterion development. Although such decision rules may be more or less reasonable, this trimming of the content universe of necessity creates interpretive difficulties. The problem is to draw a sample of tasks while preserving the ability of the job performance measure to reflect an incumbent's performance on the entire job.

At the extremes, there are two distinctly different sampling strategies that might be adopted. The first is to sample randomly from all tasks that define the job in question. An alternative would be to select tasks in some purposive way to represent certain a priori parameters. It is the second strategy that best characterizes the JPM Project. The question becomes whether this purposive task selection plan describes performance (through the hands-on medium) in a way that satisfies the goals of the JPM Project. To put the question more directly: Did the method of task selection for hands-on development create a definition of job performance that would permit one to conclude reasonably from a significant ASVAB validity demonstration that someone who did better on the ASVAB would do better on the job? A second, perhaps more intimidating issue is related to the linking of enlistment standards to job performance (and the desired mix of performance). Did the tasks chosen for hands-on test performance permit the assessment of the extent to which requisite performance mixes would be realized, i.e., could one be safe in inferring that a particular mix of CAT I through IV recruits would produce an acceptable mix of eventual performance? To the extent that the tasks chosen were not representative of relevant aspects of the job, both of these inferences (validity and performance mix) would be in jeopardy. In Chapter 7, we consider this issue of task sampling at some length. For purposes of this chapter, however, it should be kept in mind that the manner by which we create definitions of job success (including our operational definitions of success—i.e., the hands-on tests) will ultimately determine the strength of the inferences that can be made. If the tasks selected for hands-on development are not representative in some important way, then the technical and administrative qualities of those measures are almost irrelevant.

Specification of Test Content

By whatever route the sample of tasks is drawn, it defines the range of "stimulus materials" and acceptable responses that might be used to construct a job performance measure, as well as the alternative methods that might be used to score performance. Stimulus material refers to the items—tasks, problems, questions, situations—that might be presented in the performance test (e.g., using a grenade launcher). The form of probable or permissible responses refers to the steps, problem solutions, answers, or actions taken in response to the stimulus material (e.g., the steps required to load, aim, adjust sights, and fire a grenade launcher). The method of scoring the responses might entail counting the number or proportion of steps successfully completed in carrying out a task, or the number of correct answers to a set of questions, or an expert's evaluation of a verbal description of a procedure provided by the incumbent.

Guion (1979:23) provides an example of test content specification using a mapping sentence (following Hively et al., 1968) that completely specifies the test domain for electronics repair tasks:

> Given *(diagnostic data)* about a malfunction in *(product)*, and given *(conditions)*, candidate must *(locate and replace)* malfunctioning *(part)* with the work or response evaluated by *(method of observation or scoring)*.

Test content specification also identifies the modifications needed to translate the stimulus material and responses into a standardized form for measurement purposes (Guion, 1979).

Task Editing

Inevitably the domain of testable tasks contains a number of tasks that are trivial or repetitive that would, if included, provide little information about job performance and take up precious testing time. For example, the total time required for the Marine Corps to test the tactical measures duty area was estimated at 368 minutes. "Two-thirds of this time would be required for the subtask of 'construct fighting hole.' Certainly, there are required techniques and specifications for digging fighting holes and these concepts could be tested, but actually digging a hole would not be an efficient use of testing time" (Mayberry, 1987:24). All of the Services eliminated such tasks.

Moreover, some tasks involved equipment that, if damaged, would be expensive to fix or replace. Such was the case in the Air Force's performance test for jet engine mechanics. The solution was to create an assessment format that circumvented the problem, in this case a walk-through performance test. The walk-through performance test "has as its foundation the work sample philosophy but attempts to expand the measurement of critical tasks to include those tasks not measured by hands-on testing . . . through the addition of an interview testing component. . . ." (Hedge et al., 1987:99).

The interview portion of the test has the incumbent explain the step-by-step procedures he or she would use to complete a task. The interview is conducted in a show-and-tell manner that permits the incumbent to visually and verbally describe how a step is accomplished (e.g., that bolt must be turned five revolutions). "For example, an interview item may test incumbents' ability to determine the source of high oil consumption . . . . While the incumbent is explaining how to perform the task, the test administrator uses a checklist to indicate whether the steps necessary for successful performance are correctly described and scores overall performance on a 5-point scale" (Hedge et al., 1987:100).

Finally, tasks may need to be translated into test items in a way that eliminates dangerous elements. For example, all Services eliminated some "live fire" subtasks and only one, the Marine Corps, included any such subtasks. The Army infantryman task cluster "to shoot" included all of the components other than firing the weapons: load, reduce stoppage, and clear an M60 machine gun; perform maintenance on M16A1 rifle; prepare a Dragon for firing, and so on.

In sum, the domain of testable tasks is not synonymous with the job content universe. Some tasks may have to be eliminated entirely for want of practical assessment procedures. All remaining tasks (perhaps with associated behaviors or, in a task-by-trait system, with relevant traits) need editing for testing purposes. The "stuff" of the performance measure, the content of the test, is distilled from the domain representing job content. This entails a further reduction of the original job content universe, the universe to which, ultimately, decision makers will draw inferences from the job performance measurement. As can be seen, there is a fine art to the science of performance measurement.

An Example: Marine Corps Infantryman

Mayberry (1987) provides a good summary of the entire process beginning with job universe specification and ending with the development of a job performance measure for the infantryman occupation. The job content universe is specified by Marine Corps doctrine through its Individual Training Standards (ITS) and its Essential Subject Tasks (EST), the former specifying job-related tasks and the latter basic tasks required of all Marines. In order to accomplish the reduction of the job as a whole to a sample of that job, a series of disaggregations was adopted. First, the researchers adopted the ITS designation of 13 duty areas for the basic infantry job (e.g., land navigation, tactical measures, M16A2 rifle, communications, grenade launcher, hand grenades) each with its tasks, subtasks, and behavioral elements specified (e.g., Figures 4-2 and 4-4). This job content universe was reduced in size to the job content domain by applying the following rules of elimination (Mayberry, 1987:21):

- The subtask is hazardous or expensive, such as live firing of most weapons (except the M16A2 service rifle) and crossing a contaminated area for the NBC [Nuclear-Biological-Chemical] duty area.
- Experts judge that the subtask provides little or no information. This [criterion] was applied to trivial or repetitive subtasks (it did not translate into the exclusion of simple subtasks).

From the job content domain, a set of tasks/behavioral elements was sampled with the constraint that "Total testing time for the . . . [basic infantry portion of the test] will be limited to about four hours" with the testing time for any duty area ranging from 10 to 30 minutes (Mayberry, 1987:21). To accomplish the sampling, several steps had to be carried out. First, heterogeneous tasks and subtasks had to be defined as discrete units with clearly defined boundaries and limits of about equal size. Yet "[j]obs can not readily be decomposed into discrete and independent units of performance. . . . The solution involves extensive analyses to refine the tasks into equivalent performance units that are amenable to sampling . . ." (Mayberry, 1987:20). This was accomplished using job experts.

The second step in sampling focused on deciding how much time to allocate to each duty on the performance measure. To this end, job experts' ratings of importance and criticality were collected. Testing time was allocated to each duty area according to its importance ranking. Duty area served as a stratification variable for drawing a weighted random sample of subtasks (Mayberry, 1987:25):

> To maximize test content coverage across the behavioral elements [e.g., see Figure 4-4], each subtask . . . was weighted with respect to its behavioral elements. . . . For the first round of . . . sampling . . ., the sampling weight for each subtask was merely the number of behavioral elements that it contained. The subtasks with the greatest number of behavioral elements had the highest likelihood of being sampled.
>
> Sampling weights for the remaining subtasks were then recomputed so that a second subtask could be sampled . . . . Random sampling of weighted subtasks continued until the testable units exhausted the allotted testing time for the duty area [p. 27].

The selection of subtasks established the general test content domain. Next, a detailed analysis was done of each subtask. This analysis revealed the exact steps necessary for performance of the subtask. These steps became the actual go/no go or pass/fail test items. For example, the task "inspect the grenade launcher" includes the subtask "visual inspection," which is broken down into the following steps that were translated into the scorable units of the hands-on test:

Clearing the M16A2
- pointing the weapon down range
- placing the selector on SAFE
- removing the magazine
- engaging the bolt catch
- moving the charging handle forward
- checking for ammunition
- moving the bolt forward

Clearing the Launcher
- placing the launcher on SAFE
- sliding the barrel forward
- checking for ammunition

The criteria used to screen tasks and subtasks (see above) were also applied to the steps required to accomplish each of the subtasks in the sample. Steps were deleted "if they were hazardous or too expensive to test or, in the opinion of job experts, provided little or no information concerning one's proficiency level" (Mayberry, 1987:25). The remaining "testable" subtask units were reviewed by both job experts and incumbents to ensure that what remained was representative of the subtask on the job.

Since each subtask test had a different number of steps, the individual's score was determined as the percentage of steps successfully completed. These subtask scores were then weighted according to the relative importance of the duty area that they represented. Note that neither subtasks nor steps were differentially weighted. Each step and each subtask counted equally in the determination of hands-on scores. The performance test, then, was composed of a stratified, weighted, and "pruned" random sample of subtasks from the basic infantry job in the Marine Corps.

This description of the Marine Corps method of test construction is useful for illustrative purposes. First, it was clear that for administrative reasons they had limited time available for testing. For the grenade launcher duty area, task analysis indicated that the subtask of "maintaining the grenade launcher" was estimated at 32 minutes. Since there were 13 duty areas in the basic infantry job and a total of 4 hours to be allocated for testing (with a constraint of 10-30 minutes for testing an entire duty area), this subtask occupied too much time for inclusion. The actual time allotted to testing a single duty area depended on the relative importance of that duty area (as judged by subject matter experts) and the number of subtasks into which the duty area could be decomposed. Thus, an important duty area (e.g., land navigation in the basic infantry job) with a substantial number of subtasks (16) would be allocated 30 minutes of testing time in the hands-on test but a less important duty area (e.g., use of the night vision device) with a small number of subtasks (5) might be allocated only 10 minutes. Keep in mind, however, that *every* duty area was measured. The difference was in the amount of time allocated to the duty area in the hands-on test and the percentage of subtasks in the duty area sampled.

SCORING HANDS-ON TESTS

Test items in the JPM Project were designed to be scorable using a go/no go format. That is, each task or partial task was broken down into some number of steps that an observer could evaluate dichotomously. The scoring sheet for each task listed a sequence of steps, with a place beside each step to indicate *go* or *no go*. A critical requirement of the hands-on assessment format is that it requires that the test administrator be able to see whether the step was performed correctly.

Scoring Performance on Tasks

Deciding how to compute an overall score for a given task required the JPM researchers to consider a number of small but important points. One of these had to do with the importance of sequence to task performance. Often the list of steps on the scoring sheet mirrored the steps found in the technical manual for the occupational specialty. The question of whether the exact sequence had to be followed was task dependent. In some cases, any change in sequence meant a *no go* for that step and perhaps for the remainder of the task because in real time the lapse would result in, for example, erroneous judgments (e.g., if pressure gauges were read in the wrong order).

Similarly, procedural rules have to be established for when to abort a test item. In some instances, if a step has been done incorrectly, the remainder of the task cannot, or for reasons of safety should not, be attempted. In the JPM Project, if the step could be easily done or corrected by the test administrator (who in most cases was an expert in the job), it was done and the administrator proceeded with the remaining steps. Otherwise, the task was aborted.

Perhaps the most important decision to be made is how to derive a score from performance on the task's constituent steps. The score might be defined as the number of successive correct stages before the first error or before some critical step. Or the task score might be computed as the proportion of steps done correctly—this strategy was followed for the most part in the JPM Project. It has the benefit of expressing task performance on a standard scale even though tasks vary greatly in the number of steps they include. Within this framework it would also be possible to weight steps differentially on the grounds that some steps are more critical than others, although this was not typically done in the JPM Project.

Computing Test Scores

In arriving at a score that is to be an informative indicator of performance on the job, two issues present themselves. First is the question of combining scores from various parts of the test. Second is the question of what constitutes a "passing" score.

For a concrete example, consider the tank crew position in the Army. The current hands-on test includes several task clusters. One set of tasks involves using the radio, another navigating, and a third using the cannon. Suppose an individual did well on the first two yet poorly on the third. How is that person to be described psychometrically? How many and which tasks must the individual "pass" in order to be considered competent as a tank crewman?

There are three operational scoring models that might be considered in combining task scores. We label these models the *compensatory model*, the *noncompensatory model*, and the *hybrid model*. The compensatory model allows for an individual to make up for a poor performance in one area with a good performance in another. Task performance can be scored either dichotomously (pass/fail) or continuously. In the former case, a pass might be defined as correctly performing two of three tasks; this means that failure on any one task could be compensated by a pass on the other two. A tank crewman might have serious difficulties operating the radio but be proficient in navigation and engaging the target with the cannon and still be considered to have passed the hands-on test. Simply averaging the task scores to obtain a total proportion of steps performed successfully is another form of the compensatory model.

A noncompensatory model implies that an individual must reach an acceptable level in each and every task. In the hybrid model, there is some limited compensation but also some sine qua non requirements. It might be reasonable to assume that each crewman must be able to adequately perform two of the tasks involved in tank operation and that these tasks are logically associated. Thus, we might require the crewman to be proficient at either radio operations or navigation *and* proficient at either driving operations or cannon operations. In this instance, radio operations could compensate for navigation (or vice versa) and driving could compensate for cannon operations, but an individual who was proficient in neither radio nor navigational operations would not pass, regardless of how good that person was on driving and cannon operation tasks. In this model, the individual receives a discrete score (i.e., pass or fail) on each of the events.

These models illustrate the types of decisions that must be made in coming to some final determination of how performance will be represented psychometrically. Of course, the actual impact of the models will vary widely in terms of how many test takers would be considered competent. The noncompensatory models are more demanding (i.e., fewer individuals will be considered competent); the continuous score compensatory model is the least demanding or restrictive; and the hybrid model occupies the middle ground.

In addition to choosing a method of combining task scores, it would also be possible to weight tasks differentially, depending on criticality or difficulty. The Marine Corps studied the possibility of differential weighting in combining live-fire task scores with other infantry tasks. In that event, the differential weighting schemes were not thought to add enough to the reliability or validity of the performance measure to warrant the extra complications of execution and of interpreting the test scores.

These scoring issues are not peculiar to the JPM Project. Whenever there are multiple pieces of information about an individual that must be combined, similar choices must be made. In the current case, however, the importance of these decisions is more substantial as a result of the necessity to make statements and inferences about competency and performance standards.

CONCLUSION

The JPM Project set out to measure proficiency in job performance. A job was defined as a collection of tasks and associated behaviors. After eliminating redundant, hazardous, time-consuming or expensive tasks, a small set of representative tasks was selected from which to constitute each job performance measure. Traditional task analysis from documents and task inventories was used to identify job tasks, break them down into subtasks, and specify the individual steps required to accomplish the task. The individual steps in the task constituted the units that were scored, typically as *go* or *no go*. In general, task scores were computed as the proportion of steps successfully completed; performance on the test was an aggregate (usually a sum) of the task scores.

The methods used to analyze the jobs, select tasks, and construct and score the hands-on tests representing these jobs inevitably raise questions about the extent to which the tests accurately represent the essence of the job. It is clear from descriptions of the strategies of the four Services that the job analysis and task selection were driven by test construction goals, in particular by the desire to identify tasks that would be amenable to hands-on testing. Furthermore, in most instances, small groups of individuals made decisions about what tasks would be included in the final task domain. Each Service used a different set of decision rules and a different set of parameters for assembling the tasks that would define the occupational specialties in question.

For the most part, the Services relied on the judgment of subject matter experts to characterize the importance, criticality, and frequency of job tasks. These judgments were used to select tasks that would ensure that the job performance measures "look like" the job. When subject matter experts are used, particularly as respondents to questionnaire items, there are always the concerns about completeness of coverage and carefulness of response. Perhaps the most striking finding by several Services was that subject matter experts disagreed considerably in their judgments. In part, this disagreement arises out of local definitions of a job—those aspects of the job that are most closely attended to and therefore best understood by the subject matter expert. Variations in job definition reemphasize the point made earlier that the essence of a job is in some sense a negotiated essence, and that great care is needed in defining the construct and testing it against alternative interpretations.

With some exceptions, the JPM Project is characterized by a purposive sampling approach to task selection, which on at least one occasion deteriorated into ad hoc selection by policy makers. Moreover, in progressing from task descriptions to the development of hands-on tests, a number of limiting criteria were imposed, including the time to perform the task, safety considerations, cost of equipment, etc. As a result, the potential lack of representativeness at the task description level was compounded at the level of hands-on test design.

After examining this process, one is left with some uneasiness regarding the extent to which the essence of each job has been articulated. To be sure, each of the processes employed by each of the Services was a useful heuristic device, helping them to achieve a foundation for test development. This was certainly a manifest goal of the project. However, in the ideal case, the job would not have been defined in terms of what was amenable to a particular testing format. If the essence of the job is in some sense a negotiated essence, it was negotiated in this instance with goals unrelated to job description in mind. As a result, some might find it difficult to accept the proposition that performance on these measures can be extrapolated to overall job performance. It is also likely that each Service discovered a different essence by virtue of the use of different methodologies and different decision rules for task selection and test development.

A further concern is raised by the absence of any consistent attempt to determine the human attributes that might contribute to the successful accomplishment of each task or task group. The specification of attributes was less important to the JPM Project than it might have been in a developmental validation study in which new predictors were being constructed. But the decision to ignore attributes had its costs. For purposes of a more general discussion of job analysis, prediction, and construct validity, it is fair to say that a full attribute analysis would prove valuable in building a theory of job performance. It is through such a broadened perspective that results become more widely useful and generalizable—and generalizability of JPM results to other military jobs has proved to be a very difficult matter. It is useful to know more than the *fact* of a correlation between a predictor and criterion—one needs to know the *reason* for that correlation. One also needs to know which attributes that are useful on the job are tapped by the test under consideration. We need to know as much as possible about the constructs involved in both the criterion and the predictor. Of course, researchers can return to the JPM data and flesh out the attributes in greater detail. The results of the project would then make a greater contribution to the personnel research community as a whole rather than the more limited (but equally important) military accession community.

The JPM Project is not alone in depending on task analysis as the major component of job analysis. Task analysis is a common method in the private sector as well. It is tempting to speculate why task analysis techniques are given primacy over attribute analysis. One possibility may be that modern job analysis techniques were most frequently applied to jobs having a low cognitive composition; as a result, the job consisted of what was observed. This luxury is not available for cognitively loaded jobs, however, or for the cognitive components of work dominated by physical action. Regardless of the reason for this state of affairs, it is clear that job analysts have given little attention to human attributes in their job analysis strategies.

The JPM Project data base provides researchers the opportunity to restore this balance between tasks and attributes. As an example, it seems clear that the project's data base will permit a careful articulation of the relationships between the attributes represented by the 10 subtests of the ASVAB and the various facets of performance (measured by both hands-on tests and other devices). In addition, several of the Services (most notably the Army) have developed additional predictors to supplement the ASVAB. These enhanced attribute data sets could lead the way to an enriched understanding of the construct of job performance.

These observations and questions are raised not so much as criticisms of the JPM Project, but to convey the complexities of performance-based assessment, complexities insufficiently understood and as yet incompletely addressed.

5

The Testing of Personnel

In an ideal world, empirical evaluation of job performance would involve measuring the performance of a large, representative group of job incumbents, all on the same day, at the same time, and under the same conditions. The ideal can seldom be attained, however, so some realistic accommodations are required. This chapter discusses issues in specifying the sample of personnel to be tested as well as the logistical and standardization problems that can arise in attempting to measure job performance, particularly hands-on performance. It also discusses steps that can be taken to obviate or minimize any adverse effects such problems may have on the quality of the data collected. As the JPM Project evolved, project scientists and committee members came to realize the magnitude of these problems when large-scale test administration of hands-on tests is required. It is hoped that future researchers will profit from what the Services learned about sampling and standardization and from the solutions that emerged from conduct of the project.

Examples from the JPM Project are used to illustrate some of the more important sampling, training, and logistical issues, although the concerns discussed are generic and apply to any attempts to measure performance on the job. Our discussion assumes that the job tasks to be used for hands-on testing have been selected and the procedures for testing and scoring have been developed—the sampling of jobs and job tasks is discussed in Chapter 4 and again in Chapter 7.

SAMPLING PERSONNEL

Specifying the Personnel to be Tested

Specifying the target population to which measures will be administered depends fundamentally on the planned uses of the performance data. If, for example, the goal is to determine the value of the ASVAB as a predictor of future performance, then the target population would be individuals who finished training in the relatively recent past (before years of experience mask the contributions of ability). If the purpose is to examine the relative effects of ability and experience, then one wants people at all stages of experience, and performance would be analyzed as a function of experience. If, however, the issue is an assessment of the present quality of performance in the occupational specialty, then a sample of job incumbents across the whole range is needed, and the relation to experience is of secondary interest.

In the JPM Project, a central concern was the linking of enlistment standards to job performance. A problem that plagues all validation research of this type is the practical necessity of being able to obtain criterion performance data only from job incumbents rather than from the entire pool of job applicants. In addition to the restriction in the range of ability that this condition imposes (for a full discussion, see Chapter 8), there is the further complication that experience gained on the job may affect estimates of the relationship between selection instruments and job performance in complex and unknown ways. In some situations, on-the-job experience might reduce the correlation between job performance and selection tests. This could happen, for example, if the supervisory policy is to expend disproportionate energy on slower-developing employees and to leave the better employees on their own. In other situations, the correlation might increase if, because of the pressures of "getting the job done," below-average employees are given unimportant or minor tasks and the better employees are always assigned the important or critical tasks. It is even conceivable that on-the-job experience could result in an underestimate of the relationship between predictor scores and job performance for one test in a battery and an overestimate of the relationship for another.

No statistical adjustments can remedy this situation without making assumptions that generally will be untestable. The effects of experience gained on the job can be minimized, however, by carefully selecting the interval during which performance measures are administered. Testing should be delayed long enough for genuine and reliable individual differences in job performance to emerge, but not so long that supervisory practices and the passage of time distort relationships. Hence, in the JPM Project, job incumbents in their first term of enlistment who have at least six months of service were designated as the target population. This cohort was expected to be reasonably well versed in the job and would not yet have been promoted to largely supervisory or management functions. In addition, the amount of time between entrance testing and the administration of the job performance measures (a maximum of 36 or 45 months, depending on the Service and the terms of enlistment) was not so long as to completely vitiate the predictive power of the test.

Selecting the Personnel to be Tested

Although researchers would always prefer to test all personnel in the target group who fit the population specifications, it is possible to obtain quite stable regression results from samples of 200 to 300 cases, and results from as few as 50 can provide useful indications of trends. When only a few cases are available, however, interpretation must be tentative, unless bolstered by replications, possibly in conjunction with Bayesian statistical methods (Rubin, 1980).

When many more incumbents are available than can be tested economically, a representative sample of the total population can be used. A sample is representative of the population from which it is drawn if it reflects (within the limits of sampling error) the characteristics of the population. If the sample of incumbents from which performance information is obtained is not representative of the population of interest, any conclusions about the relationship between performance measures and selection tests would be subject to serious question. A representative sample does not mean selecting those people that some manager would like to have tested; almost always, that would mean testing those who are available. People are often available for reasons related to performance: they might be available because they are a crack group who finished some work assignment early, or they might be a group of poorly motivated personnel who were excluded from more advanced work. Using such "available" people is likely to bias the results in one way or another. Rather, each incumbent should have an equal chance of being tested.

Project researchers should be given the authority to select those individuals to be tested, or at least to specify the selection procedures in accordance with statistical methods of randomization. It is important to avoid sources of bias such as those introduced by selecting individuals recommended by a manager. Several methods are typically used to select a representative sample of incumbents. All such methods have the property that every person in the target population has the same probability of being included in the sample. The most straightforward and least used procedure is simple random sampling in which individuals are selected by some kind of lottery. For logistical purposes, the selected individuals can then be organized by unit, and the units visited in some order. Even so, the obvious problem with this scheme is the strong likelihood that the selected individuals will be dispersed at many different sites, making testing difficult and expensive.

A more advantageous regimen involves multistage sampling. Large organizations like the military are already divided into units. In multistage sampling, units are picked at random, with probabilities proportional to their size. Then individuals are selected at random from each of the selected units with probabilities inversely proportional to group size. Such a procedure is especially economical in the military, in which the units are geographically dispersed. In organizations that have a hierarchy of organization, sampling can be done at each level. For example in the Navy, with bases, squadrons, and ships within squadrons, bases can be selected at random, then squadrons within bases, and then ships within squadrons. If required, individuals can be sampled within each ship, but there are many advantages to testing all qualified people in the target population in the selected unit.

If the planned data analysis involves comparisons of subgroups, some adjustments in the sampling plan may be needed to accommodate subgroups that represent a small fraction of the population. That is, if members of a given subgroup, such as women, blacks, or ethnic minority groups, are relatively scarce in the target population and are sampled at the overall rate, subgroup comparisons may be based on numbers of cases that are too small to be meaningful. If this outcome is anticipated, the subgroup can be oversampled—members of the subgroup in question are simply given a higher probability of being selected and their data are weighted inversely by this differential probability in computing statistics for the total group.

One of the advantages of random sampling is that uncontrolled variables are not likely to influence the outcome unduly, as they might when any subjective selection elements are permitted. But randomness works only on the average; any one sample can still be unrepresentative. It is always wise to record background information on all selected persons, including age, education, and any other similar data that might be relevant. A comparison of the population and sample values for these background variables can establish the extent to which the sample's characteristics match those found in the population. With random sampling, the group is not likely to be far off the population average, but it may diverge on some variables. Whenever other considerations force a departure from the purely statistical randomization procedures, such background comparisons are especially important.

The Services varied considerably in the ease with which they could identify and select a representative sample of job incumbents. For the Navy, the sheer difficulty of obtaining access to a vessel for testing precluded any thought of preselecting a representative sample of, say, machinist's mates.

Availability sampling was the only possible option. In such a situation it is important to collect as much descriptive information on the sample as practical to determine the similarity of the sample to the population. The Army research team found that the central personnel locator could not be used to draw the sample. The largest of the Services by far, with soldiers scattered across the United States, Europe, and much of the rest of the world, some number of whom are in transit between duty stations at any given time, the Army cannot maintain the level of currency in its central data system that was required for purposes of this project. As a consequence, the sample had to be selected at each base chosen for testing.

The Marine Corps is a much smaller institution and has the bulk of its troops at a few locations, making for a more manageable task of tracking personnel. The researchers were able to design and select a stratified random sample prior to arrival at the testing sites and be assured that the Marines would be available for testing. For the infantry position of rifleman, for example, three rosters of potential examinees were prepared at Marine Corps Headquarters: a primary roster; an updated roster of recent graduates from the School of Infantry, from which the first replacements were to be drawn; and a supplementary roster. The sampling criteria used in creating the rosters were education level, time in service, and rank. Decision rules for selecting from the supplementary roster, were that to become necessary, matched the supplementary candidates as closely as possible to the riflemen being replaced. The desired size and composition of the rifleman sample are described in Table 5-1.

The problems of creating a representative sample were particularly difficult in those occupational specialties that were performed differently at different sites. The Navy radioman rating provided the most extreme example. Contextual and equipment differences between shore-based and

TABLE 5-1 Marine Corps Sampling Plan for the Infantry Occupational Field

Level of Education	Months of Service	Rank			
		Private-Private First Class	Lance Corporal	Corporal	Total
Non–High School Graduate	1-48	50	200	50	300
High School Graduate	≤9	150	150	—	300
High School Graduate	≥10	100	50	250	400
Total number		300	400	300	1000

shipboard radio telecommunications systems were considerable. In addition, restrictions on the assignment of female radiomen produce large demographic differences between the two locations in which the job is performed.

THE IMPORTANCE OF STANDARDIZATION

Most research employing psychological tests begins with the postulate that *observed* differences among individuals (i.e., the test scores they obtain) are representative of *true* differences among those same individuals (i.e., how much of the attribute tested they really possess). In other words, if a sample of individuals completes a reasoning test and if there is variation evident in the resulting score distribution, it is assumed that this observed variation is the result of real variation in the capacity of these individuals to reason efficiently.

The central hypothesis of most validation research is that differences in test scores are associated with differences in performance. Another way of stating it is that people who do better on the test will do better at the task in question. This generalization is equally applicable to aptitude tests used to predict performance and achievement tests used to measure performance.

Standardization and Prediction

A problem arises whenever the general testing postulate described above cannot be accepted. Unless we can assume that the observed score differences reflect true differences in the test takers' abilities, then the inference that people who do better on the test will do better at the task makes no sense. As an example, consider an instance in which two samples of individuals take reasoning tests. In the first sample, the tests are administered in a noisy environment, full of distractions associated with a rock band practicing next door. In the second sample, the tests are administered in a quiet environment, free of these distractions. In comparing the mean scores of the two samples, we note that the "noisy" sample performed less well than the "quiet" sample. Given the probable effect of noise on intellectual performance, it would be inappropriate to conclude that, on the average, individuals in the quiet sample have more reasoning ability than those in the noisy sample. In this instance, it would be fair to say that observed differences in reasoning scores are probably influenced by variables (e.g., noise) in addition to the reasoning abilities of the subjects.

When the basic testing postulate does not hold, the effects are far-reaching. In such circumstances, any observed relationship between the test score in question and other test scores or the particular test score and observable behavior becomes difficult to interpret. Consider adding a second test—a vocabulary test—to the reasoning test administered to the quiet and noisy samples. As was the case with reasoning performance, we note that vocabulary performance of the quiet sample is better than that of the noisy sample. Ignoring the noisy/quiet conditions, we might be tempted to conclude that those who do well on reasoning tests also do well on vocabulary tests. But it might be more appropriate to conclude that environmental noise affects intellectual performance.

In the example above, we have illustrated how an observed association between two test scores could be unrelated to attributes of the people taking the tests. An equally serious problem can be seen when certain conditions obscure a *true* relationship. Consider the quiet/noisy example once again. This time assume that we want to examine that relationship between reasoning test scores and the efficiency with which subjects make difficult judgments. As before, assume that some subjects take the reasoning test in quiet conditions and other subjects take the test under noisy conditions. Further assume that both groups of subjects are asked to make judgments in quiet conditions. Now we have an instance in which the reasoning test scores vary as a function of the environment in which the subject was tested but the judgment (performance) scores do not. In this instance, the test scores are influenced by a variable other than the underlying ability of the subject and, as a result, there will appear to be a lower relationship between the test score and performance than is actually the case.

Standardization and Performance Standards

Thus, it can be seen that when the basic testing postulate does not hold, it is possible to observe a spurious relationship or to ignore a real relationship. There is one additional problem that might arise from distorted test scores. In order to interpret test scores for individuals or groups, it is necessary to have some standard of comparison. In testing, standards of comparison are often called norms, and norms are developed by administering the test to a selected sample. The adequacy of these norms depends on the extent to which all members of the norm group or sample are exposed to identical conditions. To use our noise example, if we were constructing a reasoning test and wanted to develop norms to aid in test score interpretation, it would be unwise to allow variation in noise and quiet in our normative sample. Similarly, if the norms had been appropriately developed, they would have interpretive value only to the extent that a set of scores under consideration was gathered in conditions similar to those present when the norms were developed.

The ASVAB norms are good examples of the value of standardization in testing. The fact that they have been carefully developed allows one to interpret the score of any single test taker compared with a sample of earlier test takers. It allows us to infer that the person in question is above average on one ASVAB ability or below average on another. Furthermore, it permits us to determine if particular recruiting strategies are identifying candidates who are more capable than those produced using a different recruiting strategy. If the norms had been developed without standardization of conditions, or if the actual ASVAB testing was done under conditions that varied greatly from those present when norms were developed, these inferences would not be possible.

An associated problem arises when one attempts to link predictor test scores to performance standards. As an example, consider the implied relationship between ASVAB scores and job performance. It is assumed that it is reasonable to attempt to identify a minimum ASVAB score (or score profile) in terms of predicted performance in the Services. In other words, if there is a link between the abilities tested by the ASVAB and the abilities required to perform various military jobs, it should be possible to identify an ASVAB score (or score profile) below which successful performance is improbable. In order to identify such a score, it will be critical that the performance scores be true scores and relatively unaffected by systematic distortions. If the performance norms are too high or too low because of extraneous influences in developing these norms, then the cutoff scores on the ASVAB will be similarly too high or too low. This is a calibration challenge that can be met only through standardization.

This is the conceptual foundation for test standardization. In the JPM Project, the challenge is exaggerated by the fact that the performance tests of most interest are not standard paper-and-pencil, multiple-choice examinations but performance tests with various complex interactive mechanisms. In the sections that follow, we consider the standardization issue as it affects the hands-on tests.

STANDARDIZATION ISSUES IN HANDS-ON TESTING

Hands-on tests are work samples. It is therefore necessary to move to field environments for testing purposes. The typical hands-on test is administered to a single subject in a field setting by a trained administrator or scorer. By extension, this means that tests are administered in many settings by many different administrators. This, in turn, means that there is an opportunity for variance other than true score variance to enter into the hands-on test scores. To the extent that this unwanted variance is present in the test scores, inferences both about the capacity of the ASVAB to predict performance and about individual recruit performance predictions (i.e., performance standards) will be in error.

There are three general classes of variables that are of particular concern in the use of hands-on tests. They include test administrators, administrative and scoring procedures, and physical testing conditions. Each of these classes of variables has the potential for distorting the hands-on test scores and any inferences that might be based on them. The issue is not only developing the "best" set of circumstances but also making sure that all people who take the hands-on tests experience the *same* circumstances.

Standardizing the Test Conditions

With hands-on performance testing, which requires one-on-one test administration, attention must be given to standardizing the interactions between administrator and test taker. Usually test developers provide a definite protocol to be followed, including instructions to be read for each task being tested and procedures to be used for verifying the execution of each step of task performance. Part of the test development includes preparing standard instructions, as well as standard responses to the most common questions raised by test takers. In effect, the test administration procedures attempt to reduce the test administrator to a completely neutral presence; the best administrators are those who follow the protocol, maintain a pleasant demeanor, and avoid giving verbal or facial cues.

Some of the details of test development become critical only in the context of actual test administration and scoring. For example, all tests should have some kind of time limit, if for no other reason than to rescue the examinee who is so hopelessly lost as to be immobilized. Other details include clear specifications of what constitutes acceptable performance of each step, and how performance should be scored—go/no go versus rating on a continuum. The difficulties of the actual testing situation, in which the administrator must simultaneously time the performance, observe and evaluate the performance, grade the observable units, and handle any questions in a nondirective manner, led the JPM Project planners to prefer a dichotomous scoring system because it involves simpler judgments.

The locale of the testing must also be specified. If a task is to be performed outdoors at one site, it should be performed outdoors at all sites. There is a natural conflict between finding a quiet, relatively isolated place for the administration and having the task performed under realistic conditions. For example, some aircraft maintenance tasks are normally carried out on the flight line rather than in a hanger or shop, but conditions on the flight line make viewing the performance extremely difficult for examiners, and there are elements of risk to equipment and personnel on the flight line that are better controlled in the shop. The details of the JPM Project should be a source of valuable information about striking the best possible balance between the scientist's need for a controlled and replicable environment and the realities of measuring performance in a real-world environment.

The schedule of the testing sessions and the arrangement of the various testing stations are also candidates for standardization. Testing schedules must be set up so that trained administrators can do the testing. In the JPM Project, there were relatively few administrators and, since each test involved one test taker and at least one test administrator, testing had to be done sequentially. Moreover, in many cases, certain scarce equipment was required, and its use had to be carefully scheduled so as not to interfere with the unit's other scheduled activities.

One inevitable consequence of having to test seriatim is that individuals tested later in the sequence may gain an advantage by learning about the test from those who had been through the process earlier. Efforts to minimize this type of information transmittal by exhortation did not seem particularly effective in the military project, but careful logistical preparations so that troops were not waiting together in groups for the next activity reduced on-site communications substantially. However, since the hands-on testing typically extended over days, if not weeks, at a given location, discussion among the test takers of test tasks had to be assumed and controlled for analytically.

In the usual standardized test, all examinees perform each of the tasks to be evaluated; however, they are not required to perform the tasks in the same order. During early trials of JPM performance tests, it quickly became clear that imposing the same order on each test taker created large inefficiencies, with many individuals waiting at each station to begin testing and others waiting upon completing the final task. An important lesson in the logistics of mass performance testing gained from the project is that testing order should be counterbalanced across test takers to eliminate these inefficiencies as well as potential sources of performance variation due to the sequence in which the tasks are performed.

In the JPM Project, the Marine Corps hands-on test administration, in large part because it came last and benefited from the experiences of the other Services, was the most carefully controlled. For the infantry specialty, each of the testing stations involved approximately the same amount of time (about 30 minutes), and a daily schedule was set up in which the order of the testing stations was carefully counterbalanced across examinees. Moreover, each examinee had a printed schedule showing which station to do at which time. This kept every examinee and every test administrator busy throughout the day. Thus, examinees did not have free time while waiting their turn in which to discuss their experiences with each other.

Finally, the several testing stations were carefully isolated and/or insulated from each other so that examinees waiting to be tested could not view the test as it was being administered. This degree of control was possible because the testing site was physically separate from other activities on the base. Some of the testing locations in the JPM Project did not have sufficient space to permit the necessary degree of isolation (on shipboard that was simply impossible to achieve). As a result, individuals not being tested were undergoing training and/or performing their normal activities in close proximity to those who were. Clearly, such external activity has the possibility of adding to the error variance in the test performance. In particular, the comments of informal observers about a colleague's performance are likely to have a deleterious influence on the test taker's performance.

Not all threats to standardization are amenable to control by researchers. Hands-on tasks for many jobs must be performed outdoors, prey to weather and other differences in local environment. At one European site at which Army researchers were testing tank crewmen, the base was suddenly put on alert. Although testing proceeded, the formerly quiet and tranquil test site was now filled with equipment and soldiers awaiting further orders. While the hectic and tense atmosphere created by the alert no doubt provided an element of authenticity to the hands-on testing, it also introduced unaccountable variability to the testing environment that will make it hard to interpret the scores of the soldiers tested on that occasion.

Selecting and Training the Test Administrators

Individualized performance measurement requires trained administrators to observe and score the performance. These administrators need to understand the job fully, or at the very least to understand the tasks being tested; in the absence of careful selection and adequate training, the test administrators themselves could become sources of error variance. In the JPM Project, administrators were either past supervisors of the job under study or related jobs, or they were incumbents in supervisory positions. Navy, Air Force, and Marine Corps researchers hired former servicemen who had served as supervisors in the relevant occupations. The Army researchers, in some instances, used supervisors on the same bases as the individuals being tested; however, individuals were never tested by their supervisors.

Training of the supervisors was necessary to be sure not only that they were knowledgeable about the tasks being tested, but also that they had a common understanding of the behavior that constituted correct performance of each step of the task, and how these various behaviors were to be rated. Training videos were very useful in showing the correct and incorrect ways to do the task. Use of the videos, coupled with group discussion, provided a common basis for scoring the performances. Administrators also took turns role playing as examinees to provide experience for each other. There are many ways to provide effective training; it is important to understand that a considerable amount of such training is always necessary to ensure standardization of test administration and scoring.

One problem that arises when administrators are not accustomed to laboratory studies is their tendency to help the examinees and even act as teachers. One of the roles of a supervisor, especially in the armed forces but elsewhere as well, is to provide feedback to correct and improve the work of those under their supervision. On-the-job training is more or less continuous for new workers. By contrast, the test administrator is supposed to take an impassive, nonreactive role. Not only is this mode extremely difficult for those who have spent their working lives as first-line supervisors, but also they may not even see its importance. Certainly, there were some associated with the military project to whom it seemed more important that a serviceman learned the job than that a true study result was obtained. Such administrators had to be weeded out. Even when the administrators understand that they are not to train, it is often impossible for them to forgo the opportunity completely. Avoiding inappropriate examiner interaction with the test taker requires constant vigilance.

Calibrating the Test Administration

One-on-one testing shares some characteristics with grading test papers, such as essays written by students. When this is done professionally, as by a testing organization like the Educational Testing Service, not only is there considerable training and group discussion about standards but also, from time to time, sets of papers are rescored and careful records are kept of scores given by each scorer, so that agreed-on standards can be maintained.

Ideally, similar quality control should be used in collecting job performance data: daily records can be obtained on the scoring patterns of each administrator; periodically a second administrator or shadow scorer can watch the same performance and provide independent scoring; videotapes of the test session can be obtained for later checking. When quality control procedures are applied daily, it is possible to correct situations that might otherwise get out of control—e.g., with different administrators using different standards.

In the JPM Project the Marine Corps developed the most elaborate quality control system. Part of the success of its system came from the fact that just two teams of test administrators were used for data collections, one for the East Coast and one for the West Coast. For the infantry specialty, each team trained together for two weeks and then spent six months administering the hands-on tests. As a consequence, the scoring teams became experienced and developed a professional ethos. In addition, despite many complications, a computerized data analysis system was set up at the test sites. Each day, the scoring data were keyed in and reports were generated so that the test site manager could assess scoring trends for each administrator. In cases in which an administrator was clearly out of line—either more lenient or more stringent than the others—corrective action could be taken via group discussions of task performance, role playing, and so forth.

CONCLUSION

Because of the massive size of the JPM Project and the diversity of the jobs being tested, prodigious efforts were needed to surmount logistical and standardization obstacles. The problems encountered in field testing by the Services as well as their approaches to solutions provide a wealth of insight for others concerned with these issues. And because standardization of hands-on performance measurement presents much greater challenges than traditional written tests, this topic is worthy of far more attention than it is usually given in setting up data collection plans.

6

Evaluating the Quality of Performance Measures: Reliability

Previous chapters have discussed the development and administration of formal measures of job performance in the psychometric tradition. Much of the emphasis has been on building quality into the measures and into the measurement process. The discussion turns now to the results—the performance scores—and to a variety of analyses used to provide evidence that the measurements mean something. Traditionally this has meant examining the reliability and validity of the test or measure—which, broadly put, means in the first instance whether the test measures anything at all, and in the second, the extent to which it measures what it was intended to measure. This chapter looks at reliability, which is a property of the measurement process itself. Our discussion of the quality of job performance measures continues in Chapter 7 with an examination of content representativeness, and in Chapter 8 with analyses of the predictive validity and construct validity of the measures, which entail statistical analysis of their relations to other variables.

RELIABILITY

The first question to ask of any assessment instrument is whether the scores can be relied on, or whether they are so haphazardly variable that they cannot be said to signify anything. If a test taker is tested, and then tested again with an equivalent test, we would expect his or her score to be about the same. In principle, we could contemplate testing an individual repeatedly, with measures considered to be equivalent, so that we could then examine the resulting distribution of test scores for that person. Ideally the scores would be identical, but few measures are that good. Even measures of a person's height will typically vary by a few millimeters. With complex, performance-based measures, the scores might vary because of the choice of tasks for the tests, because of differences between test scorers, as well as other, chance factors. Still, the scores would be useful if their standard deviation were small relative to the score distribution of the population of incumbents, or relative to the potential score range of the test.

The Classical Formulation

The standard deviation of the potential scores of an individual on a test is called the *standard error of measurement*; it is an important psychometric property of the test. Expressed in the units of the score scale, it indicates how much the score would be expected to change if the measurement were repeated countless times. Assuming normally distributed measurement errors, roughly two-thirds of the scores for a person would be within one standard error of measurement from his or her mean score. Of course repeated testing is usually out of the question, but one repetition is often possible, especially in a research setting. The correlation between the scores on two equivalent testings for a representative group of test takers is called the *test reliability*. If one is willing to assume that errors are independent of score level—that is, all test scores are subject to about the same kind and amount of potential variation—then a formula can be developed relating the test reliability to its standard error of measurement.

The relation of test reliability to the standard error of measurement is based on the very simple model of classical test theory, in which an individual's test score, x, is made up of a systematic or consistent ("true") part, t, that is invariant over equivalent tests, and an error part, e, that varies independently of t: $x = t + e$. Across individuals, the standard deviation of e is the standard error of measurement. It is assumed to be the same for all individuals. On an equivalent test (which might be the very same test on another occasion or a different version of the test), the theory says that the individual would have exactly the same true score, t, but a different and independent error, which we might here call e'. It is assumed that the standard deviation of e' is also the same for all individuals. It then follows that

$$\sigma_e = \sigma_x \sqrt{1.0 - r}$$

where σ_x is the standard deviation of the representative population of test takers and r is reliability—the correlation of the two equivalent testings in the same population. The details of this classical model can be found in Lord and Novick (1968) or Gulliksen (1950), along with many variations, and need not concern us here.

For our purposes it is sufficient to say that the reliability coefficient provides a way of estimating the standard error of measurement. Reliability has the disadvantage of being population-dependent, whereas, in theory, the standard error of measurement is independent of the population being tested. Also, the standard error of measurement, being expressed in the units of the test score scale, is therefore useful for interpreting test scores. It is, however, inconvenient as an index, just because it is expressed in score units. The test reliability is a much more useful index, being a unitless correlation coefficient varying between 0 and 1.0. Accepted standards in the field are vague and depend on the characteristic being measured: generally speaking, reliabilities of .6 to .7 are considered marginal, .7 to .8 acceptable, .8 to .9, very good, and above .9 excellent.

Approaches to Reliability Analysis

Test reliability and the standard error of measurement are both global concepts. In practice, the reliability of a test or measure can be examined in a number of ways, each of which involves repeated observations on the same group of people to determine how much their scores fluctuate. For example, the correlation of scores obtained by giving a group the same test on two separate occasions provides an index of test-retest reliability, sometimes called *test stability*. This index indicates how much error is due to occasion-to-occasion fluctuations. Consistency in a person's scores on the two test occasions represents the true part of the performance score. Fluctuations in the person's scores from one occasion to the next are attributed to error. If the pair of scores is very close, error is small. If this holds for all people in the group, then the differences in scores from one person to another are considered to be due to consistent performance differences between them—that is, due to true-score differences, not error. If each person's pair of scores fluctuates widely, however, the differences among all peoples' scores are attributed primarily to measurement error.

Similarly, if two raters view and score the performance of each examinee on a job performance test, then the consistency of the raters can be evaluated by intercorrelating their scorings, providing an index called interrater reliability. A third approach to reliability analysis is to compute the correlation of scores on two equivalent or "parallel" versions of a test given to a group of examinees, either at the same time or within a short time span. Differences between scores on two parallel forms of a test or measure provide an index of how much error is introduced by the particular set of items used in a given form.

If resources do not permit repeated test administrations, multiple scorers, or the administration of parallel forms, so that the data are limited to just one occasion, one rater, and one form, it is still possible to get a reliability estimate by looking at the consistency of responses to items or tasks internal to the test. In essence, the average interitem score correlations can be manipulated to provide an estimate of parallel-form reliability in what has come to be called an index of *internal consistency reliability.* This procedure depends on all the items being interchangeable; i.e., it assumes that all items are measuring the same thing, and that any set of items is equivalent to any other set. Item heterogeneity is interpreted as error. Of course, when performance is legitimately multidimensional, not all item inconsistency is error, and the internal consistency reliability index can be a misleading tool.

Plainly, each method of assessing reliability addresses a different aspect of measurement error. Parallel-form reliability assesses error due to selection of items. The test-retest method assesses differences introduced by the occasion of testing. Interrater reliability investigations consider errors deriving from the observers who score the performance, and internal consistency focuses on item-to-item variation as a possible source of error.

Reliability Analysis in the JPM Project

Each of these approaches was used by one or more Services in the JPM Project to learn about the reliability of hands-on job sample tests. Given the central role played by observers in this assessment format, the question of consistency in scoring among raters was of particular interest. And the problem of small numbers of test items (tasks) that characterizes performance assessments made some sort of parallel-forms reliability analysis especially salient.

In the Navy study, for example, the reliability of hands-on performance scores for machinist's mates was evaluated in a separate study by having two examiners observe the performance of a subset of 26 machinist's mates as they carried out 11 tasks in the engine room of a ship similar to that on which they serve. The examiners, retired Navy machinist's mates, observed each incumbent perform all 11 tasks. The examiners had been given extensive training (see Bearden, 1986; Kroeker et al., 1988) and were accompanied by other trained personnel at all times. The hands-on tasks included reading gauges, operating equipment, and carrying out casualty control. Each task had multiple steps, ranging in number from 12 to 49, that were scored in a go/no go format by each of the two observers. A task score was the proportion of steps correctly completed, and the total performance score was the average across tasks.

The consistency of the observers' scoring was calculated by correlating the machinist's mates scores given by examiner 1 with their scores from examiner 2, after averaging over all 11 tasks. Table 6-1 presents a schematic of the data collected. Based on the full data set for the two examiners, 26 machinist's mates and 11 tasks, the Navy reported a median interrater reliability coefficient of .99, with a range of .97 to .99. This extraordinarily high reliability reflects the fact that there was near-perfect agreement in the total scores assigned by the observers. (The agreement among raters using performance appraisal rating forms, a far more common assessment technique, typically has not been nearly so close.)

The Navy study also focused on tasks, although the development costs and the large amount of time required by hands-on performance testing dictated an internal consistency analysis rather than the more satisfying parallel forms approach. The internal consistency reliability was calculated by averaging over the two examiners' scores to produce an average proportion correct for each machinist's mate on each of the 11 tasks. The machinist's mate's performance on the 11 tasks was then intercorrelated for all task pairs: $r_{1,2}, r_{1,3} \ldots, r_{10,11}$. The average internal consistency reliability of the hands-on performance measure for single pairs of tasks was .19, and the reliability based on all 11 tasks was .72. This relatively modest value means that some machinist's mates performed well on certain tasks and some performed well on other tasks. It could be taken to mean that the measurement instrument is of rather low quality, with scores fluctuating haphazardly, or it could indicate that the tasks in the hands-on performance measure are heterogeneous—that they measure different facets of performance on which the job incumbents would exhibit stable differences in skill or ability over time.

In the JPM Project, internal consistency was used as the main index of reliability. Table 6-2 summarizes the internal consistency reliabilities obtained by the Services for their various hands-on job performance tests. By

TABLE 6-1 Schematic of the Actual Data Collected on Machinist's Mates' Hands-On Performance

Machinist Mate/Examiner	Task 1		2		11	
	E_1	E_2	E_1	E_2	E_1	E_2
01	.93	.93	.93	.93	.78	.78
02	.57	.64	.67	.80	.78	.67
.	.	.	.	.	.	.
.	.	.	.	.	.	.
.	.	.	.	.	.	.
26	.79	.79	.60	.60	.67	.67

TABLE 6-2 Internal Consistency Reliability of Hands-On Performance Measures

Service	Number of Specialities	Median Reliability	Range of Reliabilities
Marine Corps	4	.87	.82 to .88
Army	9	.85	.75 to .94
Navy	2	.81	.77 to .85
Air Force	8	.75	.65 to .81

contemporary standards, the reliabilities of most of these tests are very good, but not outstanding. Widely used paper-and-pencil tests like the ASVAB have similar reliabilities of the subtest scores. According to classical test theory, a test can be made more reliable by increasing the number of items, since true-score variance grows faster than error variance. This theoretical result is easily verified in practice; for example, the composites of ASVAB test scores used for selection and placement, like the AFQT, are scores from many more items and have reliabilities over .90. Here, the job performance tests would have had to be lengthened—including up to twice as many tasks—to reach reliabilities of .90. Since the tests were already very long, one task sometimes taking 30 minutes, adding more tasks was generally seen as impractical.

UNDERSTANDING MULTIPLE SOURCES OF ERROR[1]

Traditional approaches to reliability analysis present researchers with an obvious dilemma: Which reliability coefficient should be used to characterize the performance measurement? The Navy analyses cited above, showing interrater reliabilities of .98 and an internal consistency coefficient of .72, tell quite different stories about hands-on job performance measures. Which one is the more compelling? The former gives a more optimistic accounting than the latter, but magnitude is no reason for preferring it. Classical test theory provides no help since it lumps all error together. Total test variance is simply taken to be the sum of true and error variance, and reliability is simply the ratio of true-score variance to total test variance. What is needed is a method for taking the variability of both raters and tasks into account simultaneously. Cronbach et al. (1972) extended classical test theory to the consideration of multiple sources of error by the

---

[1] This section draws on the work of Noreen Webb and Weichang Li at the University of California, Los Angeles. We are indebted to them for providing results of a number of analyses prior to their publication.

simple and elegant use of the analysis of variance paradigm, following earlier work by Lindquist (1953). This procedure, although straightforward, is not widely known nor much used in the testing community. Shavelson (Vol. II) provided the committee and the JPM Project with a detailed account of this method, which Cronbach et al. called generalizability theory, or simply G theory.

G-Theory Analysis

The term generalizability stems from the premise that the purpose of assessing reliability is to determine to what other circumstances the scores can be generalized. If one wants to generalize beyond the particular tasks on the test, then variability of individuals' scores across tasks (items) should be considered a component of error. If one wants to generalize beyond the particular examiners used, then variability of scores across examiners should be considered to be error. If time of day were thought to contribute to error, then each test taker would have to be tested at two or more different times of the day, to generate a temporal error component. Instead of asking how accurately observed scores reflect their corresponding true scores, G theory asks how accurately observed scores permit generalization about people's behavior in a defined universe of generalization—in our example, generalization of an individual's score across tasks, examiners, and time. More specifically, it examines the generalization of a person's observed score to a "universe score"—the average score for that individual in the universe of generalization.

Just as classical test theory decomposes an observed score into true-score and error components ($x = t + e$), G theory decomposes an observed score into a number of components. For the machinists' mate hands-on performance data, G theory would (roughly) define an individual's observed score as follows:

Observed score = universe score effect + examiner effect + task effect + [universe-score effect by examiner effect] + [universe-score effect by task effect] + [examiner effect by task effect] + [universe-score effect by examiner effect by task effect].

The multiplicative terms, or interactions, reflect the unique contributions of a combination of components.

Each of the effects underlying observed scores has a distribution. One can calculate a variance associated with each of the components that defines the expected observed-score variance (for technical details, see Shavelson, Vol. II). Generalizability theory permits a reliability index (called a generalizability coefficient) to be constructed as the ratio of the sum of universe-score variance components to the expected observed-score variance. The statistical mechanism used to estimate each of the variance components underlying a person's observed score is a variance component model of the expected mean squares in a standard analysis of variance (ANOVA). Usually the random-levels model for variance components is used.

It is necessary here to distinguish between random error and systematic measurement error. Very little measurement error can be simply interpreted as random error in the strict sense of mathematical statistics. If some examinees are relatively better at some tasks whereas other examinees perform better on others, a person-by-task interaction will be found; this is not random error, but would be considered measurement error in most contexts. A person's score depends on the particular task sampled on a test, something systematic but not predictable since tasks are randomly sampled. If one wishes to generalize an individual's score on a performance test to other tasks in the job, which one will almost always want to do, then a person-by-task interaction contributes to measurement error. A large variance component for this term reduces the generalizability of the scores to other tasks. Likewise, generalizing to other raters is problematic if the analysis reveals a main effect of rater, indicating that some raters are more lenient than others. A substantial variance component for the rater-by-task interaction would indicate that raters vary in their lenience in scoring different tasks, which would certainly be considered measurement error in most score interpretations.

None of these effects is simply random error, but all of the effects can be considered to be measurement error. If one's score depends on which tasks were done, or which raters evaluated which tasks, then generalizing to other tasks and other raters can be done only with considerable uncertainty. The score represents effects due not only to job performance but also to other unwanted effects.

Generalizability theory allows for different interpretations of what constitutes measurement error. For example, a main effect of rater is of no consequence if all raters rate every test taker, provided that the score is interpreted only in a relative ("norm-referenced") sense (comparing one test taker to another). If the score is to be interpreted in an absolute—or competency—sense, then rater effects do contribute to measurement error. That is, had there been different raters, the level of competency might have appeared to be different. Thus it is common in a G-theory analysis to identify all sources of variance and then to decide which variance components are to be considered part of the measurement error.

In constructing the G coefficient, it is necessary to recognize that the variance components are initially determined at the level of the item or, in the JPM case, at the level of the task. When, as is usual, the total score is the average of several pieces of data, the variance components in the reliability index must be weighted inversely by the number of such items in the average score. The amount of error in one task or item is typically large. If one neglects to account for the fact that the test score is an average of several item scores, then the reliability will seem very small, as indeed the reliability of a one-item test would be.

JPM Applications of G-Theory Analysis

Because of the character of hands-on job sample tests, the committee was especially interested in raters and tasks as probable sources of measurement error. At the committee's urging, two Services conducted G-theory analyses of such effects with some surprising results. The Navy used ANOVA techniques to look again at the machinist's mate data described above and the Marine Corps did some fairly elaborate G-theory analyses of the measurement of infantry performance (Webb et al., 1989).

The list of terms in the analysis of variance of task scores for Navy machinist's mates is shown in Table 6-3. Note that there were 26 mates (M), 2 examiners (E), and 11 tasks (T) in a completely crossed analysis of variance. The levels of all three variables were considered to be a few out of many possible, leading to the random-effects model for variance components. The table shows the variance components calculated from the mean squares in the analysis (multiplied by 1,000 for convenience.) From these component estimates, the theory permits calculation of the average reliability of a task score as the ratio of the M component to the sum of $M + ME + MT + MET$ components. For an absolute score, the effect of the particular task means, T, and examiners, E, and the ET interaction would have to be considered measurement error as well and added to the denominator. For the test as constituted, all terms except M are divided by the number of items, since the test score is, in effect, an average of task and examiner scores. For two raters, terms involving raters would be divided by the number of examiners to be used in the actual test. In this instance, nothing would change because the raters introduced no measurement error. It is possible to extrapolate to the potential use of more tasks, assuming that new tasks would be sampled from the same universe. The reliability for relative (norm-referenced) interpretation of scores was .80 using 18 tasks rather than 11.

The Marine Corps study involved 150 infantrymen at two sites, Camp Pendleton and Camp Lejeune. The Marine Corps hands-on test had 35 scorable units. For this study, performance was rated by two raters, who were retired Marines. The study was quite complicated, with many special design features (see Shavelson et al., 1990). For our purposes, a simplified version of the results is shown in Table 6-4. In this version, the Marine

TABLE 6-3 Estimated Variance Components and Generalizability Coefficients for the Hands-On Job Performance Test of Machinist's Mates by Examiner by Task

Source of Variation	Degrees of Freedom	Estimated Variance Component ($\times$ 1,000)
Machinist's mates (M)	25	6.26
Examiners (E)	1	0.00
Tasks (T)	10	9.70
$M \times E$	25	0.00
$M \times T$	250	25.84
$E \times T$	10	0.03
$M \times E \times T$ (error)	250	1.46
Generalizability coefficients		
	One Examiner One Task	Two Examiners Eleven Tasks
Relative	0.19	0.72
Absolute	0.14	0.65

Generalizability is the ratio of true to true plus error variance.
The true variance component is M in all cases.
The error variance components are:
  Relative, 1E, 1T: $M \times E + M \times T + M \times E \times T$
  Absolute, 1E, 1T: $M \times E + M \times T + M \times E \times T + E + T + E \times T$
  Relative, 2E, 11T: $(M \times E)/2 + (M \times T)/11 + (M \times T \times E)/22$
  Absolute, 2E, 11T: $(M \times E + E)/2 + (M \times T + T)/11 + (M \times E \times T + E \times T)/22$

SOURCE: Webb et al. (1989).

TABLE 6-4 Estimated Variance Components in Generalizability Study of Performance Test Scores for Marine Infantrymen, Replicated at Camps Lejeune and Pendleton

| Source of Variation | Variance Components | |
	Lejeune	Pendleton
Marines (M)	11.69	9.13
Examiners (E)	0.00	0.00
Tasks (T)	33.05	35.56
$M \times E$	0.35	0.28
$M \times T$	72.91	67.38
$E \times T$	0.07	0.02
$M \times E \times T$	11.69	12.70
Generalizability Coefficients for 35 Tasks		
Relative	.81	.78
Absolute	.76	.72

Corps study was parallel to the Navy study: the similarity of the Marine Corps and Navy results is startling. Reliability for a 35-item test, for relative scores, was .83 for Camp Pendleton and .80 for Camp Lejeune. There was marked heterogeneity in the tasks and virtually no disagreement between the raters.

In both studies the size of the reliability is satisfactory, but the main result of interest is the relative size of the variance components. Note that the variance components for raters or interactions involving raters are so small as to be essentially zero. The Marine Corps study is replicated at two sites, Camp Pendleton and Camp Lejeune. There can be no denying that the result is real. Some observers worried that the raters were not independent but were adjusting their ratings to be consistent. Others felt that monitoring by project staff and by occasional observers avoided collusion between the raters. Probably some inadvertent or intentional cooperation occurred, especially in the tight quarters on shipboard—but it was not widespread. What appears to be happening in these studies is that careful development of scorable items, daily monitoring of results by the research team, and careful and detailed scoring criteria left almost nothing to chance. In each case, tasks were comprised of several steps, each of which was scored in the go/no go format, and the steps occurred in a predefined order. With such a format, either a step is done successfully or not, and there appears to be little room for disagreement. In achievement tests such as the College Board English Essay Test, when graders have to give a qualitative grade for each essay, more disagreement is generally found. With care, discussion, and occasional negotiation, such disagreement can be managed. But apparently the JPM design of hands-on task tests is such that discrepancies among raters can be eliminated.

The Services evolved different strategies for obtaining qualified raters. A careful comparison of the Service results would be instructive. A comparison of the reliabilities of the hands-on tests with the various surrogates would likewise be instructive.

Although more elaborate studies of error sources were done, with complex results, the main findings continued to emerge. Raters appeared to introduce very little measurement error. Tasks, however, regularly turned up as large contributors to measurement error, indicating the need for more tasks to get a clearer picture of the stable performance differences among the Service personnel in the study.

It should be noted that some committee members were surprised that the hands-on tests turned out to be as reliable as they are. Their expectation was that 10 to 15 tasks would be woefully inadequate. That would probably have been true had each task been scored dichotomously. But each task score is the proportion of steps completed satisfactorily, so the score for a task has more information than a dichotomously scored multiple-choice test item.

It should also be noted that some of the tests were assessed for other sources of error. For example, the Marine Corps found a test-retest reliability of about .90, and a parallel-form reliability of .78 for their infantryman performance test that did not include live fire; with live fire the parallel form reliability was .70. Note that these results are entirely consistent with the earlier conclusion that item heterogeneity, which contributes to error in the parallel-form assessment but not in the test-retest assessment, is the main contributor to measurement error.

The Navy and Marine Corps studies of multiple sources of measurement error briefly reported here show the promise of the G-theory approach for getting a better appreciation of the properties of complex, performance-based measures. As this measurement method seems to be becoming more prevalent for educational and employee assessment purposes, the traditional approaches to reliability and validity will not suffice. These early G-theory analyses indicate that, with care and good design, quite reliable hands-on performance measurements can be made.

7

Evaluating the Quality of Performance Measures: Content Representativeness

Having established that scores on well-developed hands-on assessment instruments are not simply haphazard, we now begin to examine the question of determining whether the scores are a meaningful indicator of the job performance the instruments were intended to assess. As a first approach, we examine the concept of content representativeness, frequently called *content validity*, as it relates to job performance measures and present some criteria and tools for evaluating whether a given performance sample can adequately represent an entire job. Chapter 8 further explores the meaningfulness of hands-on test scores by examining their relationships with other variables of interest.

Job performance tests attempt to replicate the full job as faithfully as possible within the constraints of time, cost, and assessment technique. Due especially to time and cost, not all job tasks and the behavior that accomplishes them are used for the measurement. Rather, a sample is chosen to represent the job and turned into a standardized assessment device. The scores produced by this assessment are used to characterize an incumbent's performance on the entire job. One of the greatest challenges posed by performance-based measurement is found in the matter of sampling job content. It is difficult technically to provide a scientifically supportable basis—either judgmental or empirical—for extrapolating from performance on a subset of job tasks to performance on the job as a whole. And there is the added complication (not unknown in other forms of testing) of the expectations of decision makers. From their perspective—and this is as likely to be true of civilian-sector managers as the JPM Project showed it to be true of military officials—a performance measure must "look like" the job to be deemed credible.

From Concept to Practice

The content representativeness of a hands-on performance measure is the extent to which the content of the measure represents the tasks and required performance on the entire job (see Wigdor and Green, 1986:40-44; see also Guion, 1975). In other words, content representativeness refers to "how well a *small* sample of behavior observed in the measurement procedure represents the whole class of behavior that falls within the boundaries defining the content [job] domain" (Guion, 1977:3). This attribute is of particular importance in a test of job performance that purports to say something about competence.

Content representativeness can be logically argued on the grounds that (1) the hands-on performance measure was constructed by systematically sampling a set of tasks/behaviors from a universe of tasks defined by a job analysis and (2) the translation of those job tasks/behaviors into the test preserved the important features of the tasks themselves and the behaviors they require.

A practical example of the process of selecting representative tasks is provided by Lammlein (1987; see also Laabs and Baker, 1989) for the first-term Navy radioman hands-on performance measure (see Table 7-1). First, from among the universe of possible radioman tasks, the job domain for purposes of this research project was defined. Note that "Navy-wide" tasks were eliminated from the domain of interest, as were certain job-unique tasks based "upon such factors as feasibility of testing, operational requirements, availability of equipment, testing time, etc." (Lammlein, 1987:25). Second, the domain of tasks was stratified by content area (e.g., preparing and processing messages) to help ensure that the tasks sampled for the hands-on performance measure covered the wide range of tasks on the job. Third, a job analysis survey and judgments of job experts were used to identify "critical" tasks: tasks important for mission success, tasks complicated to perform, and so on. And fourth, the most critical tasks, paying attention to content strata, were systematically selected. The resulting job sample was evaluated by subject matter experts; four tasks were dropped and a new four were included as more appropriate. This resulted in a sample of 15 tasks on the radioman hands-on performance measure.

Not surprisingly, practice deviates from theory. Trade-offs had to be made in what tasks could reasonably be used in the radioman hands-on performance measure, how those tasks were selected, and the fidelity with which the hands-on performance measure replicated the tasks as they are

TABLE 7-1 Selection of Tasks for the First-Term Navy Radioman Job

Step	Description
1	Develop *task list* (i.e., define job in terms of universe of tasks) based on:
	Review of training and job documentation (pay grades E2-E4).
	Two earlier job analyses.
	Judgment of subject matter experts (experienced supervisors and trainers).
	Job observation by project staff to ensure completeness of list.
2	Identify job *content* categories based on:
	Experts (N = 16) sorting 124 cards, each representing a task, into "piles of similar task content" (Lammlein, 1987:9) and labeling each of those piles.
	Factor analyzing a 124 by 124 matrix of similarities among tasks.
	Labeling the four interpretable factors—(I) preparing and processing messages (69 tasks), (II) setting up equipment (23 tasks), (III) maintaining equipment (21 tasks), and (IV) handling secure messages (11 tasks).
3	Identify task *criticality* by:
	Using job analysis survey to define criticality along dimensions of (1) importance for mission success, (2) percentage of time each task is performed, (3) how complicated each task is to perform correctly, and (4) how often the task is performed incorrectly.
	Defining respondents for survey: (a) first-term radiomen and (b) supervisors.
	Stratified random sampling of 1,042 incumbents and experts to collect criticality data (53% usable return rate).
4	Select 15 *critical tasks* based on:
	Mean criticality rating.
	Expert judgment as to whether the tasks fit within operational requirements, call for available equipment, fit within testing time, and reflect future operational needs.

actually performed on the job. Such trade-offs, however, may compromise content representativeness.

In the JPM Project, each of the Services eliminated certain tasks from its definition of the domain of tasks defining the job. For example, all Services eliminated tasks involving live fire because of safety, cost, or some combination of the two; only the Marine Corps retained a live-fire task. Likewise, all Services eliminated tasks that job experts judged to be redundant, too time-consuming, or trivial. The Navy and the Air Force eliminated hands-on performance of certain tasks performed on jet aircraft engines because of the potential cost of an examinee's error. They substituted incumbents' oral explanations of how they would perform those tasks.

Some restrictions of the universe of possible tasks are less problematic than others. Proper wiring down of screws on an aircraft engine is critical to aircraft safety, but the skill need be demonstrated but once, not the 20 or 30 times a maintenance task might actually call for. However, some omissions, although understandable or even necessary, are inherently threatening to the concept of representativeness—for example, the hands-on performance measure for a grenade launcher that does everything but test the accuracy with which the enlistee can actually fire a grenade. When the full task domain of interest is reduced to a *convenient* task domain, content representativeness may be seriously compromised. At the very least, such reductions must be clearly documented and explained to users of the performance data with accompanying cautions regarding the interpretation of a hands-on performance score as representing on-the-job performance.

Sampling Issues

There are two schools of thought on drawing samples from a domain of tasks that define the job: one advocates purposive and the other random sampling. We examine each in turn.

Purposive Sampling

The purposive sampling school holds that samples should be chosen by job experts exercising informed judgment as to which tasks should be included in a hands-on performance measure that, because of cost and time constraints, can contain only a small number of tasks from a considerably larger domain (e.g., Guion, 1975, 1979). This approach was put into practice widely in the JPM Project, as it is in the private sector.

Purposive sampling is justified on a number of grounds (see, e.g., Wigdor and Green, 1986:49-51; see also Guion, 1979). One justification is that because hands-on performance measures contain a very limited sample of tasks (e.g., 15), each task must be carefully selected to reflect an important (or critical or difficult or frequent), nonredundant job task. To leave task selection to a haphazard procedure, or to a random sampling procedure, according to this argument, would be to risk creating a test that does not cover the essential job elements. When one considers that military jobs contain up to 800 tasks, that job tasks appear to be markedly heterogeneous, and that only 15 to 30 tasks could be tested in the 6 to 8 hours allotted, the intuitive appeal of the argument is clear.

A second reason for the popularity of purposive sampling is the face validity of the resulting test. Adherents argue that random sampling is too likely to produce an instrument that policy makers will reject as not looking like the job. This reasoning was powerful for the designers of the JPM Project. The degree of congressional interest and the enormous investment of resources by the Services convinced most of the JPM researchers that the stakes were simply too high to risk anything other than purposive sampling.

The untoward character of certain tasks might also incline one toward purposive sampling. Some tasks are simply too lengthy, intricate, dangerous, or costly to include in a hands-on performance measure. Leaving such tasks to chance selection through a process of random sampling strikes many as unwise and unwarranted.

Those involved in the JPM Project advanced another argument for purposive sampling that was related to their goal of validating the ASVAB. By selecting tasks of moderate difficulty that are frequently performed on the job and that are judged to be important by experts, the variance of hands-on performance scores would be maximized and the potential correlation between predictor (e.g., the AFQT) and criterion (job performance measurement) increased.[1]

Random Sampling

The second school of thought holds that the better scientific ground for arguing content representativeness is provided by random selection of tasks from the job domain, because only random sampling permits one to make, with known margins of error, statements that can be generalized to the entire domain of tasks. In other words, random sampling techniques provide a strong inferential bridge from test performance to performance on the job. The key consideration is that each task have a known and nonzero probability of selection into the sample (Wigdor and Green, 1986:46). To increase precision, an initial stratification of tasks (e.g., manual versus nonmanual) might be employed prior to selection. Expert advice can also be incorporated into a random sampling scheme through stratified random sampling. The strata reflect experts' judgments as to the most salient content areas of the job. In this way, the best of purposive sampling and the best of random sampling can be merged.

The random sampling school points out that purposive sampling falls prey to selection bias. That is, what experts judge to be representative of the job may be more a function of their most recent experience supervising the job, or it may conform to their conception of the job, which may not encom-

---

[1] Note that, although the correlation may increase, it may not provide the correct estimate if it is based on an unrepresentative sample of tasks/behaviors.

pass the job's full range. Put another way, the random sampling school holds that human judgment may contain predictable errors, and job experts are human. This concern gains credence from reports from the Army and the Navy that panels of job experts disagreed substantially on their judgments of important or critical tasks or samples of tasks for hands-on performance measures (e.g., Lammlein et al., 1987).

Adherents of random sampling hold, in contrast to the purposive sampling school, that the purpose of a hands-on performance measure goes beyond rank ordering individuals in correlational analyses (relative decisions). The purpose also includes interpretations about the levels of performance or competency represented by scores on the hands-on performance measure (absolute decisions). As Cronbach (1971:453) pointed out:

> Content validation . . . looks on the test as an instrument for absolute measurement, though a test validated in this way may have differential [relative-decision] uses also. From an absolute point of view the score on a task indicates that the person does or does not possess, in conjunction, *all* the abilities required to perform it successfully.

The committee was convinced that, on balance, the stratified random sampling approach to the construction of hands-on performance measures is preferable. The conviction was partly a matter of encouraging the most defensible procedures scientifically, but it was also linked to our espousal of a competency approach to the measurement of military performance. We argued (largely unsuccessfully) for absolute scores, which are interpretable in terms of the level of an incumbent's performance, not in terms of how well he or she performed compared with others. We recommended this approach because it corresponds to decisions policy makers must address (e.g., What is the least costly way to fill Service personnel needs and still maintain readiness?) and to the development of personnel assignment algorithms that attempt to maximize some performance-level criterion (discussed in Chapter 9; see also Green et al., 1988).

Although the Marine Corps adopted random sampling techniques and attempted to construct its hands-on tests to permit a competency interpretation of test scores (Mayberry, 1987, 1989), purposive sampling is far more prevalent in practice. Thus, the committee turned its attention to the problem of building an interpretive framework for purposive samples.

How Representative Are Purposive Samples?

Having espoused a random sampling perspective for arguing content representativeness and recognizing that most hands-on performance measures are constructed with purposive samples, we are in a position to ask: From this perspective, how representative is a purposive sample? Our approach to answering the question is based on the following conceptualization of the problem.

To begin with, the purposive sample of tasks/behaviors used for a hands-on performance measure is but one of many possible samples that might be chosen from the domain of interest. The sample could be characterized by its critical features, such as the average importance of the tasks contained in the hands-on performance measure, by the average frequency with which the hands-on performance tasks are performed on the job, by the average difficulty of the tasks, by the average number of errors made while performing the tasks, and so on. A 2nd, 3rd, 4th, . . . 2,000th sample of tasks could also be chosen from the job domain and their critical features characterized.

Now, focusing on the average importance of each of the 2,000 job samples drawn from the domain, a frequency distribution can be constructed with mean importance on the x-axis and frequency on the y-axis. This frequency distribution can be called a *sampling distribution of means*, or *sampling distribution* for short. The next step is to consider where the mean importance of the purposive sample falls within this sampling distribution. If it falls in the center of the distribution, the sample can be considered representative, at least in terms of the *importance* feature. If it falls within plus or minus two standard deviations (standard errors) from the mean of the sampling distribution (roughly at the mean for the entire domain of tasks if 2,000 samples were really drawn), it can still be considered representative. However, if it is more than two standard deviations from the mean, then it is among the 5 percent least probable samples with respect to the characteristic being evaluated. In that case, it would be considered an extreme sample, not representative of the job on the particular feature (importance). This process could be repeated for each of the other critical features of the job; a decision could then be made as to how representative the purposive sample is from a random sampling perspective.

The above process could be simulated on a computer, but there is no need. It has a long history and a straightforward analytic solution. The sampling distribution of means described above will be normally distributed, especially with increasing task sample size. It will have a mean equal to the domain mean and a standard deviation equal to the domain standard deviation divided by the square root of the sample size.

Finally, recognizing that the critical features of a job are most likely correlated, the features could be characterized not only one at a time, but also simultaneously. In this case, a set of mean feature scores (one each for importance, frequency, difficulty, and errors) would be sampled. Each hands-on measure, then, could be characterized by a set of four mean scores, or by a point in a multivariate space that corresponds to the set of four mean scores. By drawing repeated hands-on measures, a multivariate frequency distribution—a multivariate sampling distribution—could be constructed. This sampling distribution can be modeled by the multivariate normal distribution, just as the normal distribution characterized the sampling of mean scores for a single feature. And just as areas of the normal distribution can be marked off to characterize representative samples, so too can areas in the multivariate normal distribution be marked off. Consequently, if one had data on each of the salient features of the domain of tasks that constitute a job, one could then determine just how representative a purposive sample is for each feature and for the features taken together.

Data collected for the Navy (Lammlein, 1987) can be used to illustrate the univariate portion of the analysis. Lammlein collected experts' (incumbents' and supervisors') ratings of the salient features of the tasks that defined the radioman job domain. For each of the 124 tasks, job incumbents indicated whether they had performed the task (PCTPERF) and rated the frequency with which they performed each (FREQ) and how complicated each is to perform correctly (COMP). For each task, supervisors indicated whether they had supervised it (PCTSUP) and rated its importance for mission success (IMPORT) and how often it is performed incorrectly (ERROR).

Using these data, the mean and standard deviation were calculated for each of the six features; the correlations among the features are reported in Table 7-2. Domain parameters are presented above the main diagonal; purposive sample statistics are presented below.

TABLE 7-2 Means, Standard Deviations (SD), and Correlations Among the Salient Features of the Navy Radioman Job

	Feature							
	PCTSUP	PCTPERF	IMPORT	ERROR	FREQ	COMP	Mean	SD
	Domain (124 Tasks)							
PCTSUP		.94	.11	−.10	.59	−.49	42.31	21.30
PCTPERF	.88		−.03	−.06	.70	−.57	36.19	21.47
IMPORT	−.37	−.37		−.20	−.07	.16	3.42	0.56
ERROR	.25	.31	−.25		−.04	.43	1.50	0.27
FREQ	.40	.51	.04	.27		−.65	3.00	0.78
COMP	−.40	−.44	.14	.48	−.46		1.80	0.27
	Purposive Sample (22 Tasks)							
Mean	65.27	59.68	3.54	1.56	3.53	1.71		
SD	11.95	15.26	0.51	0.29	0.56	0.24		

NOTE: Domain parameters are presented above the main diagonal, purposive sample statistics below.

The job domain correlations among the salient features of the radioman tasks follow a predictable pattern. The features that reflect how often the tasks are performed correlate highly with each other (correlations among PCTSUP, PCTPERF, and FREQ). The correlation between supervisors' ratings of how often an error is made on a task and the incumbents' ratings of how complicated the task is to perform (.43) seems reasonable. And the negative correlations between performance frequency and the error and complicated-to-perform variables suggest either that complicated tasks occur less frequently than do easier ones or that tasks are complicated because they are not performed frequently. Finally, the importance feature tends to be unrelated to the other features.

The purposive sample correlations preserve the relationship among the frequency-of-performance task characteristics, somewhat underestimating their magnitude in the job domain. The same is true for correlations between performance frequency and the complicated-to-perform variable. However, the relationship between frequency variables and error are in the opposite direction of the domain relationships. This flip-flop may be due, in part, to small sample size ($n = 22$) and to small magnitudes of the domain correlations (−.10, −.06, and −.04). The sample accurately reflects the magnitude of the domain correlation between error and complicated-to-perform. Finally, the sample correlations between importance and the other features do not accurately reflect the domain correlations due, in part, to the low magnitude of the domain correlations and small sample size.

In sum, the correlational structure of the purposive sample tends to follow that in the universe. The exceptions can be explained by sampling error arising from small sample size and low domain correlations.

The question still remains: How representative is the purposive sample from the random sampling perspective? To complete the answer, we next measured the distance between the features of the sample tasks on the hands-on performance measure and the features of all tasks in the job domain. To do this, we calculated, for each feature, the difference between the sample mean (over 22 tasks) and the domain mean. We then divided this difference by the standard deviation of the sample means, the standard error. This produced a measure of the distance between the purposive sample and what would be expected with random sampling, in standard deviation (standard error) units (Table 7-3).

The results of these calculations for the six features characterizing the radioman's tasks are presented in column 1 of Table 7-3. The distance scores indicate that the purposive sample, as intended, included tasks that very much look like the job if "look like" is defined as "performed frequently." Put another way, the purposive sample is not representative of the job domain; it disproportionately contains frequently performed tasks. Another important piece of information is that the purposive sample tended to in-

TABLE 7-3 Evaluation of Purposive Sampling from the Perspective of Random Sampling: Navy Radioman Rating

	Domain/Sample Center		
Task Feature	Infinite, Simple Random	Finite, Simple Random	Finite, Stratified Random
PCTSUP	5.06	6.29	3.11
PCTPERF	5.06	6.25	3.25
IMPORT	1.00	1.20	1.06
ERROR	1.00	1.20	0.29
FREQ	3.12	4.08	1.50
COMP	−1.50	−1.80	−0.89

NOTE: Distance between purposive and random samples in standard deviation units.

clude tasks that incumbents rated as less complicated to perform than the average task on the job.

Also included in the table is information based on somewhat different assumptions about the size of the job domain and the sampling process. The second column of data provides distance scores assuming that a simple random sample was drawn from a finite domain (124 tasks) rather than from an indefinitely large (infinite) universe. Under this assumption, the interpretation does not change; the increase in the magnitudes of the distances emphasizes that the purposive sample contains "unrepresentative" tasks in terms of frequency.[2]

The last column in Table 7-3 provides distance scores based on the assumption that tasks were selected by stratified random sampling from a finite domain. The stratification reflects the process used by the Navy in creating content categories to ensure that the full range of critical tasks was included in the hands-on performance measure (see Table 7-1, Step 2). Once again, the magnitudes change because the content categories are weighted proportionally to the number of tasks in that category with respect to the number of tasks in the domain. Nevertheless, the story told by the last column, although somewhat less dramatic, remains unchanged.

From a random sampling perspective, then, the hands-on performance measure is not representative of the job. It consistently overemphasizes frequent tasks, as measured by the percentage of supervisors supervising the tasks, the percentage of incumbents performing the tasks, and the incumbents' ratings of how frequently the tasks are performed. One way to re-

---

[2] The magnitude is greater because the domain standard deviation is reduced in magnitude by a factor relating the sample size (n) to the domain size (N): $(N - n)/N$.

solve the representativeness problem is to stratify on frequency as well. (From a purposive sampling perspective, the hands-on performance measure may well do just what it was intended to do. It overemphasizes frequent tasks so that, from a face validity perspective, the hands-on performance measure "looks like" the job.[3])

Rapprochement

This evaluation of a purposive task sample from a random sampling perspective leads to a possible rapprochement between the two methods. If the critical features of the domain of tasks are known, random or stratified random samples can be drawn from the domain of interest, and the representativeness of each of a large number of samples can be evaluated, as we have just done. This procedure could easily be performed on a computer, and unrepresentative samples could be eliminated. At this point, several options arise for incorporating the judgments of subject matter experts. One option is to have experts choose a particular sample for the hands-on test from the set of representative samples. The limitation of this approach is that it may not be possible to make probability statements about inferences to performance on the total job. A second option is to ask experts to remove from the representative set those samples that they find unacceptable, up to some percentage of the samples (say 10 percent). Then, a single sample would be randomly selected for the hands-on test. This approach would allow a probability statement, but the exact formulation of the statement might be difficult to determine. Either approach significantly reduces the risk of erroneously inferring total job performance from a sample of tasks, however. With these options then, the complementary strengths of both the purposive and random approaches can be used to reduce the weakness of each.

Even if a rapprochement is reached with regard to task sampling, however, content representativeness is still limited. By virtue of translating job tasks into assessment devices, some aspects of the job are ignored, which is the subject of the next section.

PERFORMANCE MEASUREMENTS AS JOB SIMULATIONS

Job performance measurements attempt to replicate job tasks as faithfully as possible within constraints imposed by time, cost, and assessment

---

[3] That purposive samples tend to overrepresent frequently performed tasks in a job performance measure makes sense in light of the literature on judgment bias. One heuristic that is frequently used in judging representativeness is how easily something is recalled. Frequent tasks will be easily recalled, thus giving the impression that the performance measure is representative of the job (see Tversky and Kahneman, 1974).

techniques and contexts. But since a hands-on performance measure does not replicate tasks and their variation as encountered day to day on the job, it is a simulation of the job, albeit as concrete a simulation as possible. Consequently, hands-on performance measures can be thought of as job simulations (see Guion, 1979).

In characterizing hands-on performance measures and other measurement devices as simulations of a job, interest centers on whether it is helpful to distinguish simulations along two dimensions: fidelity and abstractness (e.g., Shavelson, 1968). *Fidelity* refers to how closely the simulation incorporates the real-world variables of interest. *Abstractness* refers to how concrete or abstract the simulation is.

A mathematical model of the trajectory of a missile provides a high-fidelity simulation because it incorporates relevant real-world variables. Likewise, a hands-on performance measure provides a high-fidelity simulation by including content-representative measurements. The mathematical model of the missile trajectory, however, is quite abstract, and looks nothing like the actual missile trajectory. In contrast, the hands-on performance measure is quite concrete; an attempt is made to replicate the job task on the test.

Hands-on performance measures tend to be concrete representations, the fidelity of which is reduced in a number of ways. First, military hands-on performance measures are carried out under peacetime conditions even though decision makers ultimately want to know how incumbents would perform in combat. Second, hands-on performance measures are standardized so that, to the extent possible, the tasks presented to one incumbent are the same as those presented to a second incumbent. But on the job, a single task is performed under a myriad of conditions by one incumbent, and it is performed in myriad ways by different incumbents. Third, hands-on performance measures, by their very nature, place incumbents under the watchful eye of examiners, a condition rarely encountered on the job. Consequently, one assumes incumbents are motivated to perform the hands-on tasks; one does not know what they actually would do on the job. Fourth, hands-on performance measures present a sequence of tasks to incumbents that may not fit the sequence of tasks typically encountered on the job. Changing the typical sequence of tasks, although necessary to sample job tasks adequately and to standardize the job performance measurement, introduces an artificiality into the hands-on performance measure. Fifth, hands-on performance measures sometimes remove incumbents from direct performance of a sequence of tasks because of the cost, time, or danger involved. Finally, the job performance of individuals, not units of individuals, as normally occurs on the job, is the focus of the hands-on performance measures.

If hands-on performance measures are simulations of the job that vary in fidelity, even more so do their surrogates, such as pencil-and-paper tests, supervisory ratings, computer simulations, and the like. For example, cognitive paper-and-pencil tests are highly abstract simulations of the job with arguably low fidelity. Pencil-and-paper job knowledge tests move closer to the real world, but only moderately so. Computer simulations and walk-through tests move along the abstractness continuum toward the concrete pole; they tend to be of higher fidelity than paper-and-pencil tests.

Because hands-on performance measures can provide high fidelity, concrete representations of jobs, the JPM Project considers them to have a certain inherent credibility. In interpreting hands-on performance measures, however, it must be remembered that the measure is itself an approximation—a simulation—of the reality one wants to know about. Although it is the closest thing to the job, it still is an abstraction from the job.

8

Evaluating the Quality of Performance Measures: Criterion-Related Validity Evidence

Investigations of empirical relationships between test scores and criterion measures (e.g., training grades, supervisor ratings, job knowledge test scores) have long been central to the evaluation and justification of using test scores to select and classify personnel in both civilian and military contexts. Such investigations, commonly known as criterion-related validity studies, seek evidence that performance on criteria valued by an organization can be predicted with a useful degree of accuracy from test scores or other predictor variables. The implications of a criterion-related validity study depend only secondarily, however, on the strength of the statistical relationship that is obtained. They depend first and foremost on the validity and acceptance of the criterion measure itself.

As summarized by the Office of the Assistant Secretary of Defense—Force Management and Personnel (1987), the program of criterion-related validity studies conducted by the Services in the past was generally based on the statistical relationship between aptitude test scores (i.e., the ASVAB) and performance in military training. Performance in basic and technical training has been the traditional criteria with which the Services validate their selection and classification measures because the data are credible, reasonably reliable, and available.

Training criteria are certainly relevant to the mission of the Services. Failures in training are expensive, and a logical case can be made that training outcomes should be related to performance on the job. The weakness of training outcomes, however, is that they tend to be primarily scores on paper-and-pencil tests of cognitive knowledge that do not tap many of the important aspects of job proficiency, such as psychomotor ability or problem-solving skills (Office of the Assistant Secretary of Defense—Force Management and Personnel, 1987:1-2).

Concerns about the criterion measures that were most commonly used to validate the ASVAB in the past provided much of the motivation for the JPM Project, the goals of which, as has been noted, "are to (1) develop prototype methodologies for the measurement of job performance; and (2) if feasible, link enlistment standards to on-the-job performance" (Office of the Assistant Secretary of Defense—Force Management and Personnel, 1987:3). Realization of the first of these goals would make possible the use of measures of job performance in criterion-related validity studies, the results of which are a necessary, albeit not sufficient, condition for realizing the second goal of the project.

OVERVIEW OF CRITERION-RELATED VALIDATION

Criterion Constructs: Measurement and Justification

Given an adequate criterion measure, the criterion-related test validation paradigm—though subject to a variety of technical complications that will be considered below—is conceptually straightforward. Basically, empirical evidence is needed to establish the nature and degree of relationship between test scores and scores on the criterion measure. But the opening phrase of this paragraph assumes away the "criterion problem," which is the most fundamental problem in criterion-related validation research. Indeed, as Gottfredson (Vol. II:1) points out, it is one of the most important but most difficult problems of personnel research.

Some 40 years ago, Thorndike (1949) defined the "ultimate criterion" as "the complete final goal of a particular type of selection or training" (p. 121). Thorndike's ultimate criterion is an abstraction that is far removed from actual criterion measures. The notion of the ultimate criterion, however, provides a useful reminder that measures that can be realized in practice are only approximations of the conceptual criteria of interest. The value of a criterion-related study depends on the closeness of the criterion measure to this conceptual ultimate criterion.

The conceptual criterion of interest for the JPM Project is actual on-the-job performance. The reasons for this choice are evident. Among the justifications that might be presented for the use of a test to select or classify applicants, none is apt to be more persuasive or intuitively appealing than the demonstration that test scores predict actual on-the-job performance. Like Thorndike's ultimate criterion, however, actual on-the-job performance is not something that can be simply counted or scored and then correlated with test scores. Rather, as described in Chapters 4, 6, and 7, measures of job performance must be developed and justified. They must be accepted as valid, reliable, and relevant to the goals of the Services before they can serve as the criteria by which the validity of aptitude tests will, in turn, be judged. It is for these reasons that previous chapters have devoted so much attention to the development, validation, and assessment of the reliability of job performance measures.

There is no need to repeat the discussion of previous chapters regarding the evaluation of the quality of criterion measures. However, two threats to the validity of any criterion measure deserve special emphasis here and will guide the discussion of specific criterion measures in subsequent sections. Criterion contamination occurs when the criterion measure includes aspects of performance that are not part of the job or when the measure is affected by "construct-irrelevant" (Messick, 1989) factors that are not part of the criterion construct. Criterion deficiency occurs when the criterion measure fails to include or underrepresents important aspects of the criterion construct.

Criterion contamination and criterion deficiency are illustrated by training criteria, whose weaknesses were acknowledged by the Office of the Assistant Secretary of Defense—Force Management and Personnel (1987). Training grades, which are based largely on written tests of cognitive knowledge about the job, may be contaminated by a greater dependence on certain cognitive abilities, such as verbal ability, than is true of actual on-the-job performance. And training measures may be deficient if they leave out tasks that require manipulation of equipment that may be crucial to successful job performance. Concerns about possible criterion contamination and deficiency are not limited to measures of training performance. A hands-on job performance measure, for example, might lack validity because it represents only a small, or atypical, fraction of the important tasks that an individual is required to perform on the job (criterion deficiency). Ratings of the adequacy of performance of a hands-on task might be influenced by irrelevant personal characteristics, such as race, gender, or personal appearance (criterion contamination).

Criterion contamination is most serious when construct-irrelevant factors that influence the criterion measure are correlated with the predictors. Similarly, criterion deficiency is most serious when the criterion measure fails to include elements of job performance that are related to the predictor constructs (Brogden and Taylor, 1950). Of particular concern are situations in which criterion deficiency or contamination "enhance[s] the apparent validity of one predictor while lowering the apparent validity of another" (Cronbach, 1971:488). An understanding of predictor constructs and criterion constructs is necessary to evaluate these possibilities.

Predictor-Criterion Relationships

The relationship between a predictor and a criterion measure may be evaluated in a variety of ways (see, e.g., Allred, Vol. II). Correlation coefficients are often used to express the relationship, but a more basic summary is provided by simple tables and graphs. In the most basic form, the data of a criterion-related validation study using a single test and a single criterion measure consist of pairs of test and criterion scores for each person or counts of the number of times each combination of test and criterion scores occurs.

Consider, for example, a simple hypothetical situation with three levels of test scores (low, middle, and high) and four levels of criterion performance (unacceptable, adequate, above average, and superior). Pairs of test and job performance criterion scores are obtained for a sample of 400 individuals. The number of people with each possible combination of test and criterion scores is shown in Table 8-1. This simple table contains all the information about the relationship between the test scores and the criterion measure. With such a small number of possible scores on the test and the criterion, this basic two-way table can also be used to summarize the findings. For example, individuals with low test scores are most likely to have performance on the criterion that is unacceptable (47 of 100 compared with 16 of 200 with test scores in the middle range or 2 of 100 for those with high test scores). Similarly, the percentage of individuals with high test scores who had superior criterion performance scores (15 percent) is nearly twice that of the total group (33 of 400, or about 8 percent) and 7.5 times as great as that of individuals with low test scores (2 percent).

Such simple frequencies provide the basis for constructing another useful summary of the data, known as an expectancy table. "Such a table reports the estimated probability that people with particular values on a test, or on a combination of predictors, will achieve a certain score or higher on the criterion" (Wigdor and Garner, 1982:53). The expectancy table corresponding to the Table 8-1 frequencies is shown as Table 8-2. As can be seen, almost all individuals with high test scores (98 percent) are predicted to

TABLE 8-1 Frequency of Test and Criterion Score Combinations

Criterion Performance	Test Score			
	Low	Middle	High	Total
Superior	2	16	15	33
Above average	11	24	30	65
Adequate	40	144	53	237
Unacceptable	47	16	2	65
Total	100	200	100	400

TABLE 8-2 Illustrative Expectancy Table: Estimated Probability of a Particular Level of Job Performance Given a Particular Test Score

Criterion Performance	Test Score		
	Low	Middle	High
Superior	2	8	15
Above average or better	13	20	45
Adequate or better	53	92	98

have adequate or better criterion performance and nearly half of them (45 percent) are predicted to have performance that is above average or superior. And almost half (47 percent; 100 percent minus the 53 percent predicted to have adequate or better performance) of the individuals with low test scores would be expected to perform at an unacceptable level.

In addition to demonstrating a relationship, an expectancy table makes it obvious that even when the relationship is relatively strong, as in the illustrative example, there will be errors of prediction. Although the vast majority of individuals with high test scores would be expected to have adequate criterion performance, 2 percent would still be expected to perform at an unacceptable level. Similarly, 2 percent of the individuals with low test scores would be expected to have superior performance on the criterion.

If the criterion categories of unacceptable, adequate, above average, and superior used for the example in Table 8-1 were given score values of 1, 2, 3, and 4, respectively, a mean score on the criterion measure for individuals in each of the three test score categories could be easily computed (Table 8-3). The tendency shown in Tables 8-1 and 8-2 for individuals with higher test scores also to have higher performance on the criterion than their counterparts with lower test scores is again apparent in Table 8-3. What is lost, however, is an indication of the degree of error in the predicted performance (e.g., the fact that 2 percent of the individuals with low test scores had superior criterion performance).

A variety of tabular and graphical summaries similar in general nature to the above tables can be useful in summarizing relationships between test scores and criterion measures. Scatter diagrams and tables or figures show-

TABLE 8-3 Mean Criterion Scores for the Total Sample and for Groups with Low, Middle, and High Test Scores

	Test Score			
	Low	Middle	High	Total Sample
Criterion mean	1.68	2.20	2.58	2.16

ing the spread as well as the average criterion scores of individuals with specified levels of test scores are particularly useful. See Allred (Vol. II) for a detailed discussion of these and other related techniques.

Although graphs and tables have considerable utility, more concise statistical summaries are more typical and can also be useful for certain purposes. The most common statistical summaries of criterion-related validity results are correlation coefficients and regression equations. A correlation coefficient summarizes in a single number ranging from −1.0 to 1.0 the degree of relationship between test scores and a criterion measure (or between other pairs of variables). A correlation of .0 indicates that there is no linear relationship between the two sets of scores, while a correlation of 1.0 (or −1.0) indicates that there is a perfect positive (or negative) relationship.

For simplicity, only linear relationships are considered here. Linear relationships are commonly assumed and widely used in criterion-related validity studies. It is important, however, to keep in mind the possibility that relationships are nonlinear; a variety of techniques is available to investigate the possibility of nonlinearity (see, e.g., Allred, Vol. II).

The correlation between test scores and scores on the criterion for the data in Table 8-1 is .40. In practice, an observed correlation (validity coefficient) of this magnitude between test scores and scores on a criterion would not be unusual.

A linear regression equation expresses the relationship between the test and the criterion scores in terms of a predicted level of criterion score for each value of the test score (low = 1, middle = 2, and high = 3). For the example in Table 8-1, the regression equation is as follows: predicted criterion score = 1.265 + .45 × the test score. Thus, the predicted criterion scores are 1.72, 2.16, and 2.62 for individuals with test scores of 1, 2, and 3, respectively. These predicted values may be compared with the mean criterion scores of 1.68, 2.20, and 2.58 for the three respective score levels (see Table 8-3). The small differences between the two sets of values are due to the use of a linear approximation in the regression equation.

This general overview has ignored a number of complications that must be considered in criterion-related validity studies. For example, the effects of the reliability of the criterion measure, the effects of basing coefficients only on samples of job incumbents who have already been selected on the basis of test scores and successful completion of training, and the possibility that validities and predictive equations may differ as a function of subgroup (e.g., men and women or blacks, whites, and Hispanics)—are all important considerations in a criterion-related validity study. Issues of how multiple criterion measures should be combined, the degree of generalization of validities across jobs, and the degree to which different combinations of predictors yield different validities across jobs are also critical considerations. Some of these complications are considered in this chapter.

Because they are better dealt with in the specific context of the JPM Project, we now turn to a discussion of some of the specifics of the project that are most relevant to an evaluation of the criterion-related validity evidence.

THE NATURE AND INTERRELATIONSHIPS OF CRITERION MEASURES

As discussed in previous chapters, hands-on performance measures are viewed as providing the "benchmark data to evaluate certain surrogate (less expensive, easier to administer tests and/or existing performance information) indices of performance as substitutes for the more expensive, labor intensive hands-on job performance" (Office of the Assistant Secretary of Defense—Force Management and Personnel, 1987:3). Consequently, the quality of hands-on measures takes on special importance within the context of the JPM Project.

It is reasonable to consider hands-on performance measures as benchmarks only to the degree that they are valid and reliable measures of job performance constructs. The threats to validity of criterion contamination and criterion deficiency apply as much to hands-on measures as to alternative criterion measures, such as job knowledge tests, ratings, or administrative records. As is also true of other types of measures, the quality of hands-on measures also depends on the reliability of the measures, that is, the degree to which the scores that are obtained can be generalized across test administrators, tasks, and administration occasions. Further, as Gottfredson (Vol. II) has noted, "job performance can be measured in many ways, and it is difficult to know which are the most appropriate, because there is generally no empirical standard or 'ultimate' criterion against which to validate criterion measures." Thus, it is important to consider the strengths and weaknesses of each of the criterion measures investigated in the JPM Project as well as their relationship.

Hands-On Measures

The development of hands-on measures and the evaluation of their reliability and content representativeness were discussed in previous chapters. Here our focus is the construct validity (see Chapter 4) of the measures. The scoring weights given to steps and tasks, the correlations of part-scores with total scores, and the correlations of hands-on measures with other criterion and predictor measures—all contribute to the evaluation of the construct validity of a hands-on measure. Consider, for example, the hands-on measures developed for the occupational specialty (MOS) of Marine Corps infantry rifleman. The total hands-on test score (TOTAL) for an infantry rifleman consisted of a weighted sum of the score from the hands-on basic infantry core (CORE) and scores obtained from MOS-unique (UNIQUE1) and supplementary (UNIQUE2) tasks (Mayberry, 1988). The CORE was a weighted sum of scores obtained from tasks in 12 basic infantry duty areas. The UNIQUE1 task involved live fire with a rifle; the UNIQUE2 task consisted of more advanced versions of two of the tasks in CORE (squad automatic weapon and tactical measures).

The task weights, test-retest reliabilities, correlations of task scores with the hands-on TOTAL score, and correlations of task scores with GT, the General Technical aptitude area composite from the ASVAB used for classification into infantry occupational specialties, are shown in Table 8-4. The pattern of correlations of task scores with the TOTAL is consistent with what would be expected from knowledge of the scoring weights and the test-retest reliabilities. The land navigation task score, for example, would be expected to have a relatively high correlation with the TOTAL

TABLE 8-4 Task Scoring Weights, Test-Retest Reliabilities, and Correlations with Hands-On Total Score (TOTAL) and General Technical (GT) Aptitude Area Composite (Marine Infantry Rifleman)

Basic Infantry Core (CORE) Duty Area/Task	Scoring Weight	Reliability	Correlations TOTAL	GT
Land navigation	3	.73	.64	.51
Tactical measures 1	3	.61	.58	.38
Squad automatic weapon 1	2.5	.20	.44	.18
Communications	2.5	.47	.48	.30
NBC defense	2	.39	.53	.29
First aid	2	.27	.48	.29
Security/intelligence	1.5	.22	.42	.22
Grenade launcher	1.5	.48	.40	.21
Mines 63	1.5	.25	.32	.20
Night vision device	1	.22	.30	.13
Light antitank weapon	1	.48	.40	.26
Hand grenades	1	.25	.13	.02
MOS unique and supplementary tasks				
Rifle, live fire	*	.45	.66	.13
Tactical measures 2	*	.45	.49	.32
Squad automatic weapon 2	*	.17	.33	.11

* The hands-on total score is defined by: TOTAL = .60 (CORE) + .25 (UNIQUE1) + .15 (UNIQUE2) where CORE is the weighed sum of the basic infantry core duty area/task scores, UNIQUE1 is the score from the rifle live fire task, and UNIQUE2 is the score from the MOS supplementary tasks (tactical measures 2 and squad automatic weapon 2).

SOURCE: Based on Mayberry (1988).

hands-on score because it is one of the two basic infantry duty area tasks with the highest-scoring weights and it has the highest test-retest reliability. The observed correlation of .64 between land navigation and TOTAL is consistent with this expectation. The fact that rifle, live fire, has the highest correlation (.66) with TOTAL of any of the tasks despite its marginal test-retest reliability is due in part to the fact that it has the largest weight for any single task used to define TOTAL. As noted in Table 8-4, UNIQUE1, which is the single rifle live fire task, has a weight of .25 in the computation of TOTAL. The CORE score, which is given a weight of .60 in computing TOTAL, is a composite based on 12 tasks; the UNIQUE2 score, with a weight of .15, is a composite based on 2 tasks.

From an inspection of the correlations of the task scores with TOTAL and a review of the actual measures for each duty area, it is clear that TOTAL measures a relatively complex job performance construct. It involves a combination of tasks that depend heavily on cognitive knowledge of duty area responsibilities (e.g., land navigation, tactical measures 1 and 2, nuclear, biological, chemical (NBC) defense, and communications). TOTAL is also strongly related to tasks requiring complex psychomotor skills, most notably live fire with a rifle. This apparent complexity and the differential dependency of subtasks on cognitive ability are supported by an inspection of the correlations of the task scores with GT, the General Technical ASVAB composite score. As would be expected, tasks judged to have a greater cognitive component have relatively high correlations with GT, and the duty areas that generally involve manipulation of weapons (rifle, live fire, squad automatic weapon 1 and 2, and hand grenades) have correlations of less than .20 with GT.

It is evident that the predictive validity that can be obtained using scores based on the ASVAB for the Marine infantry rifleman MOS depends not only on the way in which hands-on task measures are obtained but the way in which an overall composite hands-on score is defined. Increasing the relative weight that is given to such tasks as land navigation and tactical measures could be expected to increase the criterion-related validities of ASVAB composites. Conversely, increasing the relative weight that is given to such tasks as rifle, live fire, and squad automatic weapon would be expected to decrease ASVAB validities.

We do not mean to suggest that the Marines should use weights other than the ones reported in Table 8-4. Those weights are based on judgments of subject matter experts regarding the importance of each task to the job of a marine rifleman. The point is, however, that, before a hands-on measure is accepted as a benchmark or even as the most important criterion measure to consider, it is critical that the construct validity of the hands-on measure be evaluated and the relevance of the construct as measured to the mission of the Service be judged.

Job Knowledge Tests

Written job knowledge tests are sometimes used as performance criteria. Compared with hands-on performance tests, they are relatively inexpensive to construct, administer, and score. The rationale for using written tests as a criterion measure is generally based on a showing of content validity (using job analyses to justify the test specifications) and on arguments that job knowledge is a necessary, albeit not sufficient, condition for adequate performance on the job. Some have suggested more elaborate justifications for paper-and-pencil tests of job knowledge. Hunter (1983, 1986), for example, has argued that very high correlations between job knowledge and job performance measures are to be expected (on the assumption that knowing how and being able to do something are much the same) and has reported estimated correlations based on corrections for reliability and range restriction as high as .80 between job knowledge and work-sample measures of job performance. Such estimates are obtained only after substantial adjustments for reliability and range restriction, however, and those adjustments depend on strong assumptions. Moreover, as noted by Wigdor and Green (1986:98), written tests "require a much greater inferential leap from test performance to job performance" than do job-sample tests.

Paper-and-pencil job knowledge tests are widely criticized as criterion measures on the grounds of contamination and deficiency. The written format itself introduces a factor of vocabulary-grammar-verbal facility into the performance test that may not be a part of the job—or, even if relevant to the job, not the object of measurement. In multiple-choice tests, a small set of alternatives is identified for the examinee, a situation that is unlikely to be reproduced in the actual work setting. The major deficiency, of course, is that such tests do not deal directly with the ability to perform a task.

One problem involved in using a written test as a criterion measure is particularly pertinent to the JPM Project. The fact that the ASVAB is also a paper-and-pencil test means that all aspects that are common to such tests will lead to high correlations between the predictor and the criterion. This represents a special evaluation problem; because the predictor and the criterion are similarly contaminated, the degree of correlation may be spurious.

Correlations of job knowledge tests with other criterion measures, particularly with hands-on job performance measures, take on particular importance due to the concern about criterion contamination that may be correlated with the predictor test scores. Results reported for 15 specialties/ratings (9 Army, 4 Marine Corps, and 2 Navy) for which hands-on performance measures and written job knowledge tests were administered are shown in Table 8-5. As can be seen, the correlations are consistently positive, ranging from .35 to .61. These correlations demonstrate that job knowledge tests are significantly related to hands-on performance measures. The degree of relationship would appear to be even stronger if adjustments were made for the less-than-perfect reliabilities of both measures. For example, the estimated reliability (relative G coefficient) for the hands-on measure for machinist's mates in the engine room is .72 (Laabs, 1988; see also the results in Table 6-3 for 2 examiners and 11 tasks). Adjusting the .43 correlation in Table 8-5 for the .72 reliability of the hands-on measure and an assumed job knowledge test reliability of .85 would yield a corrected correlation of .55. Increases of a similar order of magnitude might reasonably be expected for the other correlations in Table 8-5.

Even with adjustments for reliability, the correlations between job knowledge and hands-on job performance tests would remain substantially less than 1.0. Thus, as would be anticipated, the two criterion measures do not measure exactly the same constructs. In other words, using a strict standard of equivalence, job knowledge tests are not interchangeable with hands-on performance tests. Compared with other variables, however, the link be-

TABLE 8-5 Correlations of Paper-and-Pencil Job Knowledge Test Scores With Hands-On Job Performance Total Score

Service	Specialty (MOS/Rating)	Correlation
Army	Infantryman	.44
	Cannon crewman	.41
	Tank crewman	.47
	Radio teletype operator	.56
	Light wheel vehicle/ power generator mechanic	.35
	Motor transport operator	.43
	Administrative specialist	.57
	Medical specialist	.46
	Military police	.37
Marine Corps	Infantry assaultman	.49
	Infantry machinegunner	.61
	Infantry mortarman	.55
	Infantry rifleman	.52
Navy	Machinist's mate (engine room)	.43
	Machinist's mate (generator room)	.39
	Radioman	.54

SOURCES: Army results are based on Hanser's report to the Committee on the Performance of Military Personnel at the September 1988 workshop in Monterey, Calif. The Marine Corps results are based on tables provided for the September 1988 workshop. The Navy results are based on Laabs's report at that workshop and Office of the Assistant Secretary of Defense (1987:45-46).

tween the two types of measures is relatively strong. If it could also be shown that decisions about the choice of predictor variables and the rules used for selection and classification would be unchanged due to the choice between these two types of criterion measures, then a case might be made that paper-and-pencil job knowledge tests are adequate surrogates for the more expensive hands-on performance tests.

Interviews

Although interviews have been used most often in selecting and classifying workers, they can also be used to assess job proficiency. A worker is asked how he or she would perform a particular task, perhaps with appropriate equipment and tools at hand, and the oral responses provide evidence about the knowledge the worker can bring to bear on executing the task.

As a criterion measure, interviews are apt to be both deficient and contaminated. A person may be able to describe what would be done, for example, without being able actually to perform the task. Interview results may also be affected to a greater degree than actual performance by personality characteristics and verbal facility.

To minimize potential criterion bias due to contamination and deficiency, the interview procedures that were investigated by the Air Force as part of the JPM Project were designed to be highly structured and task specific. The Air Force task interviews were conducted in conjunction with the hands-on testing. Together, the hands-on tasks and the interview tasks defined an overall performance test, called a walk-through performance test (WTPT). By combining the interview, or show-and-tell performance tasks, with tasks requiring actual hands-on performance, it was possible to cover more tasks, even if indirectly, in a given period of time and to test tasks that were too dangerous, time-consuming, or expensive for hands-on testing.

Correlations between the hands-on and the interview portions of the WTPT for three Air Force specialties are shown in Table 8-6. As was true of the

TABLE 8-6 Correlations Between Interview and Hands-On Portions of Walk-Through Performance Tests (WTPT) and Correlations of Parts With Total WTPT Scores in Three Air Force Specialties

	Correlations		
Specialty	Interview and Hands-on	Interview and WTPT Total	Hands-on and WTPT Total
Air traffic control	.81	.96	.91
Avionic communications	.57	.80	.92
Jet engine mechanic	.54	.81	.90

job knowledge tests, the correlation between the interview and the hands-on portions suggests that they measure similar (but not identical) constructs. If it can be shown that decisions about prediction systems would not be affected by the choice of technique, the walk-through interview tasks might make reasonable surrogates for the hands-on tasks, especially in the case of the air traffic control specialty.

Ratings

Ratings by supervisors are the most widely used criterion in industrial personnel research. They are relatively easy to collect and thus are less disruptive of ongoing activities than other measures. Ratings, however, are likely to be deficient because of people's tendency to give global ratings, no matter how detailed the questionnaire. They are also likely to be contaminated by personal attitudes or individual likings. To combat these amply documented inadequacies, researchers in recent years have designed the behaviorally anchored rating scale, which provides behavioral descriptions of the kind of performance associated with each value on the rating scale.

The subjective nature of ratings also raises concerns about possible systematic biases due to rater and ratee race/ethnic group membership and gender. Research summarized by Landy and Farr (1983), for example, led them to conclude that there is a tendency for raters "to give same-race ratees higher ratings, although the degree of [racial] integration in the setting may affect this" (p. 142).

All of the Services have developed rating scales and used them in the research conducted in conjunction with the JPM Project. Behaviorally anchored ratings scales were developed for use not only by supervisors, but also by peers and by the individuals being rated (self-ratings). Ratings of job-specific and general performances and behaviors were obtained.

The correlations of MOS-specific ratings with total hands-on performance scores were lower than the correlations of paper-and-pencil job knowledge tests with hands-on total scores for each of the nine occupational specialties for which the Army obtained hands-on measures. As shown in Table 8-7, the correlations of ratings with TOTAL ranged from a low of .18 to a high of .28 for the nine Army occupational specialties. These numbers can be compared with the range of .35 to .57 reported in Table 8-5 for the corresponding correlations between job knowledge test scores and hands-on total scores. Although the correlations of supervisory ratings and hands-on performance shown in Table 8-7 for the Navy and Air Force jobs are somewhat higher in some cases than those obtained for the Army jobs, they are still lower than the correlations of interview or job knowledge test scores with hands-on performance measures.

In general, it appears that ratings are not the best available surrogate for

TABLE 8-7 Correlations of Job-Specific Ratings of Performance With Hands-On Job Performance Total Scores

Specialty (MOS)/Rating/AFS	Correlation
Army	
Infantryman	.28
Cannon crewman	.25
Tank crewman	.27
Radio teletype operator	.28
Light wheel vehicle/power generator mechanic	.18
Motor transport operator	.24
Administrative specialist	.22
Medical specialist	.22
Military police	.28
Navy	
Machinist's mates (engine room)	
Supervisor ratings	.33
Peer ratings	.45
Self ratings	.43
Machinist's mates (generator room)	
Supervisor ratings	.19
Peer ratings	.13
Self ratings	.18
Radioman	
Supervisor ratings	.35
Peer ratings	.09
Air Force	
Air traffic control operator	
Supervisor dimensional ratings	.15
Peer dimensional ratings	.21
Self dimensional ratings	.14
Avionics communications	
Supervisor dimensional ratings	.37
Peer dimensional ratings	.30
Self-dimensional ratings	.26
Jet engine mechanic	
Supervisor dimensional ratings	.32
Peer dimensional ratings	.39
Self-dimensional ratings	.14

SOURCES: The Army results are based on Hanser's report to the Committee on the Performance of Military Personnel at the September 1988 workshop in Monterey, Calif. The Navy results are based on Laabs's report and Office of the Assistant Secretary of Defense—Force Management and Personnel (1987:45-46). Air Force results are based on tables prepared for the Monterey workshop.

hands-on performance. However, ratings may, as suggested by other results reported by the Army (Campbell et al., 1987; McHenry et al., 1987; Zeidner, 1987) tap performance constructs (e.g., effort and leadership, personal discipline, and physical fitness and military bearing) that are not assessed by hands-on measures but that are of importance to the Services.

Training Criteria

The advantages and disadvantages of training measures have already been discussed. Since training criteria generally have relied on paper-and-pencil tests, they share many of the characteristics of job knowledge tests. When taken from administrative records, training grades may also suffer from problems caused by an individual's multiple attempts at the tests used to determine course grades. Training grades are also equivocal if they are the product of self-paced instruction or are based on group performance.

The Army investigated the use of specially constructed school knowledge tests as part of its larger study of job performance (Project A). These tests were designed to cover the domain of content covered in the training classes for the nine occupational specialties for which ratings, job knowledge tests, and hands-on performance measures were used. The school knowledge tests, thus, were limited in content to topics covered in training classes, whereas the job knowledge tests included areas that might be dealt with in on-the-job training.

The correlations of school knowledge test scores with job knowledge test scores and with hands-on performance were reported by Campbell et al. (1987) as part of large correlation matrices involving 24 to 30 criterion measures per occupational specialty (Table 8-8).

TABLE 8-8 Correlations of School Knowledge Test Scores With Job Knowledge and Hands-On Performance

Army Specialty	Job Knowledge	Hands-on Performance
Infantryman	.65	.40
Cannon crewman	.65	.36
Tank crewman	.64	.23
Radio teletype operator	.72	.39
Light wheel vehicle power generator mechanic	.63	.37
Motor transport operator	.43	.28
Administrative specialist	.73	.58
Medical specialist	.67	.44
Military police	.40	.14

As might be expected, the correlations between the school knowledge and job knowledge tests are higher than the correlations between school knowledge and hands-on performance for each occupational specialty. For all but two of the nine occupational specialties (motor transport operators and military police), the correlation of school knowledge and job knowledge scores is greater than .60. Although none of the correlations of the school knowledge test scores with the hands-on performance measures reaches .60, school knowledge and hands-on performance scores are clearly related.

RELATIONSHIPS BETWEEN PREDICTORS AND CRITERION MEASURES

Predictor Constructs

ASVAB

The ASVAB is the primary predictor for the JPM Project. It consists of 10 paper-and-pencil cognitive tests, which are combined into various composites by the Services for use in screening and classifying applicants. Table 8-9 lists the 10 ASVAB subtests and provides a brief description of the test contents.

As the table shows, the ASVAB includes a variety of types of test items that are intended to measure a range of cognitive abilities. Factor analyses (e.g., Hunter et al., 1985; McHenry et al., 1987) suggest that the 10 ASVAB subtests measure four broad abilities. The four correlated factors and the subtests that define each factor are (1) verbal ability (defined by WK, PC, and GS), (2) quantitative ability (defined by AR and MK), (3) technical ability (defined by EI, MC, and AS), and (4) perceptual speed (defined by NO and CS). These four broad ability factors have substantial intercorrelations with each other.

Other Predictors

The cognitive abilities measured by the ASVAB are known to provide relatively good prediction of training criteria. These cognitive abilities might also be expected to be related to certain types of hands-on performance. However, with an expanded definition of job performance, it might also be anticipated that prediction could be improved by adding predictors that measure a wider array of constructs. Notably absent from the ASVAB in the way of cognitive measures, for example, are any measures of spatial ability. Also missing, since the ASVAB consists only of cognitive tests, are any measures of psychomotor ability, personality, or interest.

Some experimental predictor measures were included in the research programs

TABLE 8-9 Subtests of the Armed Services Vocational Aptitude Battery

Subtest	Code	Contents
General science	GS	High school level physical, life, and earth sciences
Arithmetic reasoning	AR	Arithmetic word problems
Word knowledge	WK	Identification of synonyms and the best meaning of words in context
Paragraph comprehension	PC	Questions regarding information in written passages
Numerical operations	NO	Speeded numerical calculations
Coding speed	CS	Speeded use of a key assigning numbers to words
Auto shop and information	AS	Automobile, tools, and shop terminology and practices
Mathematics knowledge	MK	High school mathematics, including algebra and geometry
Mechanical comprehension	MC	Use of mechanical and physical principles to visualize how illustrated objects work
Electronics information	EI	Electricity and electronics, including circuits, inductance, capacitance, and devices such as batteries and amplifiers

of the individual Services that were related to the JPM Project. In addition to the ASVAB, for example, the Army's Project A included a wide range of experimental measures of spatial ability, perceptual/psychomotor ability, vocational interest, and temperament/personality. It was anticipated that the interest and personality measures would be useful additions to the ASVAB for purposes of predicting such criteria as attrition, discipline, and leadership. The measures of spatial, perceptual, and psychomotor ability were expected to aid more in the prediction of hands-on performance measures.

In the Army's research, six spatial ability tests (Assembling Objects, Map, Mazes, Object Rotation, Orientation, and Figural Reasoning) were combined to form a single spatial ability composite score (McHenry et al.,

1987). In addition, 10 computer tests defined a total of 21 perceptual-psychomotor scores. These computer tests included such diverse tasks as simple reaction time, short-term memory, target tracking, target shooting, and cannon shooting. The 21 scores from the computer tests were used to define 6 perceptual-psychomotor composite scores: (1) psychomotor, (2) complex perceptual speed, (3) complex perceptual accuracy, (4) number speed, (5) simple reaction time, and (6) simple reaction accuracy (McHenry et al., 1987). The perceptual-psychomotor composites and the spatial composite were combined with 4 composites from the ASVAB (verbal, quantitative, technical, and speed) to provide a total of 11 cognitive composite scores for purposes of prediction. To these, 13 noncognitive composite scores were added as potential predictors based on the Assessment of Background and Life Experiences (ABLE), the Army Vocational Interest Career Examination (AVOICE), and the Job Orientation Blank (JOB).

Problems in Linking Predictor and Criterion Constructs

Correlations of predictor scores and scores on a criterion measure are affected by the facts that criterion measures are always less than perfectly reliable and that the correlations can be computed only for people who have been selected for the job and are still on the job at the time the criterion scores are obtained. Low reliability of a criterion measure attenuates the observed correlation between a predictor and the criterion measure. Predictor-criterion correlations are also reduced in magnitude when they are based on a sample of job incumbents who have been selected for the job on the basis of the predictor or a related variable and, therefore, have predictor scores with reduced variability.

Criterion Reliability

According to classical test theory, the correlation of a test with a criterion measure cannot be greater than the square root of the product of their reliabilities. An estimate of what the correlation would be if both measures were perfectly reliable is obtained from the ratio of the observed correlation to the square root of the product of the reliabilities of the two measures. This ratio is known as the "correction for attenuation" (see, e.g., Lord and Novick, 1968).

Although the reliability of the predictor test and the criterion affect the correlation, it is the latter reliability that is generally of greater concern, for two reasons. First, the instruments used as predictors tend to have higher reliability values than the typical criterion measures. For example, the reliability of a well-constructed cognitive test is often approximately .90; at that level, dividing an observed correlation by the square root of the test reliability will have only a small effect. An observed correlation of .40, for example, would be increased by only .02, to .42, if an adjustment was made for a test reliability of .90. But criterion reliabilities are often substantially lower than those of predictor tests. Hence, adjustments for the unreliability of criterion measures can have a more substantial effect. Second, and more important, predictor and criterion unreliability have differing implications for understanding the predictive power in applied settings. Selection and classification decisions are made on the basis of actual predictor test scores, which are always less than perfectly reliable. Adjusting the predictor score for unreliability would give an inflated notion of the accuracy of the score in practice. Failing to adjust the criterion score for unreliability, however, would result in an underestimate of the actual predictive value of the predictor test in applied settings.

Although adjusting for criterion unreliability is desirable in theory, at least three problems arise in practice. First, appropriate estimates of reliabilities are often unavailable. Second, and more important, predictor and criterion unreliability have differing implications in applied settings. If the question were, "How well does ability predict performance?" we might correct for the effects of unreliability of both predictor and criterion. And if the question were simply, "How well does our particular measure of ability predict our particular measure of performance?"then no corrections are pertinent. But in practice, selection and classification decisions are made on the basis of scores on a particular measure of ability, which is always less than perfectly reliable, but the intent is to predict performance in general. Adjusting the correlation for predictor unreliability would give an inflated notion of the accuracy of the score at hand. However, failing to adjust the correlations for criterion unreliability would result in an underestimate of the actual predictive value of the particular test for performance in general. Finally, adjustments lead to less stable statistical estimates (large standard errors of estimate). Because the direction and magnitude of the effect of unreliability are known, however, the effect can be taken into consideration without actually computing adjusted estimates. For example, if investigations of reliability suggest that the criterion reliability is between .65 and .80, it can be assumed that the observed test-criterion correlations are deflated by a factor of about .10 to .20 percent. In any event, given the limitations of the adjustments, it is important that unadjusted estimates be reported along with adjusted ones if adjustments are made.

Range Restriction

Ideally, correlations for a criterion-related validity study would be based on a random sample of all applicants. Applicants are the population for which the test will presumably be used to make decisions. Hence, the value of the test is best judged in terms of that group. In practice, however, it is almost never possible to base a criterion-related validity study on anything other than an already selected group of people who were chosen for the job and have stayed on the job long enough for the criterion measure to be obtained.

As discussed by Dunbar and Linn (Vol. II), the effects of this selection, commonly known as range restriction, can be complex and, at times, severe. The test that appears to have the highest correlation with a criterion measure in a selected sample is not necessarily the same as the test that would have the highest correlation in an unselected group or a group that was selected on another basis. Indeed, in complex selection situations, the sign of a validity coefficient can even be reversed (see Linn, 1983).

The JPM Project scientists recognized the problem of range restriction and included adjustments for it in calculating validity coefficients. That decision was reasonable. It is also important, however, to report both unadjusted and adjusted coefficients, because the adjustments depend on assumptions that are only approximated in practice. For example, when the assumption of linearity is violated, the correction may be too large or too small depending on whether the slope of the regression tends to increase or decrease at the upper end of the test score distribution. See Dunbar and Linn (Vol. II) for a more detailed discussion of the implications of this and other violations of assumptions.

Summary of Relationships Between Predictors and Criterion Measures

Prediction of Hands-On Performance

The Office of the Assistant Secretary of Defense—Force Management and Personnel (1989) summarized the validity of the AFQT for predicting the hands-on performance measures of the JPM Project in its January 1989 report to the House Committee on Appropriations. Uncorrected correlations between these two variables and correlations that were corrected for range restriction were reported for 23 occupational specialties (8 Air Force, 9 Army, 4 Marine Corps, and 2 Navy). Both sets of correlations are shown in Table 8-10. Also shown in the table are the corrected validities of the appropriate aptitude area (AA) composite for the hands-on performance total scores for the two Services (Army and Marine Corps) whose correlations were included in the 1989 report to the House Committee on Appropriations.

As can be seen, the uncorrected correlations range from a low of .10 to a high of .49; the median value is .26. After correcting for range restriction, the range is from .13 to .67 and the median is .38. The aptitude area

TABLE 8-10 Correlations of Armed Forces Qualification Test (AFQT) and Appropriate Aptitude Area (AA) Composite With Hands-On Performance Total Scores (TOTAL)

Specialty (AFS/MOS/Rating)	AFQT with TOTAL Uncorrected	AFQT with TOTAL Corrected	AA with TOTAL Corrected
Air Force			
Aircrew life support spec.	.12	.21	NA
Air traffic control oper.	.10	.16	NA
Precision measuring equip spec.	.28	.66	NA
Avionic communications spec.	.32	.67	NA
Aerospace ground equip spec.	.17	.36	NA
Jet engine mechanic	.10	.29	NA
Info. systems radio operator	.32	.35	NA
Personnel specialist	.29	.53	NA
Army			
Infantryman	.25	.34	.41
Cannon crewman	.13	.15	.20
Tank crewman	.26	.31	.37
Radio teletype operator	.34	.51	.53
Light wheel vehicle/ power generator mechanic	.13	.13	.28
Motor transport operator	.24	.39	.52
Administrative specialist	.35	.49	.50
Medical specialist	.28	.46	.57
Military police	.23	.49	.57
Marine Corps			
Rifleman	.40	.55	.62
Machinegunner	.49	.66	.68
Mortarman	.33	.38	.48
Assaultman	.38	.46	.50
Navy			
Machinist's mate	.23	.27	NA
Radioman	.22	.15	NA
Median Correlation	.26	.38	.50

NOTE: AA correlations reported only for Army and Marine Corps. Uncorrected correlations and correlations that have been corrected for range restriction are reported as available.

SOURCE: Based on Office of Assistant Secretary of Defense—Force Management and Personnel (1989).

composites have higher corrected validities than the corresponding corrected validities of the AFQT in all 13 Army and Marine Corps specialties. The median corrected validity for these 13 specialties is .50, compared with a median of .46 for the AFQT (also corrected for range restriction) with the same 13 specialties. The uncorrected correlations for the aptitude area composites were not reported.

The distributions of the 23 uncorrected and 23 corrected AFQT validities are shown in Table 8-11. The stem-and-leaf plot to left of center displays the uncorrected validity coefficients. The leaf of 9 next to the stem of .4, for example, indicates that the uncorrected correlation between the AFQT and the hands-on performance total score was .49 for 1 of the 23 occupational specialties (Marine Corps machinegunner, see Table 8-10). The stem-and-leaf plot to the right of center displays the distribution of correlations after corrections for range restriction have been made.

Although the AFQT is not the optimal predictor that might be obtained from the ASVAB, much less with the addition of new predictors to the ASVAB, it is evident from the global summary of the validity results shown in Table 8-11 that the AFQT has a positive relationship with hands-on performance in all 23 occupational specialties that were studied. The median corrected correlation of .38 represents a degree of relationship that has

TABLE 8-11 Stem-and-Leaf Plots of Uncorrected and Corrected Correlations Between the AFQT and Hands-On Performance Total Scores

	Correlations		
	Uncorrected		Corrected*
	Leaf	Stem	Leaf
		.6	667
		.6	
		.5	5
		.5	13
	9	.4	6699
	0	.4	
	85	.3	5689
	4322	.3	14
	98865	.2	79
	4332	.2	1
	7	.1	556
	32000	.1	3
Median Correlations	.26		.38

*Corrected for range restriction.

considerable practical utility for the Services (Brogden, 1946; Brown and Gheselli, 1953; Schmidt et al., 1979).

Based on the results summarized in Table 8-10, the ASVAB has a useful degree of validity for predicting hands-on performance in the occupational specialties studied. The validity coefficients, while generally somewhat lower than validities that have been reported using school or job knowledge tests as criterion measures, are consistently positive and in most cases are high enough to have practical value for purposes of selection and classification. There clearly is a substantial degree of variability across specialties in the validity of the ASVAB for predicting hands-on performance. However, some of that variability is to be expected simply as the result of sampling error. Moreover, in all 13 Army and Marine Corps specialties for which validities for aptitude area composites were reported, the correlations corrected for range restriction were .20 or higher.

Job Experience

The 1989 report to the House Committee on Appropriations by the Office of the Assistant Secretary of Defense—Force Management and Personnel also covered relationships between hands-on performance and time-in-service. The AFQT scores were broken down into four score ranges (Categories I-II, IIIA, IIIB, and IV). Time-in-service was also divided into four categories (1 to 12 months, 13 to 24 months, 25 to 36 months, and 37+ months). Average hands-on performance total scores were then computed for each of the 16 cells corresponding to the 4 AFQT categories and 4 time-in-service categories.

Figure 8-1 shows a plot of the average hands-on performance score as a function of time for each of the four AFQT score ranges. The results are based on the aggregation of the hands-on performance data for 7,093 Service personnel across all 23 jobs for which validity data were reported in Table 8-10. For each job, the hands-on performance scores were first transformed to a standard scale with an overall mean of 50 and overall standard deviation of 10. Those scores were then aggregated across jobs to compute the means displayed in Figure 8-1.

As can be seen in the figure, the hands-on scores increase with level of experience for all four AFQT score ranges. The figure also shows that the level of performance is positively related to AFQT score category at each of the four levels of job experience. The mean hands-on performance score for personnel with the highest AFQT scores (Category I-II), for example, is slightly higher during the first year than the mean performance of personnel with the lowest AFQT scores after more than three years (37+ months) of job experience. That is, the lowest aptitude group never reaches the initial performance level of the highest aptitude group.

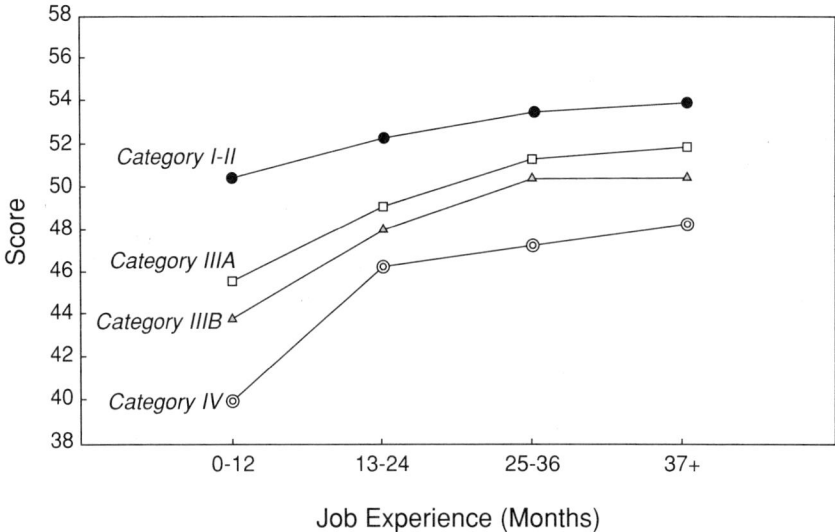

FIGURE 8-1 Mean hands-on total scores by AFQT category and job experience. SOURCE: Based on Office of the Assistant Secretary of Defense—Force Management and Personnel (1991:2-4).

The results in Figure 8-1 are quite global. The pattern of increasing hands-on performance with experience and with AFQT score is quite consistent with the detailed results that are reported for each of the 23 jobs.

Hands-On Versus Job Knowledge Criterion Measures

As discussed above, job knowledge tests were generally found to have substantial, albeit less than perfect, correlations with the hands-on performance measures (see Table 8-5). Job knowledge tests have a number of potential advantages as criterion measures. They are easy to administer and, compared with hands-on performance measures, they are relatively inexpensive. Because they are paper-and-pencil tests, however, job knowledge tests raise concerns about criterion contamination and criterion deficiency.

Questions about criterion deficiency can be addressed in part by analyzing the strength of the relationship between the job knowledge test scores and hands-on performance measures, such as those summarized in Table 8-5. Job analyses and content analyses of the tests can also be used to evaluate the degree to which the tests represent knowledge that is judged to be necessary for successful job performance. In general, the strength of the relationship between the job knowledge tests and hands-on performance measures in the JPM Project appears adequate to support some uses of the job knowledge tests as criterion measures. Assuming that the results of content and job analyses also support the use of the job knowledge tests, the primary remaining issue is that of criterion contamination.

Since job knowledge tests and the ASVAB depend on the results of paper-and-pencil, multiple-choice testing formats, it might be expected that this common method variance would inflate the correlation between the two types of measures. Comparisons of the uncorrected predictive validities of the appropriate aptitude area composite on the ASVAB using job knowledge tests and hands-on performance measures are provided in Figure 8-2 for the nine Army and four Marine Corps occupational specialties for which

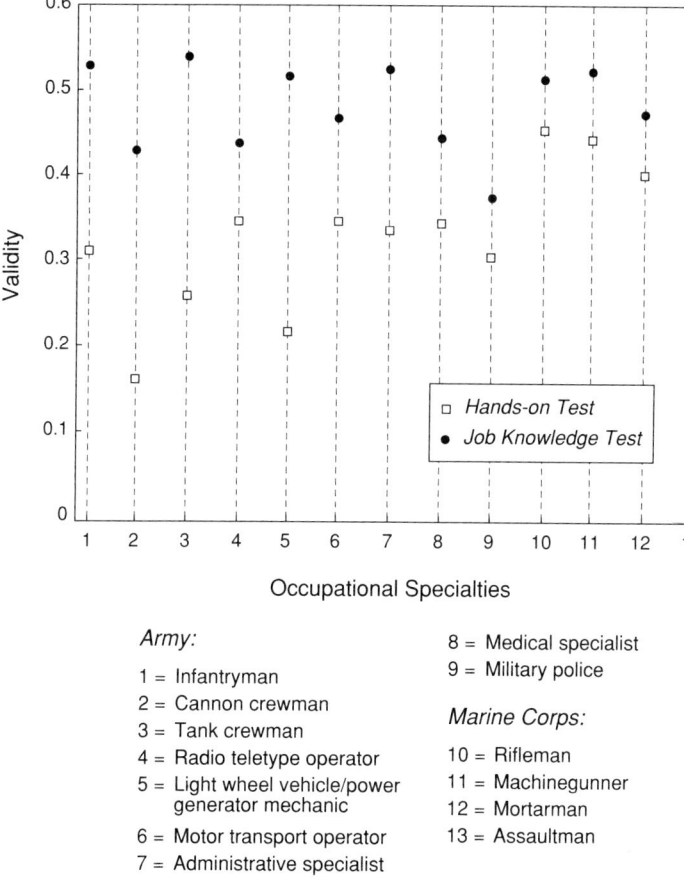

FIGURE 8-2 Aptitude area validities for hands-on and job knowledge tests for 13 occupational specialties. SOURCE: Based on table of correlations provided as part of the common data analysis plan, Monterey, Calif., September, 1988.

both criterion measures were obtained. Consistent with the expectation based on the argument of common method variance, the validity is higher for the job knowledge test criterion measure than for the hands-on criterion measure in all 13 occupational specialties.

Although the differences shown in the figure are sometimes relatively large, a given aptitude area composite appears to have a useful degree of validity for both criterion measures in all 13 jobs. Thus, it would appear that validation studies using job knowledge tests as criterion measures can provide useful indications of the predictive validity of ASVAB scores for military jobs. What results such as those shown in Figure 8-2 do not reveal, however, is the extent to which the use of one criterion measure rather than the other is likely to lead to different decisions about the best predictor for a given job. More detailed analyses of the expanded predictor sets are needed to answer such questions.

New Predictors

To investigate additional predictors, the Army used five composite job performance factors derived from the approximately 270 variables gathered from each soldier (Figure 8-3). These performance constructs are called (1) Core Technical Proficiency, (2) General Soldiering Proficiency, (3) Effort and Leadership, (4) Personal Discipline, and (5) Physical Fitness and Military Bearing (Campbell, 1986; Sadacca et al., 1986; Wise et al., 1986, McHenry et al., 1987). Core Technical Proficiency corresponds most closely to the hands-on performance total score, but it includes job knowledge and school knowledge test results. General Soldiering Proficiency also includes hands-on tasks and job and school knowledge tests. The remaining three criterion constructs are based mainly on ratings and some administrative records (see, e.g., Campbell et al., 1987).

Cognitive tests provided the best prediction for the General Soldiering Proficiency and Core Technical Proficiency criterion measures. Spatial ability and perceptual-psychomotor ability measures provided some incremental validity over that obtained from the four ASVAB aptitude composites (verbal, quantitative, and technical ability and perceptual speed) against these two criterion measures. For example, the average incremental validity for spatial ability based on correlations corrected for range restriction and adjusted for shrinkage was .02 for Core Technical Proficiency and .03 for General Soldiering Proficiency (McHenry et al., 1987). The temperament/personality, interest, and preference measures did not add much to the validity of the ASVAB for predicting those two criterion measures.

For the remaining three dimensions of performance (Effort and Leadership; Personal Discipline; Physical Fitness/Military Bearing), the noncognitive predictors not only added to the predictive validity of the ASVAB, but in

1. *Task proficiency: specific core technical skills:* The proficiency with which the individual performs the tasks that are "central" to his or her job (MOS). The tasks represent the core of the job; they are the primary definers from job to job.

• The subscales representing core content in both the knowledge tests and the job sample tests that loaded on this factor were summed, standardized, and then added together for a total factor score. The factor score does not include any rating measures.

2. *Task proficiency: general or common skills:* In addition to the core technical content specific to an MOS, individuals in every MOS are responsible for being able to perform a variety of general or common tasks—e.g., use of basic weapons, first aid, etc. This factor represents proficiency on these general tasks.

• The same procedure (as for factor one) was used to compute the knowledge and hands-on general task scores, standardized within methods, and with the two standardized scores added together.

3. *Peer leadership, effort, and self-development:* Reflects the degree to which the individual exerts effort over the full range of job tasks, perseveres under adverse or dangerous conditions, and demonstrates leadership and support toward peers. That is, can the individual be counted on to carry out assigned tasks, even under adverse conditions, to exercise good judgment, and to be generally dependable and proficient?

• Five scales from the Army-wide Behaviorally Anchored Rating Scale (BARS) rating form (Technical Knowledge/Skill, Leadership, Effort, Self-Development, and Maintaining Assigned Equipment), the expected combat performance scales, the job-specific BARS scales, the general performance rating, and the total number of commendations and awards received by the individual were summed for this factor.

4. *Maintaining personal discipline:* reflects the degree to which the individual adheres to Army regulations and traditions, exercises personal self-control, demonstrates responsibility in day-to-day behavior, and does not create disciplinary problems.

• Scores on this factor are composed of three Army-wide BARS scales (Following Regulations, Self-Control, and Integrity) and two indices from the administrative records (number of disciplinary actions and promotion rate).

5. *Physical fitness and military bearing:* Represents the degree to which the individual maintains an appropriate military appearance and bearing and stays in good physical condition.

• Factor scores are the sum of the physical fitness qualification score from the individual's personnel record and two rating scales from the Army-wide BARS (Military Appearance and Physical Fitness).

FIGURE 8-3 Performance factors representing the common latent structure across all jobs in the Army's job performance study (Project A). Note: The criterion measures that comprise each factor are as indicated. SOURCE: Campbell (1986).

some cases also had the highest validities of any of the predictors. Together, the ASVAB and the noncognitive predictors had higher validity than either had alone.

Predictor and Criterion Measure Construct Similarities

The corrected validities of the four ASVAB aptitude factors for one of the Marine Corps specialties (rifleman) are shown in Figure 8-4 using hands-on total scores and job knowledge test scores as the criterion measures. As would be expected, the validities are somewhat higher for each of the aptitude factors when job knowledge test scores serve as the criterion than when hands-on total scores are used. Of greater interest, however, is the relatively larger variation in the validities obtained for the four aptitude composites in predicting hands-on performance than in predicting job knowledge test scores. For the job knowledge test, any of the three nonspeeded apti-

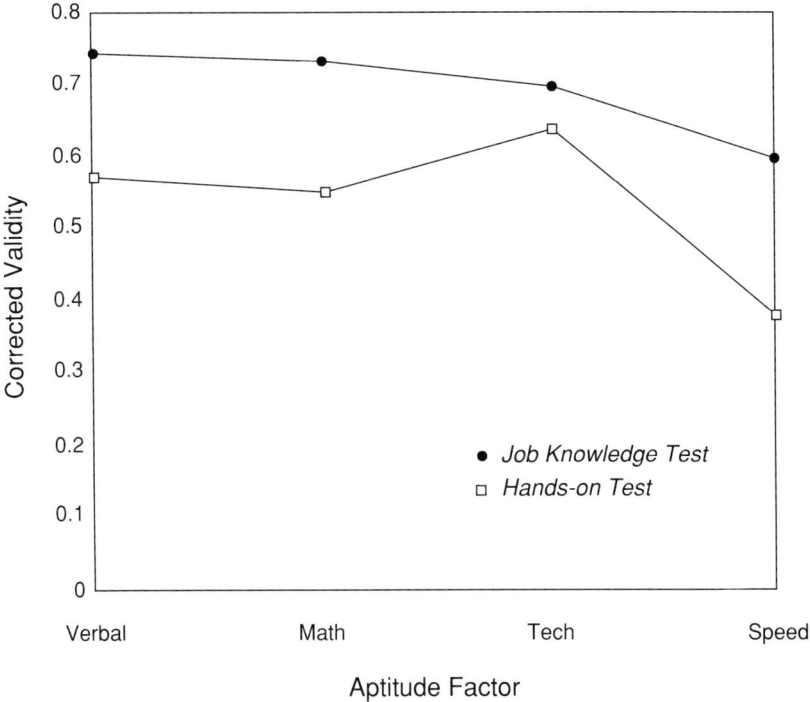

FIGURE 8-4 Validities (corrected for range restriction) of ASVAB aptitude factors for hands-on total scores and job knowledge test scores: Marine rifleman. SOURCE: Based on Mayberry (1988).

tude factors (verbal, quantitative, or technical ability) yields about equally good prediction. By a very small amount, the technical factor actually has the lowest validity and the verbal factor the highest among the three nonspeeded aptitude factors. With the hands-on measure, the variation in the validities is not only greater, but the highest validity is obtained using the technical factor.

The greater variation in the validities of the aptitude factors for the hands-on measure than for the job knowledge test shown for Marine rifleman in Figure 8-4 was also observed for the other three Marine Corps specialties (machinegunner, mortarman, and assaultman) included in the JPM Project. This greater variation in validities for hands-on measures is consistent with prior expectations. The lower verbal load of the hands-on measure and greater dependence on technical aspects of job performance result in relatively higher validities for the technical aptitude factor and relatively lower validities for the verbal factor. Such a change in the pattern of validities supports the construct validity of the hands-on measures. It also enhances the likelihood of finding variations in the patterns of validity coefficients from one job to another.

Job-to-Job Differences in Validities

In addition to demonstrating that the predictor tests have a useful degree of validity for predicting hands-on performance, it is of interest to determine the degree of differential validity and differential prediction. Unfortunately, the terms *differential validity* and *differential prediction* are used to refer to the variation in validities (or in prediction equations for various tests from one job to another) and to the degree to which validities (or predictions) for a given job differ for identifiable subgroups of the population (e.g., men and women or minority and majority group members). To avoid this possible confusion, we speak of job-to-job differences in validities or differences in prediction equations (discussed in the next section), rather than using the shorter and more traditional labels of differential validity and prediction.

Demonstrating that the ASVAB has a useful degree of validity for hands-on criterion measures in all military jobs would be sufficient if the ASVAB was used only for making selection decisions. The degree to which the pattern of predictive validities of the ASVAB subtests varies from one job to another is also important, however, for purposes of making classification decisions. Classification would be facilitated by finding that different sets of subtests provide the best prediction of performance for different jobs. If the subtests have identical validities for all jobs, then the same people will have the highest predicted performance in all jobs. However, if the pattern of validities varies from job to job, then the people who have the highest predicted performance on one job will not necessarily have the highest predicted performance on another job, and by differential assignment to jobs the overall performance across jobs can be enhanced.

Using training criteria, the differences in validities from job to job that have been obtained for the ASVAB over the years have been relatively modest. It was expected that the lack of greater variation in the pattern of validities across jobs might be partially due to the substantial general cognitive component in all of the nonspeeded ASVAB tests and in the training criterion measures. Assuming that the hands-on criterion measures reflect greater differentiation between jobs than the more cognitive training measures, it might therefore be expected that the pattern of validities would be more variable from job to job with hands-on measures than had been previously obtained using training measures. Greater variation in validities and in predictions might also be expected with an expanded set of predictors that included spatial and psychomotor tests.

Three of the Army occupational specialties can be used to illustrate job-to-job difference in validities. Observed (uncorrected) validities of the eight nonspeeded ASVAB tests with total hands-on score as the criterion measure are shown for the infantryman, light wheel vehicle/power generator mechanic, and administrative specialist occupations in Figure 8-5. Reading from left to right in the figure, the tests are arranged as follows: The first three tests (General Science, Word Knowledge, and Paragraph Comprehension) are indicators of the verbal aptitude factor, the next two (Arithmetic Reasoning and Mathematics Knowledge) are indicators of the quantitative factor, and the final three (Auto/Shop, Mechanical Comprehension, and Electronics Information) are indicators of the technical factor.

For the infantryman job, the validities for the eight tests are all relatively similar in magnitude, ranging from a low of .20 for Electronics Information and Word Knowledge to a high of .27 for General Science and Mechanical Comprehension. The pattern of validities for the two other jobs shown in the figure is much more differentiated. The three verbal tests and two math tests have relatively low validities in comparison with the three technical tests for mechanics. As might be expected, the Auto/Shop test has the highest validity (.26) for mechanics, followed by Mechanical Comprehension (.20) and Electronics Information (.19). Moving from mechanics to administrative specialists, there is a marked, and intuitively reasonable, shift in the pattern of validities. The three technical tests that provide the best prediction for mechanics have the lowest validities among the eight nonspeeded tests for administrative specialists. The two math tests have the highest validities (.31 for Mathematics Knowledge and .30 for Arithmetic Reasoning) for administrative specialists.

The contrasting patterns of validity coefficients for the three jobs in the figure suggest that there are some job-to-job differences in validities and

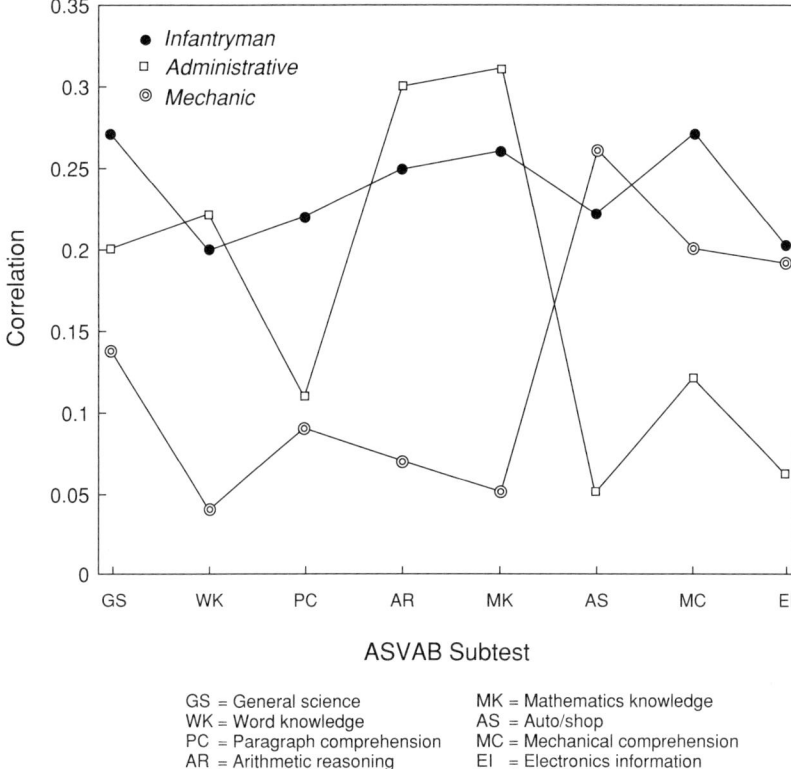

FIGURE 8-5 Correlations of ASVAB tests with hands-on total scores for three Army occupational specialties. SOURCE: Based on correlations provided by the Army for the common data analysis plan, Monterey, Calif., September 1988.

predictions that can be capitalized on for purposes of making differential assignments of personnel to jobs. These three jobs were selected to illustrate differences in patterns, however. Many jobs have more similar patterns of validities. Moreover, these simple comparisons are no substitute for more comprehensive analyses (yet to be reported by each of the Services) that identify the best predictive composites for the hands-on measures of each of the military jobs investigated and evaluate the utility of the predictive composites when used operationally to place personnel in different specialties.

FAIRNESS ANALYSIS

The discussion now turns to group differences in predictor test scores and in job performance scores. Implementation of the Civil Rights Act of

1964 challenged psychologists to develop analyses to assess the fairness of tests. As government policy focused on providing equal employment opportunity to groups formerly kept out of the economic mainstream, it was quickly realized that reliance on test scores without regard to group membership can have substantial adverse consequences because there are sizable differences in average tests scores among various population groups. Hence the need was felt to find out whether these differences in average test scores are related to real performance differences or are artifactual.

The now-conventional fairness analysis focuses on whether selection tests like the ASVAB function in the same way for different population groups, wherein it examines two questions: whether the *correlations* of test scores with on-the-job criterion measures differ by racial or ethnic group or gender; and whether *predictions* of criterion performance from test scores differ for employees who are of different racial or ethnic identity or gender. Both of these questions take test scores as their point of departure. Recently, an additional perspective on fairness has been advocated (Hartigan and Wigdor, 1989) that looks beyond whether the predictor test functions in the same way for specified groups. This approach asserts that realized job performance is the object of fundamental interest and works from performance scores back to what the predictor scores should look like. One of the important issues to emerge from this perspective on fairness concerns the size of group differences in job performance compared with group differences in predictor scores. Each of these aspects of test fairness is discussed below in turn.

Group-to-Group Differences in Prediction Systems

Although limited in various respects described below, data provided by the Services permit us to describe the degree of similarity that scores on current forms of the ASVAB have in predicting hands-on performance and job knowledge criteria for minorities and nonminorities and for men and women. The analyses presented in this section provide some insight into the magnitude of group-to-group differences in prediction systems, as well as some appreciation of the complexity of this differential prediction problem.

The principal limitation of the data on subgroup prediction systems involving hands-on performance measures is the large degree of sampling error that exists due to small sample sizes in the focal groups of the comparisons, minorities and women. Table 8-12 illustrates this problem. Seven of 21 occupational specialties had complete hands-on performance data for fewer than 25 minority recruits. The problem is somewhat worse for the hands-on measures for the gender comparisons. The size of the focal group is less of a concern with the job knowledge criterion, but even here the regression estimates in the focal group are based on far fewer observations

TABLE 8-12 Number of Studies by Focal Group Sample Size for Current ASVAB Differential Prediction Data

Sample Size in Focal Group	Knowledge	Hands-on Performance	Job
Race comparisons			
Fewer than 25	7		2
25 to 75	8		5
75 or more	6		6
Gender comparisons			
Fewer than 25	6		0
25 to 75	7		5
75 or more	3		2

SOURCE: Data submitted to the Committee on the Performance of Military Personnel.

than in the comparison groups. This degree of instability in the results for women and minorities should be kept in mind in evaluating the group-to-group differences presented in this section.

It should also be remembered that validity correlations will differ depending on the heterogeneity of the group scores. When one group has substantially less variance on either variable in the correlation, the size of the correlation will be smaller, even if, from a regression perspective, the test is equally predictive for both groups. Also, when one group has a considerably lower mean value on the predictor, and there is a substantial degree of selectivity for the job, the selection will impinge more strongly on the group with the lower mean; corrections for range restriction, which are typically made on the total population, might be inappropriate unless the same regression system is applicable to both groups.

Comparisons between minorities and nonminorities and between women and men are discussed separately below.

Minority Group Comparisons

Validity Coefficients Although comparisons of correlations can be quite misleading when concern centers on entire prediction systems, they are nevertheless useful when concern centers on groups for which it may be hypothesized that the predictor has no utility in selection. Table 8-13 summarizes correlations between criterion measures and selection composites used by the Services. (One occupational specialty with only three black

TABLE 8-13 Weighted Average Correlations Between ASVAB Predictors and Job Performance Criteria for Black and Nonminority Samples

Predictor Criterion	Number of Studies	Blacks		Nonminorities	
		N	Avg. R	N	Avg. R
Selection composite					
Hands-on	21	1,487	.22	5,557	.29
Job knowledge	12	1,304	.26	4,485	.43
AFQT					
Hands-on	20	1,118	.14	4,303	.17
Job knowledge	11	935	.20	3,231	.38

NOTE: Average correlations using within-group sample sizes as weights.

SOURCE: Data submitted to the Committee on the Performance of Military Personnel.

recruits in the validation sample was excluded from this analysis). When viewed in this global manner, these results reveal the already-noted fact that validities tend to be higher when a written job knowledge test is used as the criterion as opposed to a hands-on measure of performance (due at least in part to method effects). However, the average correlations for blacks and nonminorities are much more similar in magnitude when the hands-on measure serves as the criterion (.22 and .29 as compared with correlations of .26 and .43 on the written test). For both criteria, the average predictive validity of the selection test is lower for minorities, but only markedly so when another written test serves as the criterion. Although there is substantial variability in the size of the difference from one job specialty to another, scatterplots of correlations that had been transformed to Fisher's Z's showed that, in the majority of cases, when a predictor lacked utility for minorities, its utility for nonminorities was also questionable.

Prediction Equations The comparisons of prediction equations consider only cases for which a measure of hands-on performance served as the criterion. These were the only data in which all four Services were represented. Customary procedures were followed in this evaluation of group-to-group differences in prediction equations. The sections that follow discuss standard errors of estimates and regression slopes and intercepts, in that order, followed by direct comparisons of predicted scores using the within-group and combined-group equations.

Throughout this section, the results of the differential prediction analyses that were provided by the four Services for this study are presented without regard to the levels of statistical significance observed in individual analyses. Rather than base decisions about the extent of prediction differences among groups on individual studies, this section attempts to describe general trends that can be seen from a description of observed results from all pertinent studies. To discourage potentially misleading overinterpretations of these trends, results from studies with particularly small samples of recruits in the focal group of a comparison are identified.

Standard Errors of Prediction Studies of group-to-group differences in prediction systems have generally found regression equations to yield more accurate predictions of performance for nonminorities and women than for minorities and men (Linn, 1982). The use of hands-on performance criteria in the JPM Project, as opposed to paper-and-pencil tests, does not appear to have altered that finding to any great extent. The stem-and-leaf plot in Table 8-14 shows the distribution of ratios of mean-squared errors of prediction for blacks and nonminorities. Ratios based on samples of fewer than 25 blacks are shown in regular type, others in boldface type. Ratios above 1.0 are cases in which prediction for blacks is less accurate than those for nonminorities. Thus, in 13 of 20 occupational specialties the errors of prediction for blacks were larger than those for nonminorities, given the selection composite as predictor. The same picture emerges when the AFQT

TABLE 8-14 Stem-and-Leaf Plot of Ratios of Mean-Squared Errors of Prediction for Blacks and Nonminorities

	Leaf	Stem	Leaf	
		1.8		Predictions for Blacks
	5	1.7	4	Less Accurate
		1.6		
		1.5		
	6	1.4		
	0	1.3	29	
	2	1.2	125	
	8653	1.1	**27**	
AFQT	**50**	1.0	**046899**	Selection Composite
	8530	.9	47	
	631	.8	**23**	
	7	.7	**9**	
	9	.6	7	
		.5		
	3	.4		
		.3		Predictions for Blacks
		.2	9	More Accurate

NOTE: Leaves in boldface type are based on samples of 25 or more black recruits.

SOURCE: Based on data submitted to the Committee on the Performance of Military Personnel.

176   PERFORMANCE ASSESSMENT FOR THE WORKPLACE

is the predictor. However, the largest differences were for jobs with small sample sizes in the black cohort. Thus, the stable values in the table suggest relatively minor group differences in the accuracy of prediction.

Slopes and Intercepts Hypothesis tests of group-to-group differences in slopes were conducted for all occupational specialties with appropriate data. The t-ratios on which such tests were based are shown in the stem-and-leaf plot in Table 8-15. In this plot, t-ratios based on the selection composite form leaves to the right. Those based on the AFQT form leaves to the left. Positive t-ratios indicate that the slope for blacks was steeper than the slope for nonminorities. (There seemed to be no pattern that would indicate that the regression line for blacks was systematically flatter than that for nonminorities, as might be expected from other comparisons of this type; see Linn, 1982; Hartigan and Wigdor, 1989).

As the values in the table indicate, the t-ratios for slope differences between blacks and nonminorities tend to be larger in absolute value when the AFQT is the predictor variable in the equation. When the selection composite is the predictor, no slope differences are significant at the 10 percent level. Many of the t-ratios in the plot are instances in which the significance test had very low power due to the small sample of black recruits (Drasgow and Kang, 1984). If one were to argue that the alpha level for these tests should be raised to guard against Type II errors (here, concluding the slopes are the same when, in fact, they are not), only two slope differences involving the selection composite would be significant at the 25

TABLE 8-15 Stem-and-Leaf Plot of T-Ratios for Differences Between Slopes for Blacks and Nonminorities

	Leaf	Stem	Leaf	
	0	2.		
	7	1.	8	
	10	1.	**023**	
	9865	0.	5699	
AFQT	320	0.	**13**	Selection Composite
	10	−0.	022233	
		−0.	**6**	
	100	−1.	**001**	
	86	−1.	5	
		−2.		
	85	−2.		

NOTE: Leaves in boldface type are based on samples of 25 or more black recruits.

SOURCE: Based on data submitted to the Committee on the Performance of Military Personnel.

percent level. However, 5 of 20 slopes differences would be judged significant at the 10 percent level when the AFQT is the predictor.

The contrasting results of tests for slope differences provide a useful illustration of the possible effects of selection on the outcome of a differential prediction study. Because the AFQT is not an explicit selection variable in this context (see Dunbar and Linn, Vol. II), it is possible that the more frequent slope differences are at least a partial artifact of differing degrees of range restriction in the comparison groups. The fact that the two largest slope differences for the selection composite were from jobs with nonsignificant slope differences for the AFQT is consistent with this hypothesis of a selection effect.

Given the above results regarding slopes, within-group intercepts in jobs in which slopes were not significantly different at the 25 percent level were recalculated based on a pooled estimate of the slope. For each job, the intercept for blacks was subtracted from that for nonminorities, and the difference was divided by the standard deviation of the criterion in the black sample. These standardized differences between intercepts are given in the stem-and-leaf plot shown as Table 8-16. Although in most cases small in magnitude, the intercept differences do show a trend found in previous differential prediction studies toward positive values (Linn, 1982; Houston and Novick, 1987), which implies that the use of prediction equations based on the pooled sample in these jobs would result in overprediction of black performance more often than not. However, the amount of overprediction

TABLE 8-16 Stem-and-Leaf Plot of Ratios of Standardized Differences Between Intercepts for Blacks and Nonminorities

	Leaf	Stem	Leaf	
	2	1.		
		1.	1	
		0.		
	6	0.		
AFQT	4	0.	45	Selection Composite
	333322	0.	2223	
	11110	0.	000011	
	1	−0.	011111	
	2	−0.		
		−0.		

NOTE: Leaves in boldface type are based on samples of 25 or more black recruits.

SOURCE: Based on data submitted to the Committee on the Performance of Military Personnel.

that would typically be found appears to be smaller than in previous studies, which have used less performance-oriented criterion variables.

Criterion Predictions Perhaps a more complete picture of the magnitude of group-to-group differences in regression lines can be obtained by examining the actual criterion predictions made by group-specific and pooled-group equations. Such differences were calculated for each occupational specialty at three points on the predictor scale: one standard deviation below the black mean (–1 SD), the mean in the black sample, and one standard deviation above the black mean (+1 SD). Means and standard deviations of these differences (expressed in black standard deviation units) were calculated for groups of studies based on the size of the black sample. The results are shown in Table 8-17.

Three features of the results in the table should be noted. First, all average differences in the table are positive, which reflects once again the fact that the combined-group equations, on average, lead to overprediction of black performance (i.e., predictions that are somewhat higher on average than the performance achieved by blacks with particular scores on predictor variables). Second, the largest differences in the table tend to be those that are the least stable with respect to sampling (from jobs with data on fewer than 25 black recruits). And third, the differences tend to be larger when the AFQT is the predictor. This last result, again, may well be due to the fact that the AFQT is not an explicit selection variable for most jobs; hence, group differences in this case are confounded by differing degrees of range restriction in the comparison groups.

TABLE 8-17 Standardized Differences Between Predicted Scores from Black and Pooled Equations

Black Sample Size		Selection Composite			AFQT		
		–1SD	Mean	+1SD	–1 SD	Mean	+1 SD
Fewer than 25	(Avg.)	.12	.17	.22	.20	.27	.34
	(SD)	.37	.44	.56	.38	.47	.67
Between 25 and 75	(Avg.)	.08	.07	.05	.12	.08	.04
	(SD)	.14	.11	.20	.17	.18	.33
More than 75	(Avg.)	.07	.10	.13	.07	.15	.23
	(SD)	.10	.09	.11	.10	.09	.20

SOURCE: Based on data submitted to the Committee on the Performance of Military Personnel.

The Performance-Based Focus on Fairness

As we have seen in the previous analyses, there are small differences in the accuracy of prediction of job performance from test scores for blacks and nonminorities, but for practical purposes the same regression lines predicted performance about as well for both groups. Remembering always the thinness of the data for the black job incumbents, we observe that the ASVAB appears to fulfill that particular definition of fairness. However, this analysis does not address imperfect prediction per se as it affects the lower-scoring group. A comparison of the relative size of group differences on the predictor and criterion measures is illuminating.

Table 8-18 summarizes the mean differences between the scores of black and nonminority enlisted personnel on the AFQT and two types of criterion measure, a written job knowledge test and the hands-on performance test. In these figures, a negative difference indicates that the average black job incumbent scored *below* the average nonminority job incumbent by the given number of standard deviation units. The average group differences in scores across the 21 studies was –.85 of a standard deviation on the AFQT, –.78 of a standard deviation on the job knowledge test, and –.36 of a standard deviation on the hands-on test. In addition to these mean differences, the stem-and-leaf plot in Table 8-19, which compares group differences on hands-on and job knowledge criterion measures, shows that the entire distribution of differences on the hands-on criterion is shifted in a direction that indicates greater similarity between blacks and nonminorities on the more concrete and direct measure of job performance.

To the extent that we have confidence in the hands-on criterion as a good measure of performance on the job, these findings strongly suggest that scores on the ASVAB exaggerate the size of the differences that will ultimately be found in the job performance of the two groups. These results are in line with results for the private sector, as recently reviewed in *Fairness in Employment Testing* (Hartigan and Wigdor, 1989), which found an average score difference of 1 standard deviation between blacks and whites on the General Aptitude Test Battery compared with a one-third standard deviation on the criterion measure (typically, supervisor ratings). One might interpret the JPM Project results as meaning that the initial edge given nonminorities as a group by somewhat higher general aptitudes (as measured by verbal and mathematical reasoning tests) is greatly reduced by experience on the job. Note, however, that the written job knowledge test used as the second criterion measure in this analysis exhibits only a small diminution in the size of the average group differences. Since the AFQT and the job knowledge test are both paper-and-pencil multiple-choice tests, a strong method effect seems to be involved. This issue goes well beyond the JPM Project; it calls for the attention of the measurement profession as a whole.

TABLE 8-18 Stem-and-Leaf Plot of Standardized Differences Between: (a) Mean AFQT and Job Knowledge Criterion Performance of Black and Nonminority Enlisted Personnel and (b) Mean AFQT and Hands-On Criterion Performance of Black and Nonminority Enlisted Personnel

	Leaf	Stem	Leaf	
a.		+.0		
		−.0		
		−.1		AFQT
		−.2	11	
		−.3	2	Mean = −.85
	87	−.4	27	SD = .41
	7	−.5		
	951	−.6	568	
	7	−.7	9	
Job Knowledge	3	−.8	579	
Criterion	0	−.9		
	3	−1.0	04678	
Mean = −.78	75	−1.1		
SD = .24		−1.2	38	
		.		
		.		
		.		
		−1.8	7	
b.	55	+.0		
	3	−.0		
	85	−.1		AFQT
	9410	−.2	11	
	974222	−.3	2	Mean = −.85
	62	−.4	27	SD = −.41
	72	−.5		
		−.6	568	
		−.7	9	
Hands–On		−.8	579	
Criterion		−.9		
	0	−1.0	04678	
Mean = −.36		−1.1	3	
SD = .31	4	−1.2	38	
		.		
		.		
		.		
		−1.8	7	

NOTE: Leaves in boldface type are based on samples of 25 or more black recruits.

SOURCE: Based on data submitted to the Committee on the Performance of Military Personnel.

CRITERION-RELATED VALIDITY EVIDENCE

TABLE 8-19 Stem-and-Leaf Plot of Standardized Differences Between Mean Criterion Performance of Black and Nonminority Enlisted Personnel

	Leaf	Stem	Leaf	
		+.0	55	
		−.0	3	
		−.1	58	Hands-On Criterion
		−.2	**01**49	
		−.3	222479	Mean = −.36
	87	−.4	26	SD = .31
	7	−.5	27	
	951	−.6		
	7	−.7		
Job Knowledge	3	−.8		
Criterion	0	−.9		
	3	−1.0	**0**	
Mean = −.78	75	−1.1		
SD = .24		−1.2	4	

NOTE: Leaves in boldface type are based on samples of 25 or more black recruits.

SOURCE: Based on data submitted to the Committee on the Performance of Military Personnel.

Gender Comparisons

Data on the differences between prediction systems for men and women in military occupational specialties are limited not only by the small number of female recruits in individual jobs, but also by the number of jobs for which the relevant data are available. Accordingly, only general discussion of apparent trends in these data is possible.

Validity Coefficients Weighted average correlations between ASVAB predictors and performance criteria for men and women are shown in Table 8-20. As was true in the comparisons based on race, the average correlation is higher when the criterion is a written test than when the criterion is a direct measure of performance. However, the dominant feature of these data is the markedly higher average correlation between the AFQT and hands-on performance among women. In addition, and unlike the black/nonminority comparison, there seems to be no clear relationship between the size of the group difference between validity coefficients and the type of criterion variable.

Regression Equations Standard errors of estimate, slopes, and intercepts from the regressions of hands-on performance on the ASVAB selection composite were examined in the 16 occupational specialties for which data

TABLE 8-20 Weighted Average Correlations Between ASVAB Predictors and Performance Criteria for Samples of Men and Women

Predictor Criterion	Number of Studies	Women		Men	
		N	Avg. R	N	Avg. R
Selection composite					
Hands-on	3	814	.24	3,454	.26
Job knowledge	7	606	.41	2,318	.43
AFQT					
Hands-on	13	814	.27	3,454	.19
Job knowledge	7	606	.40	2,318	.37

NOTE: Average correlations using within-group sample sizes as weights.

SOURCE: Data submitted to the Committee on the Performance of Military Personnel.

on male and female recruits were available. Although the results from individual jobs were quite mixed, when viewed as a whole the data do suggest some inconsistencies with previous findings from gender comparisons of this type.

In general, the accuracy of prediction, as measured by the standard error of estimate, was similar for men and women. In 10 of the 16 jobs, predictions were more accurate among women than among men. This is generally consistent with findings reported by Linn (1982) in educational contexts and by Dunbar and Novick (1988) in a military training context. In instances in which the standard errors of estimate were markedly different in magnitude, sampling error appeared to be a likely cause of the difference.

Comparisons of slopes and intercepts showed mixed results. Whereas the typical finding in studies of differential prediction by gender is that slopes among samples of women are steeper than among samples of men, half of the jobs in the current data showed the opposite trend. One might suspect that the use of a performance criterion rather than a written test of job knowledge might account for this discrepancy with previous studies. However, even among the seven jobs that provided criterion data from a test of job knowledge, there were four in which the slope in the samples of women was flatter than it was in the samples of men.

A second and perhaps more notable contrast with the findings of previous studies is the difference between intercepts in instances in which slopes were judged to be similar. In 8 of 12 such instances, the intercept of the regression equation in the female sample was smaller than that of the male sample. Such findings would imply that the use of a combined prediction equation for men and women in these instances would result in the overprediction of female performance on the hands-on criterion, that is, female recruits would be predicted to perform better than they actually would. This finding is counter to the results summarized by Linn (1982), in which the dominant trend was for the criterion performance of women to be underpredicted by the use of a combined equation.

Whether this contrast can be attributed to the use of the hands-on performance criterion is only suggested by results from the seven specialties that also used a job knowledge test as the criterion. Among those seven, five showed intercept differences that would suggest underprediction of female performance on the test of job knowledge, a result more in line with the literature on gender differences in prediction systems. Given the inconsistencies reported here, further investigations of prediction differences between men and women in the military should continue to examine the role of the criterion in the interpretation of such differences.

CONCLUSION

The JPM Project has succeeded in demonstrating that it is possible to develop hands-on measures of job performance for a wide range of military jobs. The project has also shown that the ASVAB can be used to predict performance on these hands-on measures with a useful degree of validity. With the addition of measures of spatial ability and perceptual-psychomotor abilities to the ASVAB, some modest increments in the prediction of hands-on performance could be obtained. Noncognitive predictors, however, are apt to be useful for purposes of predicting criteria such as discipline and leadership but are unlikely to improve the prediction of actual hands-on job performance.

Although the 23 jobs studied to date in the JPM Project are relatively diverse, many more jobs were *not* included in the research than were. The validation task that remains to be accomplished is to develop a means of generalizing the results for these 23 jobs to the full range of jobs in the Services. Each Service is currently conducting research that seeks to accomplish this task (Arabian et al., 1988).

Another task that remains to be accomplished, building on these results, is to link enlistment standards to job performance. The Department of Defense is currently conducting research that seeks "to develop a method or methods for linking recruit quality requirements and job performance data" (Office of the Assistant Secretary of Defense—Force Management and Personnel, 1989:8-1). The hands-on job performance data are a critical aspect of that effort.

9

The Management of Human Resources

In previous chapters we have described JPM Project results showing that job performance can be measured and that it can be predicted, with varying degrees of success, by entrance tests of cognitive ability. The second major goal of the JPM Project is to develop models for setting military enlistment standards (the minimum test scores required for entry into military service) based on the information now available about the job performance that can be anticipated for given ASVAB scores.[1] Some might think that the validity correlations of tests with performance reported in Chapter 8 show that the link between entrance standards and job performance has been established, and so the work is done. But the management problem does not stop with a correlation, because higher-aptitude personnel cost more to recruit. There is a tension between the Services' desire to recruit the most highly qualified men and women possible and the equally felt need of Congress to contain costs by holding down recruiting budgets. This is a quandary familiar to private-sector employers who must balance the productivity gains from hiring highly skilled workers against the costs of positioning themselves at the high end of the labor market.

The second phase of the JPM Project is concentrating on the development of analytical tools that will illuminate for policy makers the effects of

---

[1] See Green et al. (1988) for a lengthier discussion by committee members, military researchers, and consultants of the issues involved in providing an empirical basis for military enlistment standards.

alternative decisions on performance and costs. There is no single discipline that has the analytical tools in hand to answer the questions of quality and costs fully. In personnel work, the traditional approach has been to rank applicants in order of their predicted performance. Since higher test scores indicate a probability of better performance on the job, the simple answer offered by psychological measurement is that more is better. From this point of view, performance is the essential consideration, and the costs of increased performance are not calculated.

Management specialists tend to use the econometric approach to questions of selection standards. In the military context, some interesting models for setting enlistment standards were developed in the 1970s and 1980s. These models were designed to locate the most cost-effective cutoff score; they do not help answer the question of how much performance is sufficient in some absolute sense, but rather set enlistment standards in order to minimize personnel costs per unit of productivity. From this point of view, cost is the essential consideration.

Neither the psychometric nor the econometric approach alone is satisfactory. If the military is to fulfill its mission to provide for the national defense, enlistment standards must be set at a level that will produce a first-term corps that as a group can master all of the enlisted jobs and that can also provide the next generation of leaders. Hence, in the committee's view, costs should not be allowed to drive the analysis. At the same time, a simple more-is-better policy is untenable, particularly in these times of fiscal retrenchment. Military and civilian policy makers need analytical tools that will provide a deeper understanding of the distribution of recruit quality needed to maintain adequate levels of job performance. And the policy process would benefit from better modeling of the trade-offs between costs and performance.

Phase II of the JPM Project provides an interesting opportunity to apply a fairly rich body of job performance data to the development of techniques for modeling the policy maker's need to balance performance requirements and personnel costs. Although the research is still under way and will have to be reported elsewhere, we take the opportunity here to discuss the general outlines of the problem of balancing quality and costs as it relates to setting military enlistment standards—and in the process to review some of the earlier work that provides the intellectual heritage of the Phase II efforts.

Although it draws on the JPM Project, the discussion is not limited by the design decisions made in this instance. The chapter examines, for example, how a competency approach to performance measurement could contribute important information to the setting of enlistment standards even though the JPM performance data cannot be readily interpreted along a competency scale. And because of the status of Phase II, the chapter necessarily raises more questions than it has answers to report.

The chapter begins with a brief review of personnel selection and placement procedures in the U.S. Armed Services including a discussion of current military job allocation procedures and the role of job performance information in implementing those procedures. Next it examines the notion of competency or job mastery and how this approach to measuring job performance might be pertinent to modeling cost/performance trade-offs. The discussion then focuses on existing applications of cost-benefit analysis to questions of employee selection and allocation. The last major section of this chapter addresses the problems associated with setting standards for several jobs at the same time—in the discussion, we examine the competition among jobs for the available talent and review several approaches for comparing the utility of performance across jobs.

PERSONNEL ACCESSION AND JOB ALLOCATION

Although the numbers will decline substantially in this period of military downsizing, during the 1980s the Services selected approximately 300,000 persons annually from over 1 million applicants across the country. The enlistment standards that new recruits must meet to gain entry into the Services, and to specific jobs within a Service, have evolved over many years. They are based on accumulated experience in employing and training young people, many of whom are entering their first full-time job. As described earlier, the Services base their first enlistment decision on the Armed Forces Qualification Test (AFQT), a composite of several subtests in the Armed Services Vocational Aptitude Battery (ASVAB). The minimum acceptable ASVAB scores vary by high school graduation status; they have at times also varied by gender. Additional requirements are set for the applicant's medical status and moral character as manifested in the main by record of previous illegal activities. (For details, see Eitelberg, 1988; Waters et al., 1987.) In what follows, we emphasize the assessment of skills and abilities rather than physical condition or past experiences, although the discussion applies generally to any valid predictor.

Jobs in the Services are varied and in many cases involve the performance of complex or hazardous tasks. In order to develop a cadre of well-qualified recruits, the military personnel accession system must attract a substantial number of applicants, collect information about their capabilities, and, using that information, decide who to enlist and how to allocate across jobs those that do enlist. Because applicants have the option of refusing employment, or enlistment, the system must also decide how aggressively to court applicants and how far to go in accommodating their preferences as to job, duty station, and length of service.

Large employers like the military generally have openings in a great many jobs; in such cases, it is often efficient to consider job assignment as a second decision, to be made after the primary decision to employ (or the applicant's decision to accept employment). Each job has its own minimum applicant requirements—some are at the same level as those used for employment decisions themselves, and others are higher than the first-stage requirements for employment. In the private sector, labor laws and union restrictions must also be taken into consideration.

Minimum standards are especially vital when employment decisions must be made at different times by decentralized staff for each individual, independent from others who might also be applying. Moreover, it may be prudent to hire and place prospects as they apply, rather than postpone decisions until a large pool of applicants is available, from which the best can be selected. By that time, the pool may have evaporated, as applicants find alternative opportunities. Job standards and job specifications take on added importance in such dynamic day-to-day hiring environments. The Services have introduced the added complication of the delayed entry program, whereby good prospects can be signed up immediately for entry into the military at a later time when they have completed personal commitments (e.g., high school) or when a desired position—a "training school seat"—becomes available.

JOB ALLOCATION AND MULTIPLE STANDARDS

Before considering methods for setting entrance standards, it is important to consider the practical context for such standards. In the Services, extensive computer-based systems are used for allocating recruits in ways that control for competition among the jobs in each Service.

Each Service has local recruiting stations staffed with enlisted personnel who contact prospects and try to convince them to apply. Recruiters are given quotas specifying how many of what kind of qualified recruits are needed. Upper limits are often placed on the number of non–high school graduates and the number of persons with below-average AFQT scores who may be recruited. The applicant's qualifications are evaluated in greater detail at one of the 68 Military Entrance Processing Stations (MEPS). If the applicant qualifies for entry, the Service classifier then helps the applicant to select one of the job options that the Service's computer-based allocation system presents.

Each Service uses a somewhat different system for classifying recruits. The Air Force uses its Procurement Management System (PROMIS) to assign a proportion of its recruits—some 50 percent in the mid 1980s, about 35 percent in 1991—to specific specialties before they enlist. The remainder are guaranteed an assignment in one of four general categories of jobs; the specific assignment is made early in Basic Military Training, via the Processing and Classification of Enlistees (PACE) system (Peña, 1988).

The Navy classifies recruits with its system, Classification and Assignment within Pride (CLASP) (Kroeker and Rafacz, 1983), which is very similar to the Air Force PROMIS system. The Marine Corps' Recruit Distribution Model is designed to assign recruits to the most complex specialty for which they are qualified. The Army is currently using a system called REQUEST, but it is developing a more sophisticated system, the Enlisted Personnel Assignment System, or EPAS (Schmitz, 1988).

The main function of these allocation systems is to predict the applicant's performance on each of the available jobs, determine which jobs the applicant is qualified for, and from among those select the person-job assignments that would be most beneficial to the Service. Obtaining the best performance on each job must be assessed in terms of the requirements for all jobs. For example, if one job has much higher entrance standards than the others, the recruits with superior talents may all be assigned to that job, leaving the less talented recruits for the other jobs. Such a solution would not be acceptable. Military manpower experts all stress the importance of having some superior workers assigned to each job. Such workers are said to be the best source of supervisors as well as instructors for future recruits. The relative value of these considerations is not easily quantified, but the military manpower systems start with the assumption that an adequate distribution of performance is essential in every job.

The Services' allocation algorithms have different ways of effecting an efficient distribution of talent among jobs. The Air Force and the Navy use a nonlinear aptitude/difficulty component, whereas the Army uses explicit quality goals for each job, stated in terms of proportions of incumbents in various AFQT categories. As the quality goals are or are not met, changes are made in the job priorities in the system. Minimum standards set lower bounds on talent for each specialty and have indirect effects on the talent mix.

The current military personnel accession system appears to work adequately, but many of its procedures lack a formal basis. It is reasonable to expect that the system would improve with a stronger empirical basis. Methods for measuring job performance are now well developed, and standard methods for relating entrance test scores to performance criteria are well known. But setting entrance standards, allocating applicants to jobs, and budgeting recruiting resources make up a complex and interdependent set of policy functions that could be clarified with the aid of computer-based models. With the above background concerning the military personnel accession system in mind, we now turn to some approaches to the development of the needed methods.

COMPETENCY SCALES

If performance scores are to be useful in setting entrance standards, the interpretation of the scores must be clear. The interpretive framework that would be most useful for balancing costs and performance requirements would be a competency scale indicating level of job mastery. The traditional approach of personnel psychologists to measurement is to compare people with each other. Most tests, like the aptitude tests used for Service entry, are designed to be interpreted comparatively. The scores can be interpreted only by reference to norms. In fact, the primary entry qualifier, the AFQT, reports scores on a percentile scale, which emphasizes its comparative nature: a person who scores 70 has a general aptitude that is better than about 70 percent of the people in the 1980 reference population. The score does not, however, indicate that the person is 70 percent as good as needed to do a good job.

There is another approach to measurement, one that gained vogue in education circles in the 1970s under the name of criterion-referenced testing. Such tests are designed to measure individual performance against a standard of desired performance. The measurement of job proficiency lends itself to this approach, and performance tests can be constructed in a way that permits interpreting proficiency on an absolute scale. This approach seems particularly salient to the policy question of how much quality is enough. One would like to be able to say, for example, that a person can do a job at 70 percent of the level of someone who has mastered the job, and that this represents journeyman-level performance. A scale that measures proficiency in this manner has been called a *competency scale*. The idea is familiar to the general public, and to teachers, who often have more trouble appreciating the strictly comparative scale of aptitude tests. But a performance scale with an external, fixed referent rather than a comparative norm is not usually encountered in personnel work, and thus it needs explication.

The term *competency* as used here denotes a way of interpreting scores on a performance scale. It follows that there are degrees of competency. The term has often been used in related contexts to signify a simple dichotomy that separates the competent from the incompetent. Such a dichotomy is often encountered, as in deciding whether someone has passed or failed a course of study, or deciding whether a high school student has or has not developed enough competence to be awarded a diploma. But in the job performance context, any dichotomy would be artificial and unnecessary. In selection systems, cutoffs are placed on entrance tests, not on performance measures—on the input, not on the output. Setting a particular input standard results in a consequent output distribution of job performance scores—some low, some intermediate, some high. Policy makers must decide if the resulting distribution of performance scores is acceptable.

It cannot be expected that all incumbents will become experts. All that can be expected is that a reasonable proportion of each skill level will be available. Also, because the predictor tests are imperfectly related to performance, selecting the higher scorers does not guarantee eventual high-level job performance. The minimum standard for job entry will have only an indirect effect on the distribution of job competence. Raising the minimum cutoff will raise the mean and reduce the variance of the distribution of competence, but a considerable spread will remain. Setting entrance standards must ultimately depend on a judgment about the acceptability of the resultant distribution of competence.

Consider an oversimplified illustration of the effects of setting entrance standards. The scores on the entrance test used to predict performance have a distribution. Some people will score high, others will score lower. Likewise, there is a distribution of performance; inevitably, some incumbents will not perform as well as others. Technical training schools cannot be expected to turn out only experts. A more realistic expectation is that job incumbents will develop and improve on the job. There is always a flow of personnel through a job. As some incumbents become experts, others are being promoted or released, and still others are just entering the job. There will always be some novices, some apprentice-level job incumbents, many journeymen, some masters, and a few experts. Managers of human resources would find it desirable to establish an expected or realistically acceptable distribution of proficiency in each job cadre.

Figure 9-1 shows, for a large group of applicants, predictor scores and performance scores that are related in the usual psychometric fashion, assuming a moderate validity correlation and roughly normal distributions of both scores. For purposes of discussion, we assume the availability of performance scores for people who will not be selected and therefore will have no chance to actually perform. Each person is, in principle, represented by a point on the diagram, and the entire population by a swarm of points roughly elliptical in shape. The figure indicates by an ellipse the distribution of scores on both predictor and criterion for the total population, and it shows the effect of three alternative standards on the predictor. Each standard cuts off a group of predictor scores and leads to a skewed distribution of performance scores for those exceeding the predictor cutoff.

Two major points are clear from this schematic view of the selection process. First, setting a cutoff on the predictor composite does not entail setting a corresponding cutoff on the performance measure. Second, evaluating the result of a particular predictor cutoff requires evaluating the resulting distribution of performance scores. Whether a given cutoff is acceptable depends on whether the resulting performance distribution is acceptable, as well as on the additional considerations of cost, personnel needs, and so on. Deciding whether a performance distribution is acceptable would be greatly aided if performance scores could be interpreted as competency. The interpretation of a performance test score refers to the inferences about job performance that can legitimately be drawn from criterion test performance. To the extent that a criterion measure is representative of the work

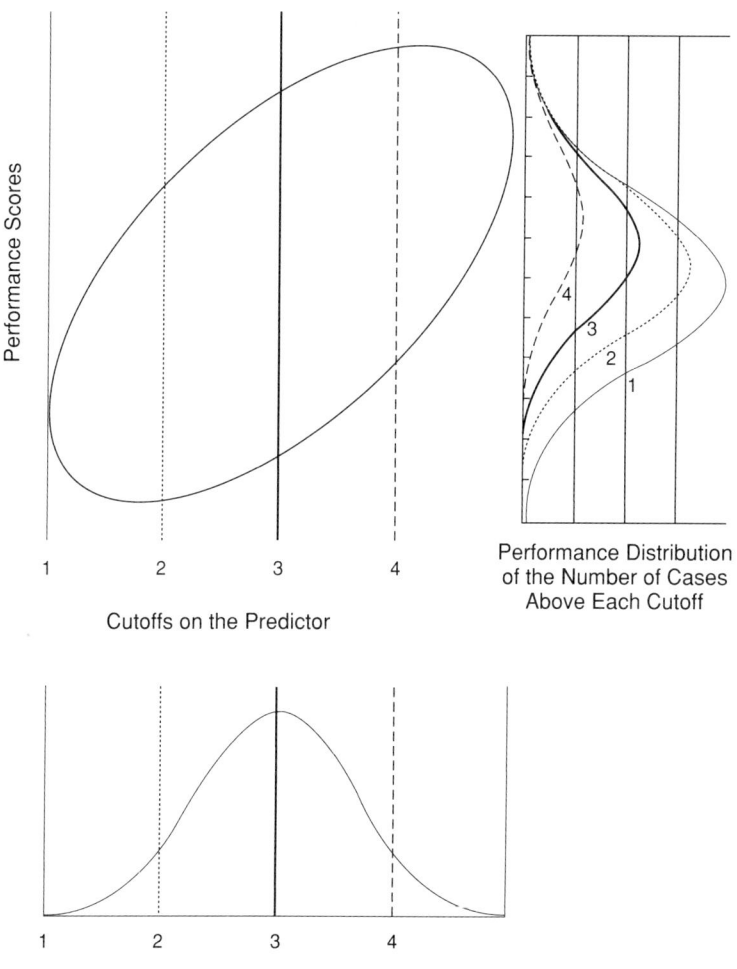

FIGURE 9-1 Schematic scatterplot of predictor and performance scores.

required on the job, some kind of inference is warranted from the test to the job domain.

Establishing a scale of competency is not straightforward by any means. The job domain must first be delineated in terms of the job's constituent tasks or in some other units. Moreover, some tasks may be more important, or more critical, than others. An incumbent who can do 70 percent of the job tasks may not be able, in some sense, to do 70 percent of the job. Green and Wigdor (Vol. II) discuss this issue in further detail.

There are many levels of proficiency and, at any point in time, any job will have some incumbents at each level. There is merit in having some sort of interpretive scale anchors making it possible to establish various levels, associated with such terms as novice, apprentice, journeyman, master, expert. They might be strongly related to the various pay grades of enlisted personnel or to the already-established skill levels associated with military jobs.

A slightly different approach would be to establish a minimum competency score on a job performance measure and to establish some acceptable proportion of incumbents who are at or above that level. Bentley (1986) reported an approach to this problem for one Air Force specialty; it involved setting minimum acceptable levels of performance on each task in a walk-through performance test. Hutchins (1986) used a similar approach, with judgments obtained through a Delphi technique, for a Navy rating. Arabian and Hanser (1986) discussed the general problem in the Army context. And Mayberry (1987) reported a systematic approach to developing a competency scale for Marine infantrymen.

SETTING MINIMUM STANDARDS FOR A SINGLE JOB

The next step in the development of methods for managing accessions is to find a rationale for setting a minimum entrance standard for a single job. Such methods are of limited practical use, since jobs usually do not exist in isolation. Still, it is wise to understand the details of a model for setting one standard before attempting to develop a method for many jobs at once.

Every job has certain minimum qualifications. Employers want to avoid hiring typists who cannot type or chauffeurs who cannot drive. Although most jobs require additional training, some initial level of knowledge, skill, and ability is needed as a starting point. Some jobs are so demanding that relatively few people can be trained to do them. Other jobs could be filled by many people if they were given very extensive training, but such training is too expensive; more highly qualified applicants are needed to keep the time and expense of training within reasonable limits. Some jobs are so critical that a poorly skilled person in the job is worse than useless and may actually be dangerous. Sometimes poor performance is merely embarrassing; sometimes it is even expected and tolerated, as when a mess hall worker cooks poorly or a sergeant types poorly. In other cases, poor performance can cost lives and in such cases misallocation is intolerable.

Determining the validity of a selection test normally does not include setting a minimum standard. Rather, it assumes that a large group of applicants is tested, all at once, and that a single decision is made to select a certain number of the top scorers. The concept of a job-success ratio refers to the proportion of accepted applicants who can be expected to achieve at some acceptable level and thus be called successful. The famous Taylor and Russell (1939) tables display, for a normal bivariate distribution, the success ratio as a function of the proportion of applicants who are accepted. It is tacitly assumed that applicants are accepted from the top scorers, that the selected applicants all have predicted performance levels well above an acceptable minimum, and that all who are offered the job will accept. Since predictions are usually far from perfect, not all those who are selected are expected to succeed. For any given score on the predictor, there is a corresponding distribution of performance. In a stable environment, this experience will recur, yielding the same "hit" rate. If the selection tests are useful, the proportion of expected successes will be higher as the selection ratio is reduced, and fewer applicants will be accepted.

In practice, an appropriate minimum standard is often critical. Some people are so unskilled that they should not be hired, no matter how severe the need. The minimum standard must be set high enough to reject most of these people. By contrast, highly talented applicants will have the choice of several jobs (or schools or other alternatives), they may not accept a job that is offered, and they will be more expensive to attract and retain. Thus, the minimum must be set low enough to ensure an adequate number of acceptances while avoiding overinvesting in applicant talent. If standards are raised, more recruiting effort—and expense—will be required to obtain adequate numbers of recruits; if standards are lowered significantly, training time will increase, and attrition may also increase (which in turn implies that a larger group of recruits will have to be trained so that an adequate number remain after the expected attrition).

In the past, the cost-benefit trade-off has been evaluated subjectively, and equilibrium has been reached by judgment, negotiation, and compromise. Not inappropriately, entrance standards have changed according to the supply and quality of recruits. They have responded to pressures to economize in lean times and pressures toward risk aversion in better times.

This system has two striking weaknesses. First, it provides little evidence as to how much additional investment in recruitment is warranted, or how much saving could be achieved as the recruit mix changes. Second, it leaves policy makers with less evidence than they would like as to the competence of the force they have recruited. With objective measures of job performance in hand, there is now a realistic possibility of developing better-informed methods for setting entrance standards, based on econometric models that pit costs against performance. Although cost-performance trade-off models are still in the development stage, they are sufficiently promising to interest policy makers and might provide attractive alternatives to the traditional method of setting standards and assessing the manpower quality of the force.

Two methods have been proposed for objectively setting a minimum entry standard for a single job. Both methods are premised on partial-equilibrium rather than general-equilibrium models. That is, they involve models that take into consideration the various competing forces of costs and performance for a particular job, but they do not consider the possible impact on other related jobs, each of which also has its own cost and performance needs. The first method, the utility difference approach, has its roots in psychometric work in personnel decision making. The other method is based on the so-called Rand model, a well-known econometric analysis. Both approaches are concerned with a cost-benefit analysis of the problem that seeks to determine the best trade-off between costs and resulting performance.

The Utility Difference Approach

Brogden (1949) suggested an approach to the cost-benefit analysis of personnel selection, which was further developed by Cronbach and Gleser (1965) and more recently extended by Cascio and Ramos (1986). The model is widely used in industrial and organizational psychology, and it is the basis for a well-known economic evaluation by Hunter and Schmidt (1982) of the U.S. Employment Service's widespread use of the General Aptitude Test Battery, GATB (see Hartigan and Wigdor, 1989).

The main purpose of the analysis is to justify the cost of applicant aptitude testing by comparing the cost of testing with the resulting increases in the value of employee performance. The increased value is taken to be the difference between the performance utility of the selected workers and the performance utility that would have been experienced if selection had been at random. The utility of performance is assumed to be a linear function of the criterion used for validating the entrance tests. The criterion is formulated as a monetary scale of performance worth. Since test scores are imperfectly related to job performance, the potential utility of a prospective employee is given by his or her predicted performance, which is derived from a linear regression function relating job performance to scores on the predictors. The model states that the marginal productivity gain due to using the selection procedure is the difference between the cost of that testing and the mean marginal gain in performance realized by selecting applicants with a valid predictor test.

The simplest version of the model has only one predictor. In this version, the mean marginal performance gain is the product of three factors: the validity correlation of the predictor, the average standard predictor score for the selected applicants, and the standard deviation of the performance measure, in dollars. The first two factors can be readily calculated, but establishing the dollar-valued standard deviation of performance is a challenge. It would seem that expensive cost accounting methods would be needed to estimate this parameter, but Cascio (1987) claims that behavioral methods are just as accurate and are cheaper and quicker to accomplish. He reviews several methods for estimating the standard deviation of performance, which specifies the unit of the scale. The simplest approach is to estimate it as 40 percent of the average salary paid to the employees in a job class (Schmidt and Hunter, 1983). This figure represents the lower bound of the 95 percent confidence interval, based on the cumulative results of studies that actually measured the dollar value of job performance of individual employees.

Such salary-based estimates of the performance scale may not be appropriate for the JPM Project because the metric of salary dollars may not be very relevant in a military context. One alternative is the Superior Equivalents Technique (SET), which was developed by Eaton et al. (1985) specifically for use in situations in which individual salary is only a small percentage of the value of performance to the organization or of the cost of the equipment operated (e.g., a jet engine mechanic or a nuclear power technician). The standard deviation is first expressed in performance units and then converted to dollar units. A subject matter expert judges how many soldiers performing at the 85th percentile would be equivalent to a fixed number of soldiers performing at the 50th percentile. Then, by assuming the value of the 85th percentile is one standard deviation higher than the value at the 50th, the standard deviation in monetary units can be obtained readily.

Several aspects of the utility difference analysis are worth noting. First, better test scores mean higher predicted performance and therefore better yield. Utility is assumed to be a linear function of test scores. A candidate with an outstanding test score is worth more than a candidate with a mediocre score. As discussed below, a linear function may not always be appropriate, however.

Second, nothing in the formulation precludes negative utilities. Since the model adds the utilities of all the incumbents, it implies that utilities differ only in degree, but in some cases, negative utilities would seem to differ in kind. Sometimes work that is detrimental to a mission can be offset by the performance of others, but sometimes it cannot. Some jobs are better not done at all than if done by someone who does harm—for example, jobs involving very delicate and costly machinery or possible endangerment of human life. Perhaps this just means that the utility scale needs changing, but in general the model is easier to accept if poor performance has low but still positive value.

Third, the economic benefit of testing is calculated as the difference between the total utility realized from those hired, minus the cost of testing all applicants. If few are hired, their combined value has to be relatively high to offset the cost of testing, whereas if many are hired even a small validity has positive value. This conclusion depends on the assumption that those with the highest test scores are hired. In the simple version of the model, no allowance is made for applicants not accepting offered employment or for rejection of applicants on other grounds, such as a significant criminal record. Such allowances can of course be made (Hogarth and Einhorn, 1976; Boudreau, 1988).

Cascio proposes extending the cost-benefit analysis to cover the setting of minimum standards. The costs of training and recruiting would have to be included with testing costs. The cutoff would be set at the point at which benefits (utility) equal cost. To our knowledge, however, this calculation has actually been done only in the private sector. A thorough review of the model in the military context is given by Zeidner and Johnson (1989).

The Rand Approach

Much of the recent military work on models for standard setting stems from seminal work done at the Rand Corporation. The basic Rand model, as described by Armor et al. (1982) was designed to set the enlistment standard for the Army occupation of infantryman as a single cutoff score on the combat aptitude (CO) composite of the ASVAB. The data base used included about 14,000 infantrymen who entered the Army during fiscal 1977.

The Rand group based its measure of performance on the Skill Qualification Test (SQT), an assessment device administered annually by the Army's Training and Doctrine Command to soldiers in the field. This work preceded the JPM Project and the Army's Project A. During the time of this study, the SQT had three components, a written test of job knowledge, a hands-on test of some job-specific tasks, and a set of supervisory ratings; Armor et al. (1982) noted that the written component was responsible for most of the variance in the test scores. (In later years, the hands-on test and the supervisor's ratings were dropped from the SQT.) Scores on the SQT ranged from 0 to 100 percent. The Army had established 60 percent as the minimum passing score, and this operational definition was accepted by Armor et al. to identify persons who had "qualified" by passing the SQT.

The Rand group then modified the performance criterion for their econometric analysis by incorporating a temporal component as well. The resulting criterion was called the Qualified Man Month (QMM) and was defined as a "month of post-training duty time contributed by a person who can pass the SQT at a minimum standard" (Armor et al., 1982:14). To contribute a QMM, a soldier had to pass basic training, pass advanced training, stay in the service long enough to take the SQT, pass the SQT by obtaining a score of at least 60, and stay in the service one month. For each additional month in the Army, this soldier would contribute an additional QMM. Soldiers who develop skills quickly, passing the SQT early in their career, are more productive and contribute more QMMs. For example, a soldier who stays in the Army for two and a half years after passing the SQT contributes 30

QMMs. In addition to rewarding early achievement, the index also incorporates retention—a soldier who leaves the Army before his or her tour of duty is up stops adding QMMs.

In the Rand analysis the criterion (QMM) was based on SQT qualification and attrition; the predictors were the AFQT, the CO (combat aptitude) composite on the ASVAB, and high school diploma status. The relation between the criterion and the predictors was established empirically through the 1977 data base of 14,000 infantrymen. The Rand group used a categorical regression system in place of traditional psychometric methods. The soldiers were cross-classified by AFQT category (7 categories), CO composite score category (10 categories), high school diploma status (2 categories), and length of time in service (5 categories). Because of the high correlations among some of the variables, some cells in the cross-classification were empty. For each cell, the proportion of soldiers retained was determined as a function of time in service. SQT scores were regressed on AFQT score, CO composite score, high school diploma status, and time in service at the individual level using a logistic regression[2] to derive coefficients for each predictor. (The regression was based on one administration of the SQT.) These coefficients were then used to derive predicted performance levels for a group with a given ability mix (e.g., AFQT CAT IIIA, CO 90-100, HSG, TIS 2-2.5 years), using the midpoint of that group's scores on the predictor variables for convenience. Except for the SQT regression, which represents a specific functional form, all relationships were unconstrained and could be nonlinear, or indeed nonmonotonic, if that is what the data indicated. In fact, the results were generally monotonic, but often nonlinear.

Having established the QMM as an index of the quality of soldier performance, and having determined its relation to the predictors, the next analytic step was to develop an expression for the various costs. The cost components of the Rand equation are the variable costs (i.e., those that vary with the number of soldiers) involved in recruiting, basic training, advanced training, and retention. Fixed costs, such as maintaining recruiting stations and training centers and paying a base number of recruiters and trainers, are not included, because they would not vary with different entrance standards. The various temporal stages were separated because they apply to different numbers of soldiers. Only those applicants who become recruits require basic training, only those recruits who get through basic training go on to

---

[2] A logistic regression of a categorical variable on continuous variables is a model relating the category proportions, p, to the variables $x_1, x_2, x_3, \ldots$, through the equation (Fienberg, 1977):

$$\log\left(\frac{p}{1-p}\right) = b_0 + b_1 + b_2 + b_3 \ldots$$

advanced training, and only those who finish training and become combat infantrymen have retention costs.

The variable costs of training were taken to be the costs of soldier pay and materials. The variable costs of retention were the costs of salary and benefits from the end of training through the first tour of service. Determining the costs of recruiting was more complex. First, it was assumed that only high-quality enlistees (AFQT Categories I-IIIA, who are high school graduates) generate variable recruiting costs. Lower-quality recruits were assumed to be available with no *additional* cost. Second, Armor et al. proposed two alternatives for obtaining more high-quality recruits, either paying bonuses to enlistees or increasing the number of recruiters. As it turned out, both alternatives led to the same conclusion about the optimal enlistment standard, but increasing the number of recruiters was more expensive.

Armor et al. decided to fix end strength, that is, to hold constant the number of soldiers completing their first tour, and to find the entrance standard that minimized the variable cost per QMM. This can be done by calculating both cost and average QMM, and their ratio, for each possible cutoff, or enlistment standard, on the predictor, which in this case was the ASVAB's CO composite. Thus, the optimal enlistment standard was the value of the CO composite for which the ratio of cost to performance was lowest. One effect of a raised enlistment standard would be that some incumbents would not have been accepted for enlistment—it was assumed that they would have been replaced by enlistees with qualifications similar to those in the remaining eligible categories. In the analysis, the numbers of individuals in each of the remaining cells was simply increased proportionally. A similar assumption was made for lowered standards.

The optimal enlistment standard determined by the model for the base year was a score of 87 on the CO composite, which was close to the then-current (fiscal 1982) operational requirement of 85, but higher than the operational level of the base year, fiscal 1977. The optimal level would vary from year to year according to the demographics of the recruit population, the economic climate, the number of positions to be filled, and so on. The optimal level would have cost more to implement in fiscal 1977 than would the actual fiscal 1977 level, but more QMMs would have been obtained. The authors stated that the increased costs would add only a small percentage amount to the total budget for recruiting and maintaining the force. The higher standards would lead to having more recruits who could do the job, that is, to having more months of qualified performance at a lower cost per month.

The authors also concluded that high school graduates in AFQT Category IV were less cost-effective (fewer QMMs per unit cost) than nongraduates in AFQT Categories I-IIIA, because low-ability graduates are less likely to pass basic training, advanced training, or the SQT. Recall that the cost equation of the model assumed that neither group required any marginal recruiting cost.

Because Armor et al. thought that their assumptions about recruiting costs were tenuous, they recomputed their model for several alternative assumptions about those costs. The resulting value of the index cost per QMM changed considerably, but the minimum was realized somewhere between a score of 80 and 90 on the ASVAB composite for combat infantrymen, for all assumptions examined, thus lending confidence to the original conclusions.

Evaluating the Models

The Rand model and the utility difference model provide important early steps toward rationalizing the standard-setting process. Each model leaves out some factors, as any model must if it is to be sufficiently understandable to be useful.

Both models maximize performance for a fixed force size and both contain the implication that fewer excellent soldiers are equivalent to a larger number of more mediocre performers, but neither model explicitly considers whether better selection could result in smaller personnel needs. Indeed, the quality-quantity trade-off implied by both models might not be realistic. This is especially true when one considers that in wartime attrition increases because of casualties. And this, in turn, affects decisions about the size and character of a peacetime force.

One technical difference between the two models should be noted. The utility difference model is a cost-benefit analysis, which has the significant disadvantage of requiring both utility and cost to be measured on the same scale—monetary utility in this case. Many find the expression of utility in dollar terms simplistic, although the monetary scale does have the advantage, at least in principle, of providing the same metric across jobs. (If the money and the utility are equivalent across different jobs, the multiple job case is simplified.) The Rand model is a cost-efficiency analysis, which uses a ratio as an index of the cost-benefit trade-off. When the difference is replaced by a ratio, such as utility per unit cost, utility and cost can each be measured on its own scale, and the only important assumption is that the utilities of the personnel can be aggregated by addition, an assumption that many find problematic as well.

Another significant technical difference between the two models is that the Rand model dichotomizes performance—one QMM is as good as another and one month served without qualifying on the SQT is as bad as another. That is surely a simplification. For example, those who passed the SQT were presumably more valuable in the preceding month than those who did not pass. (By contrast, the utility difference model views utility as improving linearly with performance, an assumption that can also be questioned.) However, for a cost-benefit analysis along the lines of the Rand model such assumptions might not be critical. Armor has performed analyses with the Rand model, using a continuous criterion. He replaced a proportion of QMMs in each cell, with the expected (i.e., average) performance of the individuals in that cell. The general nature of the results is unchanged—the location of the minimum cutoff was very similar to that found with the dichotomous criterion.

Both models are focused on setting a minimum entrance standard, or cutoff score, on a predictor. Neither considers the more complicated question of the distribution of quality above the minimum level. Setting a minimum standard does not necessarily ensure an adequate distribution of recruit quality, because there is nothing to prevent a job's being filled by people who are all just at or just above the minimum. Although this is not likely to occur, it could happen; for example, if one job has a minimum below that established for any other job, it will get all the lowest-level qualifiers, since they can qualify only for that job. Although neither model expects this, neither model prevents it. The utility difference model assumes a normal distribution of applicants and assumes that all who are offered employment will accept, in which case the distribution above the minimum would be realized. The Rand model bases its results on empirical data from individuals actually on the job, which is certainly more realistic, but it assumes that if the cutoff is raised the distribution of those remaining would be altered proportionately—not by the addition of people just at the new minimum. Although it is difficult to see how to improve on these assumptions, the lack of explicit attention to the distribution of talent remains a concern.

Mayberry (1988) and May (1986) consider the effect of minimum entrance standards on the entire distribution of performance, rather than simply the number of QMMs. They show that a low entrance standard has the effect of lowering the relative number of incumbents who perform at superior levels. They do not, however, propose any selection mechanisms other than a minimum standard that might be used to influence the distribution of performance.

SETTING STANDARDS FOR SEVERAL JOBS

The various models for setting standards for a military job are, in many respects, very sophisticated, yet models that apply to only a single job miss the major manpower problem of how to allocate scarce resources. Plainly, making personnel decisions in a multijob environment requires not only comparing one recruit with the others, but also comparing one job with other jobs. How this is done will critically affect the conclusions reached and will probably affect the minimum entry standards set for the various jobs.

A main shortcoming of an analysis of only one job is the problem of partial equilibrium. When treating only one job in isolation, it is natural to assume that, with a few exceptions, every applicant who scores above the selection cutoff will accept employment in that job. That is almost certainly never the case in a multijob system. Models must be expanded to consider not only the possibility that the applicant might reject the offered job, but also the distinct possibility that the organization might prefer to place the applicant in a different job. In the military situation, an applicant who is qualified for one job is generally qualified for, and may have a desire for, many jobs. Yet at best he or she can accept only one. Any position in which he or she is placed will have opportunity costs, and those costs will be highest when the applicant's qualification is highest. To determine where the applicant should optimally be placed requires a general-equilibrium approach.

At this stage of the analysis, differential prediction is assumed to be possible with the available predictors. If the same predictor measure (e.g., the AFQT) is used for every job and only a single dimension of skill or ability is involved, the problem of allocating talent to jobs becomes much easier than if different predictors are used or if jobs vary in types of abilities and level of difficulty. Indeed, for jobs at the same level of difficulty, job vacancies and applicant interest may play decisive roles.

There is controversy within the profession of industrial and organizational psychology about the value or even the possibility of differential predictions. Nevertheless, all the Services use different composites of ASVAB tests for predicting performance in different types of jobs.

With differential predictions and with jobs of varying difficulty, there are complex interactions among the minimum standards set for each job. Moreover, minimum standards alone do not guarantee that the allocation algorithms will provide a range of talent for each job. The interactions of the standards for different jobs and their mutual but competing need for a distribution of talent are not well understood, but it is certainly widely recognized that revising the standards for one job has immediate effects on other jobs. To study the interactions, models for standard setting must be extended.

Revisiting the Rand and Utility Difference Models

The Rand model was extended modestly by Fernandez and Garfinkle (1985) to a situation involving four jobs. The same criterion of QMMs and roughly the same evaluations of variable costs were used, although the variable recruiting costs were limited to bonuses for AFQT Categories I-

IIIA high school graduates (whereas Armor et al., 1982 had also considered increasing the number of recruiters). The main change in the extended Rand model was in the constraints on optimization. Fernandez and Garfinkle argued that since part of their multijob problem was where to assign recruits, holding numbers of incumbents constant was not reasonable in their study. Instead, they held QMMs constant and then determined cost per QMM for various levels of job entry standards. Armor et al., for their part, held force size constant and minimized cost per QMM, on the assumption that the Army planned for a force of a certain size and that quality cannot be exchanged for quantity.

An important consequence of holding the number of QMMs constant in the four jobs under study was that the status quo was thereby accepted as the relative requirements of the four jobs. The system goal was taken to be each job's actual number of QMMs during the years under study. In a sense, this sidesteps the issue of how to allocate quality by simply accepting the status quo rather than facing the complex problem of comparing the relative values of the jobs. It confines studies of personnel allocation to studies of the means while ignoring the ends.

The utility difference approach of Brogden (1949), Cronbach and Gleser (1965), and their followers can also be extended to the multijob case. With its linear evaluation of utility, the utility difference model meshes well with linear programming models of the classification problem (Charnes et al., 1953), the name given to the personnel allocation problem in the operations research literature. Such models can easily handle any number of jobs, but they are designed for batch assignment, with everyone in the batch being assigned at the same time. Assigning applicants one at a time, as they apply, is called the secretary problem, and adds considerable complexity to the linear programming approaches. However, the particular side conditions of allocation—every person must get exactly one job, and every job opening must be filled—permits use of efficient network algorithms (Schmitz and Nord, 1987).

A model for standard setting in a total system with many jobs should include some way of controlling the distribution of talent among jobs. Nord and White (1988), in their design of the Army's EPAS system, considered quality goals to be boundary conditions or constraints on their system; they explicitly studied the effect of including or not including those constraints. They found, not surprisingly, that the effect of distributing talent across jobs to match quality goals results in substantially reduced overall utility of the job assignments than when no such constraints exist.

Nord and White also pointed out a number of technical problems that have not yet been dealt with adequately. One is the effect of different validities for different jobs. If two jobs have equal importance and require equal numbers of recruits, but performance can be predicted more accurately for one job than for the other, the more predictable job will get the better recruits, because the predicted performance will be better for that job—by regressing predictions toward the mean as the degree of predictability decreases. As a result, the jobs that are not well predicted will suffer. This effect is more apparent in the utility difference model, in which utility is assumed to increase linearly with predicted performance, but it is also present in the Rand model, as pointed out by Armor et al.

Comparing Jobs

Comparing jobs is a critical part of deciding how to allocate personnel across multiple jobs most effectively. In making their job comparisons, Fernandez and Garfinkle assumed that equal performance levels could be considered equally valuable in all jobs—that is, they treated all QMMs as equivalent and optimized on the total number. In lieu of such an arbitrary assumption, a direct comparison of job value is needed. One likely candidate is to place job performance for every job on a single overall scale of utility. Sadacca et al. (1988) took an empirical approach to determining utility—they devised an elaborate procedure in which Army officers were asked to make comparative judgments of utility for various levels of performance in each of several military occupational specialties. Nord and White (1988) used the resulting utilities to compare two methods of job allocation based on different models for utility aggregation. The model in which only average group utilities were maximized led to higher utility than a model concerned with individual utilities.

Competency scales are also useful ingredients in making comparisons among jobs. With an absolute scale of competency, the same score indicates roughly the same level of performance across jobs. Placing jobs on a single scale—whether of performance utility, job difficulty, importance, or some other dimension—allows comparative judgments to be made objectively. Experts could be asked to make absolute judgments about the acceptability of a performance distribution and the possible negative value of very poor performance. This would avoid some of the pitfalls faced by Sadacca et al., who asked their experts how a soldier at the 70th percentile among motor mechanics compared in utility with a soldier at the 30th percentile among cannon crewmen. A percentile is a purely relative scale of performance, and it may misrepresent the quality of the performance. In principle, most of the motor mechanics could be no better than journeymen, whereas most of the cannon crewmen could be masters or experts. In practice, such an occurrence is very unlikely, and in fact the judges may have had an idealized distribution of performance in mind, but to some extent the known quality of the job incumbents could bias the comparisons.

Alley (1988) described an imaginative alternative to comparing jobs with respect to utility. He proposed instead that jobs be compared in terms of how difficult they are to learn. A scale of learning difficulty implies that the more time and effort needed to learn a job, the higher the abilities needed in the assigned recruits. All military jobs require intense specialized training, so a comparison of learning difficulty can be quite objective. Even though learning difficulty provides a dimension along which different jobs can be rated, the question remains: Is learning the right dimension? The fact that two such different concepts as performance value and learning difficulty might each provide a useful common scale for comparing jobs suggests that there may be other dimensions worth considering. For the present, the question must be left unanswered.

Generalizing Across Jobs

A practical hurdle to be overcome in any multiple job allocation systems is the need to consider all jobs. If job performance information is only available on a subset of jobs, as is the case in the JPM Project, some means must be found for generalizing that information to the remaining jobs. One possibility is to combine military occupations into a few large clusters of similar jobs and then to generalize from one or two jobs in a cluster to other similar jobs. Hunter and Schmidt's validity generalization model (Hunter, 1980) is a well-known approach to this problem.

Most of the work on validity generalization is concerned only with the validity correlations, including the degree of relationship between predictors and criteria. A central question is how far to generalize—to all jobs, as Hunter and Schmidt often claim, or to only closely related jobs? Sackett (Vol. II) pointed out that different types and levels of descriptors can produce very different groupings. For example, job similarity can be based on a comparison of job analyses, which in turn can focus on specific behaviors, general behaviors, or needed abilities, each providing a different basis for job clustering. Pearlman (1980) reviewed and analyzed several approaches and selected ability requirements as the best job descriptors when clustering jobs for validity purposes.

For setting standards, validity correlations alone are not enough. One has to be able to generalize performance score distributions, including means and standard deviations, or at least to generalize minimum requirements across jobs. That is, one must know not only which aptitudes are predictive of performance, but also what level of performance is predicted from a given level of aptitude.

Sackett (Vol. II) discussed three methodologies that can be used to generalize both validity and cutoff scores. One method uses job components from McCormick's Position Analysis Questionnaire (PAQ)—which would permit predictions of mean test scores as well as estimations of validity correlations. Judges would have to identify those PAQ dimensions most likely to be indicative of good performance in a given job. A second method employs an item-level analysis of the judged importance of the test item for predicting performance. This type of analysis, although useful in high school competency tests, is largely irrelevant in connecting aptitude tests with job performance. A third method scales jobs on needed ability by using paired comparisons. In all of these methodologies, the processes of judgment are fundamental, as are the sources of such judgments.

Generalizing the research on validity relationships usually assumes that predictors and criteria remain constant. Within groups of similar jobs, the Services generally use the same predictive ASVAB composites. However, an important feature of the JPM Project is the use of different types of criterion measures, including hands-on performance tests, walk-through performance tests, simulations, job knowledge tests, and ratings. These measures are more or less costly to obtain. More important, however, they measure different aspects of performance, possibly limiting the extent of validity generalization.

Another approach to generalizing is the synthetic validity project recently described by Wise et al. (1988). The research project uses a variety of job characteristics in determining how far to generalize validity and how to estimate the validity relationship. The project has the unique opportunity for extensive independent evaluation of the methodology, because the projected validities can be compared with actual validity correlations in the same and related jobs. The project plans to collect judgmental data relevant to the validity and standards issues and to connect this new data base whenever and wherever possible with the extensive criterion-related validation data base developed by the Army. The results of this project will be very useful in understanding the extent and limitations of validity generalization.

SUMMARY

Although the problem of linking entrance standards and quality goals to job performance is complex, the main outlines are now understood and much of the basic methodology seems to be in hand. There is reason to expect that important advances can be made in developing objective, empirically based methods of demonstrating the levels of quality needed in the recruit population to ensure adequate staffing of a range of first-term military jobs and to seed the next generation of leaders. Some of the work reported in this chapter also encourages optimism that cost-performance trade-off models for setting enlistment standards can be designed to handle more sophisticated performance information and a larger number of jobs.

The process of setting minimum entry standards and using job performance data must be understood in the larger setting of allocating personnel to various jobs within the military. Indeed, the modeling of optimal entrance standards must take account of the details of the algorithms themselves. In some systems, filling technical school training seats is the highest priority, leaving little room for the decision rules for estimated job performance to come into play beyond the exclusion of those below the entrance standards. But the development of multijob models for setting standards could provide a blueprint for reweighting the factors considered in allocation decisions to emphasize job performance over and above the management of the training flow. In effect, one might suggest a model in which a single minimum standard would be replaced by a set of standards keyed to the performance distribution needed to supply each job with its required mix of abilities.

Of special interest with regard to the problem of maximizing performance within a given pool of enlistees is the picture presented by Nord and White (1988) of the way in which minimum entrance standards would interact in an assignment model with the mechanisms (e.g., quality goals) used to maintain an acceptable distribution of recruit quality in all Army jobs. Clearly, any method for setting minimum entrance standards must take account of these mechanisms as side conditions on the optimization. The model cannot be given free rein to assign applicants only to optimize their aggregate individual value to the Service.

To be useful for setting standards in a complete personnel system, existing models must be extended to the situation with many jobs. When performance has not been measured for all jobs, various means are available for generalizing the validity correlations and cutoff scores from the measured jobs to other jobs.

The central problem, however, is not how to extend the models, but how to compare jobs. Not only must average performance on one job be valued relative to average performance on other jobs, but each level of performance must be comparatively valued. Performance utility and learning difficulty offer possible scales on which jobs can be ranged, and other dimensions might also be viable alternatives.

Coda: The JPM Project and Accession Policy

Selecting personnel who will turn out to be successful on the job, particularly from a youthful and inexperienced applicant population, is a complicated business. Maintaining a standing army is also expensive. At the heart of these discussions of job proficiency, quality requirements, and trade-off models is the recognition that the public purse is not bottomless. The Department of Defense has an interest in attracting the best possible people into the military. At some point, however, the quality of the enlisted force becomes a function of what the nation can afford; high-quality personnel are more expensive to recruit and, having greater opportunities elsewhere, they are less likely than others to remain in the military for their career. In order to make reasonable budgetary decisions, Congress needs to be able to balance performance gains attributable to selecting those with better-than-average scores on the ASVAB against the costs of recruiting, training, and retaining high-quality personnel. And to improve their control over performance in the enlisted ranks, DoD and the Services need to be able to make more empirically grounded projections of their personnel quality requirements.

Although the problems are complex, and there is still room for improvement at every stage of the research and development, the results of the JPM Project to date indicate that the concept of linking selection standards to objective measures of job performance is basically sound. It appears that it will be feasible for human resource planners and policy makers to incorporate empirical data derived from job performance into the decision process in a systematic way. Both for the Services' internal management purposes and for justification of Service quality requirements at the departmental level, this is desirable.

Phase I of the JPM Project has demonstrated that it is possible to develop remarkably reliable hands-on measures of job performance. This was one of the biggest unknowns at the start of the project because there was very little experience of large-scale testing in the job sample mode. Success in this regard seems to have been due to the fact that the test items were designed as a sequence of discrete steps that involved specific, observable actions. This facilitated the scoring. Obviously, the nature of entry-level enlisted jobs lent itself to this kind of test item in a way that managerial or more cognitively loaded jobs would not. In addition, the reliability of the hands-on tests depended on careful training of the test administrators so that they would not give cues or otherwise distort the testing situation. (Such results should not be expected to generalize to situations in which supervisors score the performance of their subordinates or teachers their students.) Daily monitoring of scoring trends both within and among raters seems to have been an effective way to guard against unusually lenient or stringent scoring.

The first phase of the JPM Project also demonstrated that reasonably valid measures of job proficiency can be developed. As anticipated, coverage of the total job domain is a problem with hands-on testing because the methodology is extremely time-consuming. Despite six to eight hours of testing time per individual, the analysis of measurement error due to the particular set of tasks selected for testing presented in Chapter 6 indicates that more time and more tasks would have produced better measures of job proficiency. In addition, there is still much to learn from the JPM data base about the relationships among the hands-on, walk-through performance tests, simulations, and written tests and about the substitutability of the less expensive and time-consuming measures for the hands-on tests. Nevertheless, the JPM Project has produced hands-on measures of job proficiency that are more credible than training grades and substantially more stable and accurate than the ubiquitous supervisor's rating.

One of the most important implications of these findings is that the Armed Services Vocational Aptitude Battery has been shown to be moderately related to something fairly close to actual performance in 23 military jobs (comprising some 40 percent of the enlisted force)—and by inference to many more. Although the AFQT is not the optimal predictor that could be obtained from the ASVAB, the median corrected correlation of .38 with hands-on performance reported in Chapter 8 has considerable practical utility. When one remembers the uncertainties occasioned by the misnorming episode of 1976-1980, this is an important datum—enough to justify the use of the ASVAB in setting enlistment standards, if also modest enough to encourage the search for new predictors to add to the ASVAB.

The development of cost/performance models for setting enlistment standards, now being explored by both DoD and the Services, has great potential relevance for accession policy. Until now, the standards-setting process has been largely based on an informal process of individual judgments and negotiations among the stakeholders. The manpower management models used by military planners for other purposes have simply assumed an appropriate enlistment standard or have used surrogates at quite some remove from job performance. If the JPM performance data can be successfully incorporated into trade-off models, the models will offer policy officials useful tools for estimating the probable effects on performance and/or costs of various scenarios—say a 10 percent reduction in recruiting budgets, a 20 percent reduction in force, or a downturn in the economy. The solutions provided by such models are not intended to and will not supplant the overarching judgment that policy officials must bring to bear, but they can challenge conventional assumptions and inject a solid core of empirical evidence into the decision process. One of the early runs of the DoD cost/performance model, for example, has suggested the counterintuitive proposition that, in a situation of economic downturn, it is cost-effective to increase recruiting budgets: the marginal costs of increasing the proportion of high-quality personnel under these conditions will be outweighed by their performance contribution to the downsized force.

There are a number of gaps in the JPM data that could limit the usefulness of the cost/performance methodology in operational settings. One of the most difficult challenges has been to find a satisfactory way to generalize the JPM results to performance in other military jobs. At least two lines of research might be fruitful. First, analysis of the personal attributes or traits required by a sample of military jobs (see Chapter 4) might provide clues for more homogeneous clusters of jobs around the JPM anchor jobs. In addition, a better understanding of the relative difficulty of military jobs has turned out to be of overriding importance in understanding the hands-on test scores and, by extension, in supporting the generalizability of the results to other, similar jobs.

We have spoken at some length in this volume of the need to provide an absolute, or competency, interpretation of performance in a particular job in order to set enlistment standards—so that policy makers can address the question of how much performance is enough. If policy makers are only interested in optimizing costs, then relative comparisons among people as provided by the JPM data will suffice. From that data, analysts can construct various groups or ability mixes (based on different cutoff scores), compute their costs and overall performance outcomes, and see if there is a cutoff (or ability distribution) that minimizes cost per unit of productivity.

But that analysis does not provide policy makers with a grounds for judging whether the optimal cost solution will produce an enlisted corps that can perform all first-term jobs competently. If policy makers want to be able to look at costs in the framework of the performance needed to accomplish the institutional mission, then the performance data will have to be interpretable with regard to an absolute standard of mastery or competency. By and large, the JPM measures were not developed as competency scales. However, some thought is being given to ways of providing external competency anchors for the data—say, by comparing the JPM cohort with the enlisted force in what military experts consider a very bad and a very good recruiting year and extrapolating the known job performance to the other two groups. This kind of thing seems well worth exploring.

The full implications of the job performance measurement research for military policy makers—and for civilian-sector employers—remain to be worked out in coming years. It has produced a rich body of data and a wealth of methodological insights and advances. Most important of all, the JPM Project has defined the challenges for the next generation of research on performance assessment.

References

Alley, W.E.
   1988 Occupational learning difficulty. In B. Green, H. Wing, and A. Wigdor, eds., *Linking Military Enlistment Standards to Job Performance: Report of a Workshop*. Committee on the Performance of Military Personnel, Commission on Behavioral and Social Sciences and Education, National Research Council. Washington, D.C.: National Academy Press.

Angoff, W.
   1971 *The College Board Admissions Testing Program: A Technical Report on Research and Development Activities Relating to the Scholastic Aptitude Test and Achievement Tests*. New York: College Entrance Examination Board.

Arabian, J., and L. Hanser
   1986 *Army Research to Link Standards for Enlistment to On-the-Job Performance*. RS-WP-86-05. Alexandria, Va.: U.S. Army Research Institute for the Behavioral and Social Sciences.

Arabian, J., J. McHenry, and L. Wise
   1988 Synthetic Validation Procedures for Identifying Selection Composites and Cut Scores. Paper presented at the 30th annual conference of the Military Testing Association, Washington, D.C.

Armor, D., R. Fernandez, K. Bers, and D. Schwartzbach
   1982 *Recruit Aptitudes and Army Job Performance*. R-2874-MRAL. Santa Monica, Calif.: The Rand Corporation.

Bearden, R.
   1986 Training the Machinist's Mates. Unpublished manuscript. Navy Personnel Research and Development Center, San Diego, Calif.

Bentley, B.
  1986 Determining Minimal Competence for an Air Force Performance Test. Paper presented at the annual meeting of the American Psychological Association, Washington, D.C.
Bernardin, H.
  1989 *Human Resources Management: An Experimental Approach.* New York: McGraw Hill.
Bernardin, H., and R. Beatty
  1984 *Performance Appraisal: Assessing Human Behavior at Work.* Boston: Kent.
Binken, M.
  1982 *Blacks in the Military.* Washington, D.C.: The Brookings Institution.
Blanz, F., and Ghiselli, E.
  1972 The mixed standard scale: a new rating system. *Personnel Psychology* 25:185-199.
Block, N.J., and G. Dworkin
  1976 *The I.Q. Controversy: Critical Readings.* New York: Pantheon Books.
Boring, E.
  1929 *A History of Experimental Psychology.* New York: The Century Co.
Boudreau, J.
  1988 Utility analysis for decisions in human personnel management. In M. Dunnette, ed., *Handbook of Industrial and Organizational Psychology.* Palo Alto, Calif.: Consulting Psychologist's Press.
Bowman, W., R. Little, and G. Sicilia, eds.
  1986 *The All-Volunteer Force After a Decade: Retrospect and Prospect.* Washington, D.C.: Pergamon-Brassey's.
Brogden, H.
  1946 On the interpretation of the correlation as a measure of predictive efficiency. *Journal of Educational Psychology* 37:65-76.
  1949 When testing pays off. *Personnel Psychology* 2:171-185.
Brogden, H., and E. Taylor
  1950 The theory and classification of criterion bias. *Educational and Psychological Measurement* 10:159-186.
Brown, C.W., and E.E. Ghiselli
  1953 Percent increase in proficiency resulting from use of selective devices. *Journal of Applied Psychology* 37:341-345.
Campbell, J.
  1986 *Validation Analysis for New Predictors.* RS-WP-86-09. Alexandria, Va.: U.S. Army Research Institute for the Behavioral and Social Sciences.
Campbell, J., J. McHenry, and L. Wise
  1987 Analysis of Criterion Measures: The Modeling of Performance. Paper presented at the mid-year conference of the Society of Industrial and Organizational Psychology, Atlanta, Ga.
Campbell, J., J. McHenry, and L. Wise
  1987 Analysis of Criterion Measures: The Modeling of Performance. Paper presented at the mid-year conference of the Society of Industrial and Organizational Psychology, Atlanta, Ga.

Cascio, W.
 1987 *Costing Human Resources: The Financial Impact of Behavior in Organizations*, 2nd ed. Boston: Kent.

Cascio, W., and R. Ramos
 1986 Development and application of a new method for assessing job performance in behavioral/economic terms. *Journal of Applied Psychology* 71:20-28.

Charnes, A., W. Cooper, and S. Henderson
 1953 *An Introduction to Linear Programming*. New York: Wiley.

Christal, R.
 1974 *The United States Air Force Occupational Research Project*. AFHRL-TR-73-75. Brooks Air Force Base, Tex.: Air Force Human Resources Laboratory.

Cronbach, L.
 1971 Test validation. Pp. 443-507 in R. Thorndike, ed., *Educational Measurement*, 2nd ed. Washington, D.C.: American Council on Education.

Cronbach, L., and G. Gleser
 1965 *Psychological Tests and Personnel Decisions*, 2nd ed. Urbana: University of Illinois Press.

Cronbach, L., G. Gleser, A. Nanda, and N. Rajaratnam
 1972 *The Dependability of Behavioral Measurements: Theory of Generalizability for Scores and Profiles*. New York: Wiley.

Darling-Hammond, L.
 1991 The Implications of Testing Policy for Educational Equity and Equality. Paper presented at the American Education Research Association Invitational Conference on Accountability as a State Reform Instrument: Impact on Teaching, Learning, Minority Issues and Incentives for Improvement, Washington, D.C.

Dertouzos, J.
 1989 *The Effects of Military Advertising: Evidence from the Advertising Mix Test*. Rand Note No. N-2907-FMP. Santa Monica, Calif.: The Rand Corporation.

Drasgow, F., and T. Kang
 1984 Statistical power of differential validity and differential prediction analysis for detecting measurement nonequivalence. *Journal of Applied Psychology* 69:498-508.

DuBois, P., ed.
 1947 *The Classification Program*. U.S. Army Air Force Aviation Psychology Program Research Report, No. 2. Washington, D.C.: U.S. Government Printing Office.

Dunbar, S., and M. Novick
 1988 On predicting success in training for men and women: examples from Marine Corps clerical specialties. *Journal of Applied Psychology* 73:545-550.

Dunnette, M.
 1963 A note on *the* criterion. *Journal of Applied Psychology* 47:251-254.

Eaton, N., H. Wing, and K. Mitchell
 1985 Alternate methods of estimating the dollar value of performance. *Personnel Psychology* 38:27-40.

Eitelberg, M.
 1988 *Manpower for Military Occupations.* Washington, D.C.: Office of the Assistant Secretary of Defense (Force Management and Personnel).
 1986 *Representation and Race in America's Volunteer Military.* Monterey, Calif.: Naval Postgraduate School.

Eitelberg, M., J. Laurence, and B. Waters with L. Perelman
 1984 *Screening for Service: Aptitude and Education Criteria for Military Entry.* Office of the Assistant Secretary of Defense (Manpower, Installations and Logistics). Washington, D.C.: U.S. Department of Defense.

Fass, P.
 1980 The IQ: a cultural and historical framework. *American Journal of Education* 88:431-458.

Fernandez, R., and J. Garfinkle
 1985 *Setting Enlistment Standards and Matching Recruits to Jobs Using Job Performance Criteria.* R-3067-MIL. Santa Monica, Calif.: The Rand Corporation.

Fienberg, S.E.
 1977 *The Analysis of Cross-Classified Categorical Data.* Cambridge, Mass.: MIT Press.

Fleishman, E.
 1975 Toward a taxonomy of human performance. *American Psychologist* 30:1127-1149.

Fleishman, E., and M. Quaintance
 1984 *Taxonomies of Human Performance: Description of Human Tasks.* Broedling, Fla.: Academic Press.

Freeman, F.N.
 1926 *Mental Tests: Their History, Principles, and Applications.* Boston. (Reprinted 1939)

Fullinwider, R., ed.
 1983 *Conscripts and Volunteers: Military Requirements, Social Justice, and the All-Volunteer Force.* Totowa, N.J.: Rowman and Allanheld.

Gael, S.
 1984 *Job Analysis: A Guide to Assessing Work Activities.* San Francisco: Jossey-Bass.
 1988 *The Job Analysis Handbook for Business, Industry, and Government.* New York: Wiley.

Goodenough, F.
 1949 *Mental Testing: Its History, Principles, and Applications.* New York: Rinehart and Co.

Green, B., H. Wing, and A. Wigdor, eds.
 1988 *Linking Military Enlistment Standards to Job Performance: Report of a Workshop.* Committee on the Performance of Military Personnel, Commission on Behavioral and Social Sciences and Education, National Research Council. Washington, D.C.: National Academy Press.

Guion, R.
1975 Issues for a discussion of content validity. In R. Guion, ed., *Proceedings of Content Validity II*. A conference on implications and applications of ideas of content validity in employee selection procedures. Bowling Green, Ohio: Bowling Green State University.
1977 Content validity—the source of my discontent. *Applied Psychological Measurement* 1:1-10.
1979 *Principles of Work Sample Testing: III. Construction and Evaluation of Work Sample Tests*. TR-79-A10. Alexandria, Va.: U.S. Army Research Institute for the Behavioral and Social Sciences.

Gulliksen, H.
1950 *Theory of Mental Tests*. New York: Wiley.

Hale, M.
1980 *Human Science and Social Order: Hugo Munsterberg and the Origins of Applied Psychology*. Philadelphia, Pa.: Temple University Press.

Hartigan, J., and A. Wigdor, eds.
1989 *Fairness in Employment Testing: Validity Generalization, Minority Issues, and the General Aptitude Test Battery*. Committee on the General Aptitude Test Battery, Commission on Behavioral and Social Sciences and Education, National Research Council. Washington, D.C.: National Academy Press.

Hedge, J., M. Lipscomb, and M. Teachout
1987 Work sample testing in the Air Force job performance measurement project. In H.G. Baker and G.J. Laabs, eds., *Proceedings of the Department of Defense/Educational Testing Service Conference on Job Performance Measurement Technologies*. Washington, D.C.: Office of the Assistant Secretary of Defense (Force Management and Personnel).

Hively, W., H. Patterson, and S. Page
1968 A "universe-defined" system of arithmetic achievement tests. *Journal of Educational Measurement* 5:275-290.

Hogarth, R.M., and H.J. Einhorn
1976 Optimal strategies for personnel selection when candidates can reject offers. *Journal of Business* 49:478-495.

Houston, W., and M. Novick
1987 Race-based differential prediction in Air Force technical training programs. *Journal of Educational Measurement* 24:309-320.

Hunter, J.
1980 *Test Validation for 12,000 Jobs: An Application of Synthetic Validity and Validity Generalization to the GATB*. Washington, D.C.: U.S. Employment Service, U.S. Department of Labor.
1983 A causal analysis of cognitive ability, job knowledge, job performance, and supervisor ratings. Pp. 257-266 in F. Landy, S. Zedeck, and J. Cleveland, eds., *Performance Measurement and Theory*. Hillsdale, N.J.: Erlbaum.
1986 Cognitive ability, cognitive aptitudes, job knowledge, and job performance. *Journal of Vocational Behavior* 29:340-362.

Hunter, J., and F. Schmidt
1982 Fitting people to jobs: the impact of personnel selection on national pro-

ductivity. In M.D. Dunnette and E.A. Fleischman, eds., *Human Performance and Productivity: Human Capability Assessment.* Hillsdale, N.J.: Erlbaum.

Hunter, J., J. Crosson, and D. Friedman
  1985 *The Validity of the Armed Services Vocational Aptitude (ASVAB) for Civilian and Military Job Performance.* Rockville, Md.: Research Applications, Inc.

Hutchins, S.
  1986 Developing Criterion-Based Performance Standards for a Navy Task Using the Delphi Technique. Paper presented at the annual meeting of the American Psychological Association, Washington, D.C.

Ilgen, D., and J. Feldman
  1983 Performance appraisal: a process focus. In L. Cummings and B. Straw, eds., *Research in Organizational Behavior (Vol. 5).* Greenwich, Conn.: JAI Press.

Irvine, S., and J. Berry
  1988 *Human Abilities in Cultural Context.* Cambridge, England: Cambridge University Press.

Jacobs, R., S. Kafry, and S. Zedeck
  1980 Expectations of behaviorally anchored rating scales. *Personnel Psychology* 33:595-640.

Jaynes, G., and R. Williams, eds.
  1989 *A Common Destiny: Blacks and American Society.* Committee on the Status of Black Americans, Commission on Behavioral and Social Sciences and Education, National Research Council. Washington, D.C.: National Academy Press.

Jehn, C.
  1991 Statement of the Assistant Secretary of Defense, Force Management and Personnel, on military recruiting and advertising. Hearing Before the House Committee on Armed Services, May 1, 1991.

Jenkins, J.
  1946 Validity for what? *Journal of Consulting Psychology* 10:93-98.
  1950 *The Combat Criterion in Naval Aviation.* National Research Council Committee on Aviation Psychology Report No. 6. Washington, D.C.: Division of Aviation Medicine, Bureau of Medicine and Surgery, United States Navy.

Kevles, D.
  1968 Testing the Army's intelligence: psychologists and the military in World War I. *The Journal of American History* 55:565-581.
  1985 *In the Name of Eugenics: Genetics and the Uses of Human Heredity.* New York: Knopf.

Kraus, M.
  1986 *Personnel Research, History, and Policy Issues: Walter Van Dyke Bingham and the Bureau of Personnel Research.* New York: Garland.

Kroeker, L., and B. Rafacz
  1983 *CLASP: A Recruit Assignment Model.* NPRDC TR 84-9. San Diego, Calif.: Navy Personnel Research and Development Center.

Kroeker, L., G. Laabs, R. Vineberg, J. Joyner, and R. Zimmerman
  1988 *Developing a Hands-on Performance Measure for Machinist Mate's (MM) Rating.* NPRDC Technical Report. San Diego, Calif.: Navy Personnel Research and Development Center.

Laabs, G.
  1988 The Navy's Job Performance Measurement Program. Paper presented to the JPM Data Workshop of the Committee on the Performance of Military Personnel, Monterey, California.

Laabs, G., and H. Baker
  1989 Selection of critical tasks for Navy job performance measures. *Journal of Military Psychology* 1:3-16.

Lammlein, S.
  1987 *Final Report: Job Analysis and Critical Task Selection for the First-Term Navy Radioman Job.* Institute Report No. 134. Minneapolis, Minn.: Personnel Decisions Research Institute.

Lammlein, S., N. Peterson, and R. Rosse
  1987 *Final Report: Pilot Test of a Probabilistic Sampling Critical Task Selection Model for Performance Testing.* Institute Report No. 133. Minneapolis, Minn.: Personnel Decisions Research Institute.

Landy, F.
  1989 *The Psychology of Work Behavior.* Monterey, Calif.: Brooks Cole.

Landy, F., and J. Farr
  1983 *The Measurement of Work Performance: Methods, Theory, and Applications.* New York: Academic Press.

Laurence, J., P. Ramsberger, and M. Gribben
  1989 *Effects of Military Experience on the Post-Service Lives of Low-Aptitude Recruits: Project 100,000 and the ASVAB Misnorming.* Alexandria, Va.: Human Resources Research Organization.

Lesgold, A., S. Lajoie, D. Logan, and G. Eggan
  1990 Applying cognitive task analysis and research methods to assessment. In N. Frederiksen, R. Glaser, A. Lesgold, and M. Shafto, eds., *Diagnostic Monitoring of Skill and Knowledge Acquisition.* Hillsdale, N.J.: Erlbaum.

Lindquist, E.F.
  1953 *Design and Analysis of Experiments in Psychology and Education.* Boston: Houghton-Mifflin.

Linn, R.
  1982 Ability testing: individual differences, prediction, and differential prediction. In A. Wigdor and W. Garner, eds., *Ability Testing: Uses, Consequences, and Controversies.* Washington, D.C.: National Academy Press.
  1983 The Pearson selection formulas: implications for studies of predictive bias and estimates of effects in selected samples. *Journal of Educational Measurement* 20:1-15.

Lipmann, O.
  1916 Zur Psychologischen Characteristik der 'mittleren' Beruf. Z. f. ang. Psychol., 12. (as cited in Viteles).

Loney, S.
  1890 *The Elements of Statics and Dynamics.* London: MacMillan.

Lord, F., and M. Novick
 1968 *Statistical Theories of Mental Test Scores.* Reading, Mass.: Addison-Wesley.
MacGregor, M.
 1981 *Integration of the Armed Forces.* Washington, D.C.: U.S. Army Center of Military History.
Madaus, G.F., and T. Kellaghan
 1991 Curriculum evaluation and assessment. Chapter 5 in P.W. Jackson, ed., *Handbook of Research on Curriculum.* New York: Macmillan.
Maier, M., and C. Hiatt
 1984 *An Evaluation of Using Job Performance Tests to Validate ASVAB Qualification Standards.* CNR 89. Alexandria, Va.: Center for Naval Analyses.
May, L.
 1986 *Educational Quality Requirements for Marine Corps Enlisted Personnel.* CNR 121. Alexandria, Va.: Center for Naval Analyses.
Mayberry, P.
 1987 *Developing a Competency Scale for Hands-On Measures of Job Proficiency.* Research Contribution 570. Alexandria, Va.: Center for Naval Analysis.
 1988 *Interim Results for the Marine Corps Job Performance Measurement Project.* Research Memorandum 88-37. Alexandria, Va.: Center for Naval Analysis.
 1989 *Performance of Basic Infantry Tasks.* Research Memorandum 89-45. Alexandria, Va.: Center for Naval Analysis.
McHenry, J., L. Hough, J. Toquam, M. Hanson, and S. Ashworth
 1987 Project A Validity Results: The Relationship Between Predictor and Criterion Domains. Paper presented at the mid-year conference of the Society of Industrial and Organizational Psychology, Atlanta, Ga.
Messick, S.
 1989 Validity. Pp. 13-103 in R. Linn, ed., *Educational Measurement*, 3rd ed. New York: Macmillan.
Milkovich, G., and A. Wigdor, eds.
 1990 *Pay for Performance: Evaluating Performance Appraisal and Merit Pay.* Committee on Performance Appraisal for Merit Pay, Commission on Behavioral and Social Sciences and Education, National Research Council. Washington, D.C.: National Academy Press.
Moskos, C., and J. Butler
 1987 Blacks in the Military Since World War II. Paper prepared for the Committee on the Status of Black Americans, Commission on Behavioral and Social Sciences and Education, National Research Council, Washington, D.C.
Murphy, G.
 1929 *An Historical Introduction to Modern Psychology.* London: Kegan Paul, Trench, Trubner, and Co.
Murphy, K., and J. Cleveland
 1991 *Performance Appraisal: An Organizational Perspective.* Boston: Allyn and Bacon.

REFERENCES

Murphy, K., and J. Constans
  1988 Psychological issues in scale format research: behavioral anchors as a source of bias rating. In R. Cardy, S. Peiffer, and J. Newman, eds., *Advances in Information Processing in Organizations (Vol. 3)*. Greenwich, Conn.: JAI Press.

Murphy, K., and B. Jako
  1989 Under what conditions are observed intercorrelations greater than or smaller than true intercorrelations. *Journal of Applied Psychology* 74:827-830.

Murphy, K., C. Martin, and M. Garcia
  1982 Do behavioral observation scales measure observation? *Journal of Applied Psychology* 67:562-167.

Nord, R., and L. White
  1988 The measurement and application of performance utility: some key issues. In B. Green, H. Wing, and A. Wigdor, eds., *Linking Military Enlistment Standards to Job Performance: Report of a Workshop*. Committee on the Performance of Military Personnel, Commission on Behavioral and Social Sciences and Education, National Research Council. Washington, D.C.: National Academy Press.

Office of the Assistant Secretary of Defense (Force Management and Personnel)
  1987 *Joint-Service Efforts to Link Enlistment Standards to Job Performance*. Sixth Annual Report to the House Committee on Appropriations. Washington, D.C.: U.S. Department of Defense.
  1988 *Department of Defense Manpower Requirements Report, FY 1989*. Washington, D.C.: U.S. Department of Defense.
  1989 *Joint-Service Efforts to Link Enlistment Standards to Job Performance: Recruit Quality and Military Readiness*. Report to the House Committee on Appropriations. Washington, D.C.: U.S. Department of Defense.
  1990 *Joint-Service Efforts to Link Military Enlistment Standards to Job Performance*. Report to the House Committee on Appropriations. Washington, D.C.: U.S. Department of Defense.
  1991 *Joint-Service Efforts to Link Military Enlistment Standards to Job Performance*. Report to the House Committee on Appropriations. Washington, D.C.: U.S. Department of Defense.

Office of the Assistant Secretary of Defense (Manpower, Installations, and Logistics)
  1984 *Joint-Service Efforts to Link Enlistment Standards to Job Performance*. Third Annual Report to the House Committee on Appropriations. Washington, D.C.: U.S. Department of Defense.

Office of the Assistant Secretary of Defense (Manpower, Reserve Affairs, and Logistics)
  1980a *Aptitude Testing of Recruits*. Report to the House Committee on Armed Services. Washington, D.C.: U.S. Department of Defense.
  1980b *Implementation of New Armed Services Vocational Aptitude Battery and Actions to Improve the Enlistment Standards Process*. Report to the House and Senate Committee on Armed Services. Washington, D.C.: U.S. Department of Defense.
  1981 *Department of Defense Efforts to Develop Quality Standards for Enlist-*

ment. Report to the House and Senate Committees on Armed Services. Washington, D.C.: U.S. Department of Defense.

1982a *Profile of American Youth: 1980 Nationwide Administration of the Armed Services Vocational Aptitude Battery.* Washington, D.C.: U.S. Department of Defense.

1982b *First Annual Report to the Congress on Joint-Service Efforts to Link Standards for Enlistment to On-the-Job Performance.* Report to the House Committee on Appropriations. Washington, D.C.: U.S. Department of Defense.

1983 *Second Annual Report to the Congress on Joint-Service Efforts to Link Standards for Enlistment to On-the-Job Performance.* Report to the House Committee on Appropriations. Washington, D.C.: U.S. Department of Defense.

Pearlman, K.
 1980 Job families: a review and discussion of their implications for personnel selection. *Psychological Bulletin* 87(1):1-28.

Peña, M.
 1988 Air Force person-job match: nonprior service enlisted classification. In B. Green, H. Wing, and A. Wigdor, eds. *Linking Military Enlistment Standards to Job Performance: Report of a Workshop.* Committee on the Performance of Military Personnel, Commission on Behavioral and Social Sciences and Education, National Research Council. Washington, D.C.: National Academy Press.

Peterson, J.
 1925 *Early Conceptions and Tests of Intelligence.* Yonkers-on-Hudson, N.Y.: World Book Company.

Peterson, N., and D. Bownas
 1982 Skill, task structure, and performance. Chapter 3 of M. Dunnette and E. Fleishman, eds., *Human Performance and Productivity, Vol.1.* Hillsdale, N.J.: Erlbaum.

Pinter, R.
 1923 *Intelligence Testing: Methods and Results.* New York: Henry Holt and Co.

Reed, J.
 1987 Robert M. Yerkes and the mental testing movement. In M. Sokal, *Psychological Testing and American Society, 1890-1930.* New Brunswick, N.J.: Rutgers University Press.

Rubin, D.
 1980 Using empirical Bayes techniques in the law school validity studies. *Journal of the American Statistical Association* 75:801-816.

Sadacca, R., M. de Vera, and A. DiFazio
 1986 Weighting Performance Constructs in Composite Measures of Job Performance. Paper presented at the annual meeting of the American Psychological Association, Washington, D.C.

Sadacca, R., L. White, J. Campbell, and A. DiFazio
 1988 Measurement of the Utility of Performance in Army Jobs. Technical Re-

REFERENCES

port. U.S. Army Institute for the Behavioral and Social Sciences, Alexandria, Va.

Samelson, F.
1987 Was Early Mental Testing. . . . In M. Sokal, *Psychological Testing and American Society, 1890-1930.* New Brunswick, N.J.: Rutgers University Press.

Schmidt, F., and J. Hunter
1983 Individual differences in productivity: an empirical test of estimates derived from studies of selection procedure utility. *Journal of Applied Psychology* 68:407-414.

Schmidt, F., J. Hunter, R. McKenzie, and T. Mouldrow
1979 Impact of valid selection procedures on workforce productivity. *Journal of Applied Psychology* 64:609-626.

Schmitz, E.
1988 Improving personnel performance through assignment policy. In B. Green, H. Wing, and A. Wigdor, eds., *Linking Military Enlistment Standards to Job Performance: Report of a Workshop.* Committee on the Performance of Military Personnel, Commission on Behavioral and Social Sciences and Education, National Research Council. Washington, D.C.: National Academy Press.

Schmitz, E., and R. Nord
1987 *Evaluating Improvements to MOS Assignment Policy.* MPPRG Working Paper. Alexandria, Va.: U.S. Army Research Institute for the Behavioral and Social Sciences.

Shavelson, R.
1968 Lunar gravity simulation and its effect on man's performance. *Human Factors* 10:393-402.

Shavelson, R., P. Mayberry, W. Li, and N. Webb
1990 Generalizability of job performance measurements: Marine Corps rifleman. *Military Psychology* 2:129-144.

Smith, P., and L. Kendell
1963 Retranslation of expectations: an approach to the construction of unambiguous anchors for rating scales. *Journal of Applied Psychology* 7:149-155.

Sokal, M.M.
1987 *Psychological Testing and American Society, 1890-1930.* New Brunswick, N.J.: Rutgers University Press.

Spearman, C.
1927 *The Abilities of Man.* New York: MacMillan.

Super, D., and Crites, J.
1962 *Appraising Vocational Fitness By Means of Psychological Tests.* New York: Harper.

Taylor, H., and T. Russell
1939 The relationship of validity coefficients to the effectiveness of tests in selection: discussion and tables. *Journal of Applied Psychology* 23:565-578.

Thorndike, R.L.
  1949 *Personnel Selection.* New York: Wiley.
Tversky, A., and D. Kahneman
  1974 Judgment under uncertainty: heuristics and biases. *Science* 185:1124-1131.
Tyack, D.
  1974 *The One Best System: A History of American Urban Education.* Cambridge, Mass.: Harvard University Press.
Uhlaner, J., and D. Bolanovich
  1952 Development of Armed Forces Qualification Test and Predecessor Army Screening Tests, 1946-1950. PRS Report 976. Personnel Research Section, Department of the Army, Washington, D.C.
U.S. Air Force
  1980 United States Air Force Job Inventory: Jet Engine and Turboprop Propulsion Career Ladders. Randolph Air Force Base, San Antonio, Tex.
  1987 Defense Planning Guide. Internal document. Headquarters, United States Air Force, August.
Viteles, M.
  1932 *Industrial Psychology.* New York: W.W. Norton and Company.
Von Mayrhauser, R.
  1987 The manager, the medic, and the mediator: the clash of professional psychological styles and the wartime origins of group mental testing. In M. Sokal, ed., *Psychological Testing and American Society, 1890-1930.* New Brunswick, N.J.: Rutgers University Press.
Wallace, S.R.
  1965 Criteria for what? *American Psychologist* 20:411-417.
Waters, B., J. Laurence, and W. Camara
  1987 *Personnel Enlistment and Classification Procedures in the U.S. Military.* Paper prepared for the Committee on the Performance of Military Personnel, Commission on Behavioral and Social Sciences and Education, National Research Council. Washington, D.C.: National Academy Press.
Webb, N., R. Shavelson, K-S. Kim, and Z. Chen
  1989 Reliability (generalizability) of job performance measurements: Navy machinist's mates. *Journal of Military Psychology* 1(2):91-110.
Wigdor, A., and W. Garner, eds.
  1982 *Ability Testing: Uses, Consequences, and Controversies Part I: Report of the Committee.* Committee on Ability Testing, Assembly of Behavioral and Social Sciences, National Research Council. Washington, D.C.: National Academy Press.
Wigdor, A., and B. Green, eds.
  1986 *Assessing the Performance of Enlisted Personnel: Evaluation of a Joint-Service Research Project.* Committee on the Performance of Military Personnel, Commission on Behavioral and Social Sciences and Education, National Research Council. Washington, D.C.: National Academy Press.
Wise, L., J. Campbell, and J. Arabian
  1988 The Army synthetic validation project. In B. Green, H. Wing, and A. Wigdor, eds., *Linking Military Enlistment Standards to Job Performance: Report of a Workshop.* Committee on the Performance of Military Personnel,

Commission on Behavioral and Social Sciences and Education, National Research Council. Washington, D.C.: National Academy Press.

Wise, L., J. Campbell, J. McHenry, and L. Hanser
 1986 A Latent Structure Model of Job Performance Factors. Paper presented at the annual meeting of the American Psychological Association, Washington, D.C.

Yerkes, R.M., ed.
 1921 Psychological Examining in the United States Army. Volume XV in *Memoirs of the National Academy of Sciences*. Washington, D.C.: U.S. Government Printing Office.

Young, K.
 1923 The history of mental testing. *Pedigogical Seminary* 31 (March):1-48.

Zeidner, J.
 1987 *The Validity of Selection and Classification Procedures for Predicting Job Performance*. IDA paper P-1987. Alexandria, Va.: Institute for Defense Analyses.

Zeidner, J., and C.D. Johnson
 1989 *The Utility of Selection for Military and Civilian Jobs*. IDA paper P-2239. Alexandria, Va.: Institute for Defense Analyses.

REPORTS OF THE COMMITTEE ON THE PERFORMANCE OF MILITARY PERSONNEL

1984 *Job Performance Measurement in the Military: Report of a Workshop.*

1984 *Joint-Service Job Performance Measurement/Enlistment Standards Project: Its Progress and Potential.* Bert F. Green, Jr., and Alexandra K. Wigdor, eds.

1986 *Assessing the Performance of Enlisted Personnel: Evaluation of a Joint-Service Research Project.* Alexandra K. Wigdor and Bert F. Green, Jr., eds.

1987 *Personnel Enlistment and Classification Procedures in the U.S. Military.* Brian K. Waters, Janice H. Laurence, and Wayne J. Camera.

1988 *Measuring Job Competency.* Bert F. Green, Jr., and Alexandra K. Wigdor, eds.

1988 *Analysis of Job Performance Measurement Data: Report of a Workshop.* Bert F. Green, Jr. and Hilda Wing, eds.

1988 *Linking Military Enlistment Standards to Job Performance: Report of a Workshop.* Bert F. Green, Jr., Hilda Wing, and Alexandra K. Wigdor, eds.

Appendix A

Service Bibliographies

AIR FORCE

Alley, W.E., and M.S. Teachout
   1990 Aptitude and Experience Trade-offs on Job Performance. Paper presented at the annual meeting of the American Psychological Association, Boston.

Ballentine, R.D.
   1986 Air Force job performance measurement research. Pp. 314-318 in D.A. Harris, chair, *Joint-Service Job Performance Measurement/Enlistment Standards Project. Proceedings of the Tenth Psychology in the DoD Symposium.* Colorado Springs, Colo.: U.S. Air Force Academy.
   1989 Criterion measures in selection research—case study. In M. Smith and I. Robertson, eds., *Advances in Personnel Selection and Assessment.* Sussex, England: John Wiley and Sons.

Ballentine, R.D., and J.W. Hedge
   1987 Use of job performance criteria for evaluating training technology. In H.W. Ruck, chair, Toward an Integrated Personnel System: USAF Training Research and Development. Symposium conducted at the annual meeting of the Society of Industrial and Organizational Psychology, Atlanta, Ga.

Ballentine, R.D, and M.S. Lipscomb
   1987 Developing performance measures and standards for accurate assessment. In J.W. Hedge and M.S. Lipscomb, eds., *Walk-Through Performance Testing: An Innovative Approach to Work Sample Testing.* AFHRL-TP-87-8. Brooks Air Force Base, Tex.: Training Systems Division, Air Force Human Resources Laboratory.

Bentley, B.A., K.L. Ringenbach, and J.W. Augustin
1989 *Development of Army Job Knowledge Tests for Three Air Force Specialties.* Technical paper. AFHRL-TP-88-11. Brooks Air Force Base, Tex.: Training Systems Division, Air Force Human Resources Laboratory.

Bentley, B.A., K.L. Ringenbach, J.W. Augustin, and T.M. Donnelly
1989 A comparison of three Air Force knowledge tests. In proceedings of the 31st annual conference of the Military Testing Association, San Antonio, Tex.

Bierstedt, S.A., and J.W. Hedge
1987 *Job Performance Measurement System Trainer's Manual.* Technical paper. AFHRL-TP-86-34. Brooks Air Force Base, Tex.: Training Systems Division, Air Force Human Resources Laboratory.

Bierstedt, S.A., A.H. Gillet, B.A. Bentley, and D.L. Harville
1989 Methodology to evaluate the Air Force job performance measurement system. In proceedings of the 31st annual conference of the Military Testing Association, San Antonio, Tex.

Blackhurst, J.L., and J.W. Hedge
1986 Equating Job Performance Measurement Test Scores. Paper presented at the annual meeting of the American Psychological Association, Washington, D.C.

Blackhurst, J.L., R.D. Ballentine, and M.W. Pellum
1988 Air Force job performance measurement technology applied to training. In M.S. Lipscomb and J.W. Hedge, eds., *Job Performance Measurement: Topics in the Performance Measurement of Air Force Enlisted Personnel.* Technical paper. AFHRL-TP-87-58. Brooks Air Force Base, Tex.: Training Systems Division, Air Force Human Resources Laboratory.

Borman, W.C., and G.L. Hallam
1989 *Relationships Between Individual Differences and Accuracy in Rating Air Force Jet Engine Mechanic Performance.* Technical paper. AFHRL-TP-89-2. Brooks Air Force Base, Tex.: Training Systems Division, Air Force Human Resources Laboratory.
1990 Observation accuracy for assessors of work-sample performance: consistency across task and individual-differences correlates. *Journal of Applied Psychology* 76:11-18.

Borman, W.C., M.A. Hanson, S.H. Oppler, E.D. Pulakos, and L.A. White
1991 The role of early supervisory experience in rating performance. In M.S. Teachout, chair, Understanding the Work Experience Construct in Personnel Research and Practice. Symposium conducted at the annual meeting of the Society of Industrial and Organizational Psychology, St. Louis, Mo.

Carpenter, M.A., S.J. Monaco, F.E. O'Mara, and M.S. Teachout
1989 *Time to Job Proficiency: A Preliminary Investigation of the Effects of Aptitude and Experience on Productive Capacity.* Technical paper. AFHRL-TP-88-17. Brooks Air Force Base, Tex.: Training Systems Division, Air Force Human Resources Laboratory.

Coovert, M.D., and J.P. Craiger
1991 Determining the dimensionality of work experience and the prediction of job performance. In M.S. Teachout, chair, Understanding the Work Expe-

rience Construct in Personnel Research and Practice. Symposium conducted at the annual meeting of the Society of Industrial and Organizational Psychology, St. Louis, Mo.

Craiger, J.P., and M.D. Coovert
1991 The relationship between job experience and ratings of performance. In M.S. Teachout, chair, Understanding the Work Experience Construct in Personnel Research and Practice. Symposium conducted at the annual meeting of the Society of Industrial and Organizational Psychology, St. Louis, Mo.

Dickenson, T.L.
1986 *Performance Ratings: Designs for Evaluating Their Validity and Accuracy.* Technical paper. AFHRL-TP-86-15. Brooks Air Force Base, Tex.: Manpower and Personnel Division, Air Force Human Resources Laboratory.
1987 Designs for evaluating the validity and accuracy of performance ratings. *Organizational Behavior and Human Decision Process* 40:1-21.
1987 Some comments on walk-through performance testing. In J.W. Hedge and M.S. Lipscomb, eds., *Walk-Through Performance Testing: An Innovative Approach to Work Sample Testing.* AFHRL-TP-87-8. Brooks Air Force Base, Tex.: Training Systems Division, Air Force Human Resources Laboratory.
1991 Structural analysis of aptitude, training, and job experience for predicting job performance. In M.S. Teachout, chair, Investigating the Construct Validity of a Job Performance Measurement System. Symposium conducted at the annual meeting of the Society of Industrial and Organizational Psychology, St. Louis, Mo.

Dickinson, T.L., and J.W. Hedge
1988 Predictive efficiency of the ASVAB for the Air Force's job performance measurement project. In M.S. Lipscomb and J.W. Hedge, eds., *Job Performance Measurement: Topics in the Performance Measurement of Air Force Enlisted Personnel.* Technical paper. AFHRL-TP-87-58. Brooks Air Force Base, Tex.: Training Systems Division, Air Force Human Resources Laboratory.
1989 *Work Performance Ratings: Measurement Test Bed for Validity and Accuracy Research.* Technical paper. AFHRL-TP-88-36. Brooks Air Force Base, Tex.: Training Systems Division, Air Force Human Resources Laboratory.

Dickenson, T.L., and M.S. Teachout
1991 *Structure of the Air Force's Job Performance Measurement System and Predictability of the Armed Services Vocational Aptitude Battery (ASVAB).* Technical paper. AFHRL-TP-90-85. Brooks Air Force Base, Tex.: Training Systems Division, Air Force Human Resources Laboratory.

Dickenson, T.L., C.E. Hasset, and S.I. Tannenbaum
1986 *Work Performance Ratings: A Meta-Analysis of Multitrait-Multimethod Studies.* Technical paper. AFHRL-TP-86-32. Brooks Air Force Base, Tex.: Training Systems Division, Air Force Human Resources Laboratory.

Dickenson, T.L., J.W. Hedge, and R.D. Ballentine
1987 Predictability of the Armed Services Vocational Aptitude Battery for the Air Force's job performance measurement system. Paper presented at the

Department of Defense/Educational Testing Service Conference on Job Performance Measurement Technologies, San Diego, Calif.

Dickenson, T.L., J.W. Hedge, and M.S. Teachout
1987 Accuracy of Performance Ratings: A Structural Model of Rater Attributes. Paper presented at the annual meeting of the American Psychological Association, New York.

Dickenson, T.L., J.W. Hedge, R.L. Johnson, and T.A. Silverhart
1989 *Work Performance Ratings: Rater Accuracy Training.* Technical paper. AFHRL-TP-89-61. Brooks Air Force Base, Tex.: Training Systems Division, Air Force Human Resources Laboratory.

Duncan, R.E., D.A. Hodge, and J.L. Blackhurst
1988 Inter-service technology transfer: promise and payoff. In M.S. Lipscomb and J.W. Hedge, eds., *Job Performance Measurement: Topics in the Performance Measurement of Air Force Enlisted Personnel.* Technical paper. AFHRL-TP-87-58. Brooks Air Force Base, Tex.: Training Systems Division, Air Force Human Resources Laboratory.

Faneuff, R.S., L.D. Valentine, B.M. Stone, G.L. Curry, and D.C. Hageman
1988 *Exploratory Models to Link Job Performance to Enlistment Standards.* Technical paper. AFHRL-TP-88-39. Brooks Air Force Base, Tex.: Training Systems Division, Air Force Human Resources Laboratory.

Ford, J.K., D.J. Sego, M. Quinones, and J.L. Speer
1991 A literature review of the conceptualization and operationalization of the experience construct. In M.S. Teachout, chair, Understanding the Work Experience Construct in Personnel Research and Practice. Symposium conducted at the annual meeting of the Society of Industrial and Organizational Psychology, St. Louis, Mo.

Ford, J.K., D.J. Sego, and M.S. Teachout
1991 A test of the influence of general ability, job experience, and task experience on task level performance. In M.S. Teachout, chair, Understanding the Work Experience Construct in Personnel Research and Practice. Symposium conducted at the annual meeting of the Society of Industrial and Organizational Psychology, St. Louis, Mo.

Gott, C.D.
1988 *Exploratory Models to Link Job Performance to Enlistment Standards.* Technical paper. AFHRL-TP-88-39. Brooks Air Force Base, Tex.: Training Systems Division, Air Force Human Resources Laboratory.

Gould, R.B., and J.W. Hedge
1983 Air Force Job Performance Criterion Development. Paper presented at the annual meeting of the American Psychological Association, Anaheim, Calif.

1984 Background and theoretical bases of walk-through performance testing. In S. Zedeck, chair, Walk-Through Performance Testing: An Innovative Approach to Work Sample Testing. Symposium conducted at the annual meeting of the American Psychological Association, Toronto, Canada.

1987 History, background, and theoretical bases of walk-through performance testing. In J.W. Hedge and M.S. Lipscomb, eds., *Walk-Through Performance Testing: An Innovative Approach to Work Sample Testing.* AFHRL-

TP-87-8. Brooks Air Force Base, Tex.: Training Systems Division, Air Force Human Resources Laboratory.

Hedge, J.W.
1984 The methodology of walk-through performance testing. In S. Zedeck, chair, Walk-Through Performance Testing: An Innovative Approach to Work Sample Testing. Symposium conducted at the annual meeting of the American Psychological Association, Toronto, Canada.
1986 Issues in Job Performance Measurement Research. Symposium conducted at the annual meeting of the American Psychological Association, Washington, D.C.
1987 The methodology of walk-through performance testing. In J.W. Hedge and M.S. Lipscomb, eds., *Walk-Through Performance Testing: An Innovative Approach to Work Sample Testing.* Technical paper. AFHRL-TP-87-71. Brooks Air Force Base, Tex.: Training Systems Division, Air Force Human Resources Laboratory.

Hedge, J.W., and F.J. Laue
1988 Can appraisers rate work performance accurately? In C. Lance, chair, Are People Pretty Good Judges of Others After All? Symposium conducted at the annual meeting of the American Psychological Association, Atlanta, Ga.

Hedge, J.W., and M.S. Lipscomb
1986 The Air Force Job Performance Measurement Project. Paper presented at the annual meeting of the American Psychological Association, Washington, D.C.
1986 The Identification of Surrogate Indices of Hands-On Performance. Paper presented at the annual meeting of the American Psychological Association, Washington, D.C.

Hedge, J.W., and M.S. Lipscomb, eds.
1987 *Walk-Through Performance Testing: An Innovative Approach to Work Sample Testing.* Technical paper. AFHRL-TP-87-8. Brooks Air Force Base, Tex.: Training Systems Division, Air Force Human Resources Laboratory.

Hedge, J.W., and M.S. Teachout
1986 *Job Performance Measurement: A Systematic Program of Research and Development.* Technical paper. AFHRL-TP-86-37. Brooks Air Force Base, Tex.: Training Systems Division, Air Force Human Resources Laboratory.
1990 The Development and Evaluation of an Interview Work Sample Criterion Measure. Paper presented at the fifth annual conference of the Society of Industrial and Organizational Psychology, Miami, Fla.
1991 The conceptual development and implementation of a job performance measurement system. In M.S. Teachout, chair, Investigating the Construct Validity of a Job Performance Measurement System. Symposium conducted at the annual meeting of the Society of Industrial and Organizational Psychology, St. Louis, Mo.

Hedge, J.W., R.D. Ballentine, and R.B. Gould
1985 Examining the Link Between Training Evaluation and Job Performance Criterion Development. Paper presented at the NATO defense research

Group Panel VIII Symposium on Transfer of Training to Military Operational Systems, Brussels, Belgium.

Hedge, J.W., T.L. Dickinson, and S.A. Bierstedt
1988 The Use of Videotape Technology to Train Administrators of Walk-Through Performance Testing. Technical paper. AFHRL-TP-87-71. Brooks Air Force Base, Tex.: Training Systems Division, Air Force Human Resources Laboratory.

Hedge, J.W., M.S. Lipscomb, and R.D. Ballentine
1985 Performance Assessment Research in the Air Force. Paper presented at the annual meeting of the American Psychological Association, Los Angeles, Calif.

Hedge, J.W., M.S. Lipscomb, and M.S. Teachout
1988 Work sample testing in the Air Force Job Performance Measurement Project. In M.S. Lipscomb and J.W. Hedge, eds., *Job Performance Measurement: Topics in the Performance Measurement of Air Force Enlisted Personnel*. AFHRL-TP-87-58. Brooks Air Force Base, Tex.: Training Systems Division, Air Force Human Resources Laboratory.

Hedge, J.W., M.S. Teachout, and T.L. Dickenson
1987 User acceptance as a criterion for choosing performance measures. In M. Secunda, chair, Beyond Current Performance Appraisal Research: Acceptability as a New Paradigm. Symposium conducted at the annual meeting of the American Psychological Association, New York.

Hedge, J.W., M.S. Teachout, and F.J. Laue
1990 *Interview Testing as a Work Sample Measure of Job Proficiency*. Technical paper. AFHRL-TP-90-61. Brooks Air Force Base, Tex.: Training Systems Division, Air Force Human Resources Laboratory.

Hedge, J.W., K.L. Ringenbach, M.S. Slattery, and M.S. Teachout
1989 Leniency in performance ratings: implications for the use of self-ratings. In proceedings of the 31st annual conference of the Military Testing Association, San Antonio, Tex.

Kavanagh, M.J.
1987 Issues and Directions in Measuring Job Performance in the Air Force. Panel discussion conducted at the annual meeting of the Society of Industrial and Organizational Psychology, Atlanta, Ga.

1988 *Performance Rating Accuracy Improvement Through Changes in Individual and System Characteristics*. Technical paper. AFHRL-TP-87-67. Brooks Air Force Base, Tex.: Training Systems Division, Air Force Human Resources Laboratory.

Kavanagh, M.J., W.C. Borman, J.W. Hedge, and R.B. Gould
1986 A model of performance measurement quality and its implications for research and practice. In B. Bass, P. Drenth, and P. Weissenberg, eds., *Advances in Organizational Psychology: An International Review*. Beverly Hills, Calif.: Sage Publications.

1986 *Job Performance Measurement Classification Scheme for Validation Research in the Military*. Technical Report. AFHRL-TR-85-51. Brooks Air Force Base, Tex.: Manpower and Personnel Division, Air Force Human Resources Laboratory.

Kavanagh, M.J., B.B. Kavanagh, T. Lee, and J.W. Hedge
- 1988 The Effects of the Purpose of Measurement, Acquaintance With the Job, and Research Method on Performance Measurement Rating Accuracy. Paper presented at the annual meeting of the Academy of Management, Anaheim, Calif.

Kraiger, K.
- 1988 *Generalizability Theory: An Assessment of its Relevance to the Air Force Job Performance Measurement Project.* Technical paper. AFHRL-TP-87-70. Brooks Air Force Base, Tex.: Training Systems Division, Air Force Human Resources Laboratory.
- 1990a *Generalizability of Performance Measures Across Four Air Force Specialties.* Technical paper. AFHRL-TP-89-60. Brooks Air Force Base, Tex.: Training Systems Division, Air Force Human Resources Laboratory.
- 1990b *Generalizabiity of Walk-Through Performance Tests, Job Proficiency Ratings, and Job Knowledge Tests Across Eight Air Force Specialties.* Technical paper. AFHRL-TP-90-14. Brooks Air Force Base, Tex.: Training Systems Division, Air Force Human Resources Laboratory.
- 1991 Generalizability theory as evidence of the validity of work sample tests and proficiency ratings. In M.S. Teachout, chair, Investigating the Construct Validity of a Job Performance Measurement System. Symposium conducted at the annual meeting of the Society of Industrial and Organizational Psychology, St. Louis, Mo.

Kraiger, K., and M.S. Teachout
- 1987 Generalizability theory as evidence of the construct validity of performance ratings. In G. Laabs, chair, Applications of Generalizability Theory to Military Performance Measurement. Symposium conducted at the annual meeting of the American Educational Research Association, Washington, D.C.
- 1990 Generalizability theory as construct-related evidence of the validity of job performance ratings. *Human Performance* 3(1):19-35.
- 1991 *Application of Generalizability Theory to the Air Force's Job Performance Measurement Project: A Summary of Research Results.* AFHRL-TR-90-92.

Lance, C.E., T.M. Donnelly, and M.S. Teachout
- 1991 Assessing the hierarchical structure of a job performance measurement system using hierarchical confirmatory factor analysis. In M.S. Teachout, chair, Investigating the Construct Validity of a Job Performance Measurement System. Symposium conducted at the annual meeting of the Society of Industrial and Organizational Psychology, St. Louis, Mo.

Lance, C.E., J.W. Hedge, and W.E. Alley
- 1987 *Ability, Experience, and Task Characteristic Predictors of Task Performance.* Technical paper. AFHRL-TP-87-14. Brooks Air Force Base, Tex.: Training Systems Division, Air Force Human Resources Laboratory.
- 1989 Joint relationships of task proficiency with aptitude, experience, and task difficulty: a cross-level, interactional study. *Human Performance* 2(4):249-272.

Lance, C.E., M.S. Teachout, and T.M. Donnelly
   1990   Specification of the Job Performance Construct Space: An Application of Hierarchical Confirmatory Factor Analysis. Paper presented at the annual meeting of the Southern Management Association, Boston.

Laue, F.J., M.S. Teachout, and D.L. Harville
   1990   Assessing the substitutability of surrogate measures of job performance for hands-on work sample tests. In L.S. Gottfredson, chair, How Good are Alternative Measures of Job Performance? Symposium conducted at the annual meeting of the American Psychological Association, Boston.

Lipscomb, M.S.
   1987a   A task-level domain sampling strategy: a content valid approach. In J.W. Hedge and M.S. Lipscomb, eds., *Walk-Through Performance Testing: An Innovative Approach to Work Sample Testing.* AFHRL-TP-87-8. Brooks Air Force Base, Tex.: Training Systems Division, Air Force Human Resources Laboratory.
   1987b   Criterion development and application: the Air Force Job Performance Measurement Project. In T. Watson, chair, One More Time: Means for Improving Personnel Selection Criteria. Symposium conducted at the convention of the Texas Psychological Association, San Antonio, Tex.
   1990   A Comparison of Domain Sampling Procedures for Test Construction. Unpublished PhD dissertation, University of Texas, Austin.

Lipscomb, M.S. and T.L. Dickinson
   1988   Test content selection. In M.S. Lipscomb and J.W. Hedge, eds., *Job Performance Measurement: Topics in the Performance Measurement of Air Force Enlisted Personnel.* Technical paper. AFHRL-TP-87-58. Brooks Air Force Base, Tex.: Training Systems Division, Air Force Human Resources Laboratory.

Lipscomb, M.S., and J.W Hedge
   1987   Content Selection. Paper presented at the Department of Defense/Educational Testing Service Conference on Job Performance Measurement Technologies, San Diego, Calif.

Lipscomb, M.S., and J.W Hedge, eds.
   1988   *Job Performance Measurement: Topics in the Performance Measurement of Air Force Enlisted Personnel.* Technical paper. AFHRL-TP-87-58. Brooks Air Force Base, Tex.: Training Systems Division, Air Force Human Resources Laboratory.

Moran, G.V., and R.D. Ballentine
   1986   Effects of job experience on performance scores. In J.W. Hedge, chair, Issues in Job Performance Measurement Research. Symposium conducted at the annual meeting of the American Psychological Association, Washington, D.C.

Pellum, M.W., and M.S. Teachout
   1988   Evaluating the Effectiveness of the "4-Level" Training Program. Paper presented at the annual conference on Air Force Technology in Training and Education, Biloxi, Miss.
   1988   A longitudinal evaluation of training effectiveness using multiple levels of information. In M. Teachout, chair, Understanding and Evaluating Train-

ing Effectiveness: Multiple Perspectives. Symposium conducted at the fifth annual conference of the Society of Industrial and Organizational Psychology, Miami, Fla.

1988 The Air Force Job Performance Measurement Project. In D.A. Harris, chair, The Joint-Service Job Performance Measurement Project. Symposium conducted at the annual conference on Air Force Technology in Training and Education, Biloxi, Miss.

1988 Evaluating training effectiveness: challenges and application. In H. Ruck, chair, Training Evaluation R & D in the Air Force. Symposium conducted at the third annual conference of the Society of Industrial and Organizational Psychology, Miami, Fla.

Taylor, C.J., J.L. Blackhurst, and R.D. Ballentine

1985 Walk-through performance test development: lessons learned. Pp. 306-310 in Proceedings of the 27th Annual Conference of the Military Testing Association, San Diego, Calif.

Teachout, M.S.

1986 Developing a composite measure of job performance: problems and solutions. In J.W. Hedge, chair, Issues in Job Performance Measurement Research. Symposium conducted at the annual meeting of the American Psychological Association, Washington, D.C.

1990 Understanding and evaluating training effectiveness: multiple perspectives. In M.S. Teachout, Chair, symposium conducted at the fifth annual conference of the Society of Industrial and Organizational Psychology, Miami, Fla.

1990 Determinants of Performance Rating Accuracy: A Field Study. Unpublished PhD Dissertation, Old Dominion University, Norfolk, Va.

1991 Understanding the work experience construct in personnel research and practice. In M.S. Teachout, chair, symposium conducted at the sixth annual conference of the Society of Industrial and Organizational Psychology, St. Louis, Mo.

1991 Investigating the construct validity of a job performance measurement system. In M.S. Teachout, chair, symposium conducted at the sixth annual conference of the Society of Industrial and Organizational Psychology, St. Louis, Mo.

Vance, R.J., M.D. Coovert, R.C. MacCallum, and J.W. Hedge

1988 Construct validity of multiple job performance measures using confirmatory factor analysis. *Journal of Applied Psychology* 73: 74-80.

1989 Construct models of task performance. *Journal of Applied Psychology* 74:447-455.

ARMY

Arabian, J., and J. Mason
   1986 Relationship of SQT Scores to Project A Measures. Paper presented at the annual conference of the Military Testing Association, Mystic, Conn.

Borman, W., S. Motowidlo, S. Rose, and L. Hanser
   1987 *Development of a Model of Soldier Effectiveness.* Technical Report 741. Alexandria, Va.: U.S. Army Research Institute for the Behavioral and Social Sciences.

Borman, W., L. White, and I. Gast
   1984 Factors Relating to Peer and Supervisor Ratings of Job Performance. Paper presented at the annual meeting of the American Psychological Association, Toronto, Canada.

Brandt, D., D. McLaughlin, L. Wise, and P. Rossmeissl
   1984 Adjustment for the Effects of Range Restriction on Composite Validity. Paper presented at the annual convention of the American Psychological Association, Toronto, Canada.
   1984 Complex Cross-Validation of the Validity of a Predictor Battery. Paper presented at the annual convention of the American Psychological Association, Toronto, Canada.

Campbell, C., R. Campbell, M. Rumsey, and D. Edwards
   1986 *Development and Field Test of Task-Based MOS-Specific Criterion Measures.* Technical Report 717. Alexandria, Va.: U.S. Army Research Institute for the Behavioral and Social Sciences.

Campbell, C., P. Ford, M. Rumsey, E. Pulakos, W. Borman, D. Felker, M. De Vera, and B. Riegelhaupt
   1987 Development of Project A Performance Measures. Paper presented at the conference of the Society of Industrial and Organizational Psychology, Atlanta, Ga.

Campbell, J.P., ed.
   1987 *Improving the Selection, Classification, and Utilization of Army Enlisted Personnel: Annual Report, 1985 Fiscal Year.* Technical Report 746. Alexandria, Va.: U.S. Army Research Institute for the Behavioral and Social Sciences.
   1988 *Improving the Selection, Classification, and Utilization of Army Enlisted Personnel: Annual Report, 1986 Fiscal Year.* Technical Report 813101. Alexandria, Va.: U.S. Army Research Institute for the Behavioral and Social Sciences.

Campbell, J., J. McHenry, and L. Wise
   1987 Analysis of Criterion Measures: The Modeling of Performance. Paper presented at the conference of the Society of Industrial and Organizational Psychology, Atlanta, Ga.

Eaton, N.
   1984 The U.S. Army Research Project to Improve Selection and Classification Decisions. Paper presented at the National Security Industrial Association Conference on Personnel and Training Factors in Systems Effectiveness, Springfield, Va.

Eaton, N., and M. Goer, eds.
　1983　*Improving the Selection, Classification, and Utilization of Army Enlisted Personnel: Technical Appendix to the Annual Report.* Research Note 83-87. Alexandria, Va.: U.S. Army Research Institute for the Behavioral and Social Sciences.

Eaton, N., M. Goer, J. Harris, and L. Zook, eds.
　1985　*Improving the Selection, Classification, and Utilization of Army Enlisted Personnel: Annual Report, 1984 Fiscal Year.* Technical Report 660. Alexandria, Va.: U.S. Army Research Institute for the Behavioral and Social Sciences.

Eaton, N., M. Weltin, and H. Wing
　1982　*Validity of the Military Applicant Profile for Predicting Early Attrition in Different Educational, Age, and Racial Groups.* Technical Report 567. Alexandria, Va: U.S. Army Research Institute for the Behavioral and Social Sciences.

Eaton, N., H. Wing, and K. Mitchell
　1983　Putting the "Dollars" Into Utility Analysis. Paper presented at the annual convention of the American Psychological Association, Anaheim, Calif.
　1984　Alternate methods of estimating the dollar value of performance. *Personnel Psychology* 38:27-40

Friedman, D., A. Streicher, H. Wing, and F. Grafton
　1982　Assessment of Practice Effects: Test-Retest Scores for FY 81 Active Army Applicants on ASVAB 8/9/10. Paper presented at the annual conference of the Military Testing Association, San Antonio, Tex.

Grafton, F., K. Mitchell, and H. Wing
　1983　*Final Status Report on the Comparability of ASVAB 6/7 and 8/9/10 Aptitude Area Score Scales.* Selection and Classification Technical Area Working Paper 82-7. Alexandria, Va.: U.S. Army Research Institute for the Behavioral and Social Sciences.

Hanser, L., and F. Grafton
　1983　Dusting Off Old Data: Encounters With Archival Records. Paper presented at the annual convention of the American Psychological Association, Anaheim, Calif.

Hanser, L., and K. Mitchell
　1983　Factorial Invariance of the Armed Services Vocational Aptitude Battery. Paper presented at the annual conference of the Military Testing Association, Gulf Shores, Ala.

Hough, L., and S. Ashworth
　1987　Predicting Soldier Performance: Assessment of Temperament Constructs as Predictors of Job Performance. Paper presented at the conference for Industrial and Organizational Psychology. Atlanta, Ga.

Hough, L., M. Dunnette, H. Wing, J. Houston, and N. Peterson
　1984　Covariance Analyses of Cognitive and Noncognitive Measures of Army Recruits: An Initial Sample of Preliminary Battery Data. Paper presented at the annual convention of the American Psychological Association, Toronto, Canada.

Human Resources Research Organization, American Institutes for Research, Personnel Decisions Research Institute, and Army Research Institute
  1983 *Improving the Selection, Classification, and Utilization of Army Enlisted Personnel: Annual Report.* Research Report 1347. Alexandria, Va.: U.S. Army Research Institute for the Behavioral and Social Sciences.
  1983 *Improving the Selection, Classification, and Utilization of Army Enlisted Personnel: Project A Research Plan.* Research Report 1332. Alexandria, Va.: U.S. Army Research Institute for the Behavioral and Social Sciences.
  1984 *Improving the Selection, Classification, and Utilization of Army Enlisted Personnel: Appendixes to the Annual Report, 1984 Fiscal Year.* Research Report 85-14. Alexandria, Va.: U.S. Army Research Institute for the Behavioral and Social Sciences.
  1985 *Improving the Selection, Classification, and Utilization of Army Enlisted Personnel: Annual Report Synopsis, 1984 Fiscal Year.* Research Report 1393. Alexandria, Va: U.S. Army Research Institute for the Behavioral and Social Sciences.
McHenry, J., H. Hough, J. Toquam, M. Hanson, and S. Ashworth,
  1987 Project A Validity Results: The Relationship Between Predictor and Criterion Domains. Paper presented at the Conference of the Society of Industrial and Organizational Psychology, Atlanta, Ga.
McLaughlin, D., P. Rossmeissl, L. Wise, D. Brandt, and M. Wang
  1984 *Validation of Current and Alternative ASVAB Area Composites, Based on Training and SQT Information on FY 1981 and FY 1982 Enlisted Accessions.* Technical Report 651. Alexandria, Va.: U.S. Army Research Institute for the Behavioral and Social Sciences.
Mitchell, K.
  1984 *Verbal Information Processing Paradigm: A Review of Theory and Methods.* Technical Report 648. Alexandria, Va.: U.S. Army Research Institute for the Behavioral and Social Sciences.
Osborn, W.
  1983 Issues and Strategies in Measuring Performance in Army Jobs. Paper presented at the annual convention of the American Psychological Association, Anaheim, Calif.
Oxford-Carpenter, R., and L. Schultz
  1983 *Reading Assessment in the Army.* Selection and Classification Technical Area Working Paper 83-5. Alexandria, Va.: U.S. Army Research Institute for the Behavioral and Social Sciences.
Peterson, N.
  1987 *Development and Field Test of the Trial Battery for Project A.* Technical Report 739. Alexandria, Va.: U.S. Army Research Institute for the Behavioral and Social Sciences.
Peterson, N., L. Hough, M. Dunnette, R. Rosse, J. Houston, J. Toquam, and H. Wing
  1987 Identification of Predictor Constructs and Development of New Selection/Classification Tests. Paper presented at the conference of the Society of Industrial and Organizational Psychology, Atlanta, Ga.
Shields, J., and L. Hanser
  1987 Designing, Planning, and Selling Project A. Paper presented at the confer-

ence of the Society of Industrial and Organizational Psychology, Atlanta, Ga.

Weltin, M., and B. Popelka,
- 1983 *Evaluation of the ASVAB 8/9/10 Clerical Composite for Predicting Training School Performance.* Technical Report 594. Alexandria, Va: U.S. Army Research Institute for the Behavioral and Social Sciences.

Wetrogan, L., D. Olson, and H. Sperling
- 1983 Job Performance and Assessment: A Systematic Model. Paper presented at the annual convention of the American Psychological Association, Anaheim, Calif.

Wise, L., M. Wang, and P. Rossmeissl
- 1983 *Longitudinal Research Database Plan.* Research Report 1346. Alexandria, Va.: U.S. Army Research Institute for the Behavioral and Social Sciences.

Wise, L., N. Peterson, R. Hoffman, J. Campbell, and J. Arabian, eds.
- 1991a *Army Synthetic Validity Project: Report of Phase III Results.* Volume I. Technical Report 922. Alexandria, Va.: U.S. Army Research Institute for the Behavioral and Social Sciences.
- 1991b *Army Synthetic Validity Project: Report of Phase III Results.* Volume II: Research Instruments. Research Product 91-08. Alexandria, Va.: U.S. Army Research Institute for the Behavioral and Social Sciences.

Young, W., K. Austin, J. McHenry, L. Wise, and F. Grafton
- 1989 *Sample Concurrent Validation Codebook.* Selection and Classification Draft Working Paper RS-WP-89-2. Alexandria, Va.: U.S. Army Research Institute for the Behavioral and Social Sciences.

Young, W., J. Harris, R. Hoffman, J. Houston, and L. Wise
- 1987 Large Scale Data Collection and Database Preparation. Paper presented at the conference of the Society of Industrial and Organizational Psychology, Atlanta, Ga.

MARINE CORPS

Bowes, M.
　1991 *Average Costs of Training for First-Term Marines.* Research Memorandum 90-238. Alexandria, Va.: Center for Naval Analysis.

Carey, N.B.
　1990a *An Assessment of Surrogates for Hands-On Tests: Selection Standards and Training Needs.* Research Memorandum 90-47. Alexandria, Va.: Center for Naval Analysis.
　1990b *Methods to Assess the Utility of Proxies.* Research Memorandum 90-311. Alexandria, Va.: Center for Naval Analysis.

Cooke, T.W., and J.M. Jondrow
　1990 *Costs of Improving Recruit Aptitudes: A Joint Product Approach.* Research Memorandum 89-193. Alexandria, Va: Center for Naval Analysis.

Divgi, D.R., and P.W. Mayberry
　1990 *The Role of Aptitude Factors in Predicting Hands-On Job Performance.* Research Memorandum 89-215. Alexandria, Va.: Center for Naval Analysis.

Maier, M.H., and C.M. Hiatt
　1984 *An Evaluation of Using Job Performance Tests to Validate ASVAB Qualification Standards.* Alexandria, Va.: Center for Naval Analyses.
　1985 *On the Content and Measurement Validity of Hands-On Performance Tests.* Research Memorandum 85-79. Alexandria, Va.: Center for Naval Analyses.

Maier, M.H., and P.W. Mayberry
　1989 *Evaluating Minimum Aptitude Standards.* Research Memorandum 89-9. Alexandria, Va.: Center for Naval Analyses.

May, L.J.
　1987 *Alternative Modeling Approaches for Setting Cost-Effective Qualification Standards.* Research Memorandum 87-54. Alexandria, Va.: Center for Naval Analyses.

May, L.J., and P.W. Mayberry
　1986 *The Rand Cost-Performance Model for Setting Qualification Standards: Preliminary Comments.* Research Memorandum 86-200. Alexandria, Va.: Center for Naval Analyses.

Mayberry, P.W.
　1986 *Confirming Differences in Relative-Value Proficiency Marks.* Research Memorandum 86-187. Alexandria, Va.: Center for Naval Analyses.
　1986 *Examining the Validity of Hands-On Tests as Measures of Job Performance.* Research Contribution 540. Alexandria, Va.: Center for Naval Analyses.
　1986 *From Hands-On Measurement to Job Performance: The Issue of Generalizability.* Research Memorandum 86-214. Alexandria, Va.: Center for Naval Analysis.
　1987 *Developing a Competency Scale for Hands-On Measures of Job Proficiency.* Research Contribution 570. Alexandria, Va.: Center for Naval Analyses.
　1988 *Interim Results for the Marine Corps Job Performance Measurement Project.* Research Memorandum 88-37. Alexandria, Va.: Center for Naval Analyses.

1989a *Analysis of Data Quality for the Infantry Phase of the Marine Corps Job Performance Measurement Project.* Research Memorandum 88-259. Alexandria, Va.: Center for Naval Analyses.
1989b *Performance of Basic Infantry Tasks.* Research Memorandum 89-45. Alexandria, Va.: Center for Naval Analyses.
1990 *Validation of ASVAB Against Infantry Job Performance.* Research Memorandum 90-182. Alexandria, Va.: Center for Naval Analysis.

Mayberry, P.W., and Hiatt, C.M.
1990 *Incremental Validity of New Tests in Prediction of Infantry Performance.* Research Memorandum 90-110. Alexandria, Va.: Center for Naval Analysis.

NAVY

Baker, H., and P. Alba
  1987 Measuring the proficiency of Marine Corps J-79 jet engine mechanics. In H.G. Baker and G.J. Laabs, eds., *Proceedings of the Department of Defense/Educational Testing Service Conference on Job Performance Measurement Technologies.* Washington, D.C.: Office of the Assistant Secretary of Defense (Force Management and Personnel).
  1988 *Job Performance Measurement Package for the J-79 Engine Mechanic.* NPRDC TN 88-49. San Diego, Calif.: Navy Personnel Research and Development Center.

Baker, H.G., and G.J. Laabs
  1985 Selecting Critical Tasks for a Radioman Hands-On Performance Test. Paper presented at the conference of the Military Testing Association, San Diego, Calif.
  1987 *Proceedings of the Department of Defense/Educational Testing Service Conference on Job Performance Measurement Technologies.* Washington, D.C.: Office of the Assistant Secretary of Defense (Force Management and Personnel).

Baker, H., J. Blackhurst, and P. Alba
  1987 *Interservice Technology Transfer of J-79 Jet Engine Mechanic Performance Measures.* NPRDC TR 87-22. San Diego: Navy Personnel Research and Development Center.

Baker, H., P. Ford, J. Doyle, S. Schulze, S. Lammlein, and C. Owens-Kurtz
  1988 *Development of Performance Measures for the Navy Radioman.* NPRDC TN 88-52. San Diego, Calif.: Navy Personnel Research and Development Center.
  in press *Pilot Test of Job Performance Measures for Navy Radiomen.* San Diego, Calif.: Navy Personnel Research and Development Center.

Beardon, R.
  1981 *Relationship Between the Armed Services Vocational Aptitude Battery and Aviation Warfare Operator Performance: A Pilot Study.* NPRDC SR 81-14. San Diego, Calif.: Navy Personnel Research and Development Center.

Beardon, R., M. Wagner, and R. Simon
  1988 *Developing Behaviorally Anchored Rating Scales for the Machinist's Mate Rating.* NPRDC TN 88-38. San Diego, Calif.: Navy Personnel Research and Development Center.

Bruce, D., and M. Dittmar
  in press *Developing Performance Measures for the Navy Gas Turbineman (GSM) Rating: Item Development, Pretest, and Pilot Test.* San Diego, Calif.: Navy Personnel Research and Development Center.

Chesler, D., C. Bilinski, and M. Hamovitch
  1982 *Marine Corps Job Performance Tests for Three Enlisted Specialties.* NPRDC TN 82-20. San Diego, Calif.: Navy Personnel Research and Development Center.

Dittmar, M., and R. Magnus
  1989 *Hands-On Test for the Navy Gas Turbineman (GSM) Rating*. Contractor Report. San Antonio, Tex.: Maxima Corp.
Drasgow, F., A. Martinsek, D. Gardner, M. Muyot, and L. Kroeker
  in press Task selection models for job performance measurement. *Journal of Applied Psychology*.
Ford, P., J. Doyle, S. Schultz, and R. Hoffman
  1987 *Development and Field Test of Hands-On and Knowledge Tests for Navy Radiomen*. Contractor Report. Alexandria, Va.: Human Resources Research Organization.
Grizzle, H., II
  1987 *Needs Assessment for the Prototype Job Performance Measurement Data Base*. Contractor Report. Alexandria, Va.: Federal Computer Performance Evaluation and Simulation Center.
  1988 *General Functional Requirements for a Job Performance Measurement Data Base*. Contractor Report. Alexandria, Va.: Federal Systems Integration and Management Center.
Grizzle, H., II, and J. Keeneth
  1986 *Life-Cycle Automation Management Plan for the Job Performance Measurement Data Base*. Contractor Report. Alexandria, Va.: Federal Computer Performance Evaluation and Simulation Center.
  Needs Assessment Strategy for the Prototype Job Performance Measurement Data Base. Contractor Report. Alexandria, Va.: Federal Computer Performance Evaluation and Simulation Center.
Grizzle, H., II, J. Keeneth, H. Baker, and G. Laabs
  1988 *The Navy Job Performance Measurement Program (JPM): Life-Cycle Automation Management Plan for a JPM Data Base*. NPRDC TN 88-33. San Diego, Calif.: Navy Personnel Research and Development Center.
Hakel, M., E. Weil, and L. Hakel
  1988 *The Assessment of Social Work Behaviors and 25 Navy Occupational Ratings*. NPRDC TN 88-57. San Diego, Calif.: Navy Personnel Research and Development Center.
Hiatt, C., and W. Simms
  1981 *Relating Enlistment Standards to Job Performance: A Pilot Study of Two Ratings*. CNA Report 81-0048. Alexandria, Va.: Center for Naval Analysis.
Hunt, E., R. Frick, B. Laden, and G. Larson
  1988 *Augmentation of the Armed Services Vocational Aptitude Battery*. NPRDC Special Report. San Diego, Calif: Navy Personnel Research and Development Center.
Kidder, P.
  1987 Training simulators as a source of job performance information. Pp. 193-200 in H.G. Baker and G.J. Laabs, eds, *Proceedings of the Department of Defense/Educational Testing Service Conference on Job Performance Measurement Technologies*. Washington, D.C.: Office of the Assistant Secretary of Defense (Force Management and Personnel).

Kidder, P, and G. Laabs
　1988　An Application of Videodisc Technology for Job Performance Measurement. Paper presented at the meeting of the Society for Applied Learning Technology, Washington, D.C.

Kidder P., R. Nerison, and G. Laabs
　1987　*Navy Job Performance Measurement Program: An Examination of Data Bases, Programs, and Training Simulators as Sources of Job Performance Information.* NPRDC TN 87-28. San Diego, Calif.: Navy Personnel Research and Development Center.

Kieras, D.
　1989　*A Cognitive Analysis of the Relations Between a Set of Hands-On Job Performance Test Tasks.* NPRDC Contractor Report. Ann Arbor, Mich.: University of Michigan.

Kroeker, L.
　1986　The Navy's Job Classification and Assignment System. Paper presented at the ORSA/TIMS annual meeting, Los Angeles, Calif.
　1987　*Evaluation of a Personnel Record Data Base as a Source of Job Performance Information.* NPRDC MPPLR. San Diego, Calif.: Navy Personnel Research and Development Center.
　1988a　Broadening the Navy's Classification Decision Base. Paper presented at the ORSA/TIMS Annual Meeting, Washington, DC.
　1988b　Job Performance Measurement: Lessons Learned from the Machinist's Mates Analyses. Paper presented at the Conference on Training in Technology and Education Conference, Biloxi, Miss.
　1988c　Job Performance Measurement: Lessons Learned From the Machinist's Mates Analyses. Paper presented at the Conference on Training in Technology and Education, Biloxi, Miss.
　1988d　Reliability and Validity of Performance Measurement Data. Paper presented at the ORSA/TIMS annual meeting, Washington, D.C.
　1989a　Creating a random sampling design for job performance measurement. In J.P. Pass, chair, Task Selection for Performance Assessment. Symposium presented at the annual meeting of the American Psychological Association, New Orleans, La.
　1989b　Personnel classification/assignment models. Pp. 41-73 in M.F. Wiskoff and G. Rampton, eds., *Military Personnel Measurement: Testing, Assignment, Evaluation.* New York: Praeger.

Kroeker, L., and R. Beardon
　1987　Predicting proficiency measures for machinist's mates. Pp. 193-200 in H.G. Baker and G.J. Laabs, eds, *Proceedings of the Department of Defense/Educational Testing Service Conference on Job Performance Measurement Technologies.* Washington, D.C.: Office of the Assistant Secretary of Defense (Force Management and Personnel).
　in press　*Analyses of Job Performance Data for Machinist's Mates.* San Diego, Calif.: Navy Personnel Research and Development Center.

Kroeker, L., and G. Laabs
　1986　The Navy's Contribution to Job Performance Measures and Standards. Paper

presented at the sixth annual conference on Personnel and Training Factors in Systems Eeffectiveness, National Security Industrial Association, San Diego, Calif.

1990 Relationships Among Actual and Surrogate Measures of Job Proficiency. Paper presented at the meeting of the American Psychological Association, Boston.

Kroeker, L., G. Laabs, and R. Beardon

1985 Developing and evaluating a hands-on performance test. In G. Laabs, chair, Issues in Performance Testing. Symposium presented at the conference of the Military Testing Association, San Diego, Calif.

Kroeker, L, G. Laabs, R. Vineberg, J. Joyner, and R. Zimmerman

in press *Development of a Hands-On Performance Measure for the Machinist Mate's Rating.* San Diego, Calif.: Navy Personnel Research and Development Center.

Laabs, G.

1983 Performance testing in support of Navy personnel classification and assignment. In C. Curran, chair, Development of Military Job Performance Measures. Symposium presented at the meeting of the American Psychological Association, San Diego, Calif.

1985 Issues in Performance Testing (Chair). Symposium presented at the Conference of the Military Testing Association, San Diego, Calif.

1986a Applied performance testing and transfer of training. In V.E. Holt, ed., *Issues in Psychological Research and Application in Transfer of Training.* ARI TCN 86-647. Alexandria, Va.: U.S. Army Research Institute for the Behavioral and Social Sciences.

1986b Setting Standards in Performance Measurement (Chair). Symposium presented at the meeting of the American Psychological Association, Washington, D.C.

1986c Measuring job performance. In R. Dillon, Chair, Advances in Testing and Training: Improving Prediction and Attainment of Success in Technical Programs. Symposium presented at the meeting of the American Educational Research Association, San Francisco, Calif.

1986d A Navy performance testing program to measure technical proficiency. In E. E. Diamond, chair, Measuring Up: The Role of Military Testing. Symposium presented at the meeting of the American Educational Research Association, San Francisco, Calif.

1987a Applications of Generalizability Theory to Military Performance Measurement (Chair). Symposium presented at the meeting of the American Educational Research Association, Washington, D.C.

1987b Comparing Different Procedures for Task Selection. Paper presented at the Department of Defense/Educational Testing Service Conference on Job Performance Measurement Technologies, San Diego, Calif.

1987c Panel member in R.D. Ballentine, chair, Issues in the Implementation of a Job Performance Measurement Program. In H.G. Baker and G.J. Laabs, eds, *Proceedings of the Department of Defense/Educational Testing Service Conference on Job Performance Measurement Technologies.* Washington, D.C.: Office of the Assistant Secretary of Defense (Force Management and Personnel).

Laabs, G., and H. Baker
1989 Selection of critical tasks for Navy job performance measures. *Journal of Applied Psychology* 1(1):3-16.

Laabs, G., and V. Berry
1987 *The Navy Job Performance Measurement Program: Background and Inception.* NPRDC TR 87-34. San Diego, Calif.: Navy Personnel Research and Development Center.

Laabs, G., H. Baker, L. Kroeker, and P. Kidder
1986 Navy job performance measurement program. In D.A. Harris, chair, Joint-Service Job Performance Measurement. Panel session presented at the Tenth Symposium on Psychology in the Department of Defense, Colorado Springs, Colo.

Laabs, G., V. Berry, R. Vineberg, and R. Zimmerman
1987 Comparing different procedures of task selection. Pp. 79-93 in H.G. Baker and G.J. Laabs, eds, *Proceedings of the Department of Defense/Educational Testing Service Conference on Job Performance Measurement Technologies.* Washington, D.C.: Office of the Assistant Secretary of Defense (Force Management and Personnel).

Lammlein, S., and H. Baker
1987 *Developing Performance Measures for the Navy Radioman (RM): Selecting Critical Tasks.* NPRDC TN 87-13. San Diego, Calif.: Navy Personnel Research and Development Center.

Lammlein, S., N. Peterson, and R. Rosse
1988 *Test of a Probabilistic Sampling Critical Task Selection Model for Performance Testing.* NPRDC TN 88-13. San Diego, Calif.: Navy Personnel Research and Development Center.

Mackie, R., R. Ridihalgh, M. Seltzer, and T. Shultz
1981 *Relationship Between the Armed Services Vocational Aptitude Battery and Surface Sonar Technician Performance.* NPRDC TR 81-19. San Diego, Calif.: Navy Personnel Research and Development Center.

Morris, C., B. Best, and W. McDaniel
1985 *Simulator/Device Based Performance Measurement.* NTSC SR 85-002. Orlando, Fla.: Navy Training Systems Center, Training Analysis and Evaluation Group.

Motowidlo, S.
1988 *Alternatives to Hands-On Performance Tests: Research Plan, Conceptual Framework, Theoretical Background, and Decision Criteria.* Contractor Report. Minneapolis, Minn.: Personnel Decisions Research Institute.

Murphy, K.
1988 *A Developmental Theory of Job Performance: Applications in Two Navy Ratings.* NPRDC TN 88-36. San Diego, Calif.: Navy Personnel Research and Development Center.
Predictor-Based Taxonomy of Navy Ratings: A Preliminary Study. NPRDC TN 88-35. San Diego, Calif.: Navy Personnel Research and Development Center.

Murphy, K., and L. Kroeker
- 1988 *Dimensions of Job Performance.* NPRDC TN 88-39. San Diego, Calif.: Navy Personnel Research and Development Center.

Nugent, W.
- 1982 *Ranking the Density and Criticality of Enlisted Navy Ratings.* NPRDC TN 82-27. San Diego, Calif.: Navy Personnel Research and Development Center.

Pass, J.
- 1989 Task Selection for Performance Assessment (Chair). Symposium presented at the meeting of the American Psychological Association, New Orleans.

Pickering, E., and R. Beardon
- 1984 *Job Performance Testing Research at the Navy Personnel Research and Development Center.* NPRDC TR 84-36. San Diego, Calif.: Navy Personnel Research and Development Center.

Robertson, D.
- in press *Source Data for Job Clustering with the Navy Enlisted Occupational Classification System.* San Diego, Calif.: Navy Personnel Research and Development Center.

Schemmer, F., R. Beardon, and D. Gebhardt
- 1989 Development of job samples for the Navy electrician's mate rating. In J.P. Pass, chair, Task Selection for Performance Assessment. Symposium presented at the meeting of the American Psychological Association, New Orleans.

Schoenfeldt, L.
- 1988 *Occupational Clustering: A Review and Synthesis.* NPRDC TN 88-14. San Diego, Calif.: Navy Personnel Research and Development Center.

Van Hamel, S., R. Hinde, W. Tilton, H. Baker, and V. Berry
- in press *Development of Hands-On Tests for the Navy Fire Controlman.* San Diego, Calif.: Navy Personnel Research and Development Center.

Vineberg, R., and J. Joyner
- 1982 *Prediction of Job Performance: Review of Military Studies.* NPRDC TR 82-37. San Diego, Calif.: Navy Personnel Research and Development Center.
- 1985 *Development of an Abstracted Knowledge Simulation of a Hands-On Test for Machinist's Mates.* Contractor Report. Alexandria, Va.: Human Resources Research Organization.

Vineberg, R., and R. Zimmerman
- 1984 *Selection of Job Tasks as Criteria for Performance Measurement.* Contractor Report. Alexandria, Va.: Human Resources Research Organization.

Vineberg, R., J. Joyner, and R. Zimmerman
- 1985 *Development of a Hands-On Job-Sample Test and Score-Training Materials for Apprentices in the Machinist's Mate Rating.* Contractor Report. Alexandria, Va.: Human Resources Research Organization.

Webb, N., and L. Kroeker
- 1987 A generalizability study of job performance measurements in the Navy. In G. Laabs, chair, Applications of Generalizability Theory to Military Per-

formance Measurement. Symposium presented at the meeting of the American Educational Research Association, Washington, D.C.

Webb, N., and R. Shavelson
 1987 Generalizability theory and job performance measurement. In H.G. Baker and G.J. Laabs, eds., *Proceedings of the Department of Defense/Educational Testing Service Conference on Job Performance Measurement Technologies*. Washington, D.C.: Office of the Assistant Secretary of Defense (Force Management and Personnel).

Appendix B

Biographical Sketches

BERT F. GREEN, JR. (Chair), is professor of psychology at Johns Hopkins University. He received a Ph.D. in psychology from Princeton University in 1951 and spent the next 10 years as a staff member of the Lincoln Laboratory at the Massachusetts Institute of Technology, working on human factors problems. Before joining the faculty at Johns Hopkins in 1969, Green was head of the psychology department at Carnegie Mellon University. He is past president of the Psychometric Society (1965-1966) and from 1971 to 1978 served as editor of its journal, *Psychometrika*. He has also been active in the American Psychological Association, serving as president of the Division of Evaluation and Measurement and as chair of the Committee on Psychological Tests and Assessments. From 1984-1987 he served on the Department of Defense's National Advisory Panel on Military Testing.

JERALD G. BACHMAN is program director at the Survey Research Center of the Institute for Social Research at the University of Michigan. He also serves on the advisory boards of the University of Kansas Achievement Placement Project and of the Evaluation and Training Institute. Bachman has been a member of the Executive Council of the Inter-University Seminar on Armed Forces and Society and has been principal investigator for two nationwide, longitudinal surveys of American youth. He received M.A. and Ph.D. degrees from the University of Pennsylvania.

V. JON BENTZ retired in 1985 from Sears, Roebuck and Company after 35 years as director of Psychological Research and Services. He was also a member of the Evaluation Committee of the National Manpower Commission and served on the Board of Directors of the National Assessment of Education Progress. He has been a senior fellow with the Center for Creative Leadership and serves on the advisory boards of two research foundations. Bentz received B.A. and M.A. degrees from Ohio State University.

LLOYD BOND is professor at the School of Education, University of North Carolina, Greensboro. He was a personnel specialist and labor arbitrator for the General Motors Corporation and was on the staff of the Learning Research and Development Center at the University of Pittsburgh. He has served as a consultant to the National Urban League and was a member of the Department of Defense's National Advisory Panel on Military Testing, the American Psychological Association's committee to develop revised technical standards for educational and psychological testing, and several advisory committees of the Educational Testing Service. Bond received both M.S. and Ph.D. degrees in psychology from Johns Hopkins University.

RICHARD V.L. COOPER is an economist with Ernst & Young in Chicago. Previously he was partner in charge of the Economics Studies Group for Coopers & Lybrand, and he has worked with the Department of Defense as director on a manpower policies project. He was also director of the Defense Manpower Research Program at the Rand Corporation from 1972 to 1979. He received an M.A. in economics from the University of California at Los Angeles and a Ph.D. from the University of Chicago.

RICHARD DANZIG is partner in the law firm of Latham & Watkins, Washington, D.C., and visiting professor of law at Georgetown Law School. He has served as principal deputy assistant secretary of defense (manpower, reserve affairs, and logistics) and has been on the faculty at both Harvard and Stanford Schools of Law. Danzig received a J.D. from the Yale Law School and a Ph.D. from Oxford University.

FRANK J. LANDY is professor of psychology at the Pennsylvania State University. He received M.A. and Ph.D. degrees from Bowling Green University. Landy has conducted research in Sweden and has been a NATO senior lecturer in human factors. He has served as associate editor of the *Journal of Applied Psychology* and international editor of the *Journal of Occupational Psychology*. His research interests include the psychology of work behavior and the measurement of work performance.

ROBERT L. LINN is professor of education at the University of Colorado, Boulder. His research is directed at applied and theoretical problems in educational and psychological measurement. He is a former president of the Division of Evaluation, Measurement, and Statistics of the American Psychological Association, former president of the National Council on Measurement in Education, and former vice president of the American Educational Research Association for the Division of Measurement and Research Methodology. He has served as editor of the *Journal of Educational Measurement* and was vice chair of the committee that developed the 1985 standards for educational and psychological testing. He received an M.A. degree in psychology and a Ph.D. degree in psychological measurement from the University of Illinois, Urbana-Champaign.

JOHN W. ROBERTS, USAF (ret.) received a B.S. degree from Mankato State Teachers College and an M.S. degree from the George Washington University. He is also a graduate of the Air Command and Staff College and the National War College. As well as serving as a command pilot, General Roberts served in the Office of the Deputy Chief of Staff, Personnel, as deputy director of personnel planning and as director, personnel plans. In 1973 he became deputy chief of staff, personnel, and in 1975 the commander of Air Training Command at Randolph Air Force Base, Texas.

DONALD B. RUBIN is professor and chair of the Department of Statistics at Harvard University. From 1971 to 1984 he worked at the Educational Testing Service. During that time he was also visiting lecturer in the departments of statistics and applied statistics at Harvard University, Princeton University, and the University of California at Berkeley. He has also been on the faculties of the University of Minnesota and the University of Chicago. Rubin has been a member of the board of directors of the American Statistical Association, as well as coordinating editor and applications editor of *The Journal of the American Statistical Association*. He received an M.A. in computer science and a Ph.D. in statistics from Harvard University.

MADY WECHSLER SEGAL is associate professor of sociology at the University of Maryland and faculty affiliate of the Women's Studies Program and the Center for International Security Studies at Maryland. She has been a guest scientist at the Walter Reed Army Institute of Research, a visiting professor at the United States Military Academy, West Point, and has served as chair of the Scientific Advisory Committee for the U.S. Army Research Institute's Army Family Research Program. Her research focuses on military women and military families. She received a Ph.D. from the University of Chicago.

RICHARD J. SHAVELSON is dean of the Graduate School of Education and professor of research methods in the Department of Education at the University of California at Santa Barbara. He is also past president of the

American Educational Research Association. He conducts research in the areas of social science measurement methods, psychometrics, and related policy issues. His most recent measurement research involves the development of performance assessments in mathematics and science education and their evaluation along psychometric, cost, and social impact lines. He has a Ph.D. in educational psychology from Stanford University.

HAROLD P. VAN COTT is principal staff officer and study director for the Committee on Human Factors of the National Research Council. He has a Ph.D. in experimental psychology from the University of North Carolina. Previously, he has been vice president of the Essex Corporation; division director at the National Bureau of Standards; and chief scientist at BioTechnology, Inc.

ALEXANDRA K. WIGDOR, study director of the Committee on the Performance of Military Personnel, is director of the Division on Education, Training, and Employment in the social sciences commission of the National Research Council. Her previous work as an NRC staff officer has included a study evaluating performance appraisal and merit pay for the federal pay system (1991), a study of the General Aptitude Test Battery (1989), and a 1982 study on ability testing. Trained as a historian, her research interests now include human performance assessment, the legal and social dimensions of psychological testing, and the development of government policy on testing and selection.

HAROLD WOOL received an M.S.S. from the New School for Social Research and a Ph.D. from American University, both in economics. He served as director of manpower procurement, policy and research at the Department of Defense and also as director of the Office of Research under the assistant secretary of labor for policy, evaluation and research. Wool has also been program director for energy manpower research at The Conference Board. He has also conducted projects for the National Commission for Employment Policy, the National Science Foundation, and the Human Resources Research Office.

Index

A

The Abilities of Man, 17
Administrators and administration, *see* Test administration
Age Discrimination Act, 16
Air Force, 47, 61, 64, 78, 90–91, 92, 94–95
   Black Americans in, 40
   classification, personnel, 22–23, 187–188
   occupations studied, 64
American Psychological Association, 19, 29
Analysis of variance, 122, 123, 124–126, 135
Apprenticeships, 16
Armed Forces Qualification Test (AFQT), 4, 47, 48, 50, 52–53, 54, 55, 62, 208
   cost-performance assessment, 186, 188, 189, 198–199, 201–202
   criterion-related validity, 160–164, 175–180
   enlistment standards, 52–54
   fairness, 12, 179

Armed Services Vocational Aptitude Battery (ASVAB), 3–4, 5, 11–13, 31, 49–52, 56, 57, 58, 60, 68, 73, 91, 93, 142
   classical test theory, 58
   classification, general, 51–52, 148, 169–170
   composites, 51–52
   cost-performance assessment, 184, 186, 196, 198, 201, 207
   criterion-related validity, 148–149, 156–158, 162–163, 165–170, 172–174, 179, 183, 205
   fairness, 44, 50, 52, 172–174, 179
   high schools, use by, 34, 49
   job performance, 12–13, 61–62, 104, 184, 186, 196, 198, 201, 205, 208
   minorities, 44, 50, 52, 172–174
   norms, 109–110
   reliability, 121
   subtests, 50
Army, 61, 67, 84, 95, 155, 157, 166, 188, 202
   Black Americans in, 39–40
   historical perspectives, 19–22, 39

occupations studied, 63
recruitment strategies, 37
task selection, 69–71
Army Alpha, 19–20
Army Beta, 20
Army Air Force Classification Program, 22–23
Army College Fund Program, 37
Army General Classification Test, 46, 47
Army Vocational Interest Career Examination, 158
Assessment of Background and Life Experiences, 158
Aviators, 22–23, 45

B

Benchmark measures, 60–61, 126, 147
Black Americans, 12, 173–174, 175–181
  history of participation in Services, 39–43

C

Civil Rights Act, 171–172
Classical test theory, 10–11, 17–18
  ASVAB, 58
  history, 17–18, 19
  JPM, 58
  reliability, 117–118, 121–122
  see also Generalizability theory
Classification and Assignment within Pride (CLASP), 188
Classification, personnel, 1, 3
  Air Force, 22–23, 187–188
  Army, 19–22, 39
  ASVAB, 51–52, 148, 169–170
  aviators, 22–23
  computer-aided, 35, 38, 187
  historical perspectives, 19, 22–23, 29, 46
  Marine Corps, 188
  minorities, 41–44
  Navy, 188
  recruits, 35
  skill level, 41–43, 45
  validity, 11–12, 141, 152

Cognitive assessment, 68, 170
  history, 18, 19–22
  paper-and-pencil tests, 61, 67, 121, 139–140, 142, 150–151, 153, 155–156, 164–166, 175, 196
  see also Armed Forces Qualification Test, Armed Services Vocational Aptitude Battery, Job knowledge tests
Cognitive task analysis, 84, 85–88
College Board, 20–21, 126
Combat situations, 23, 69–70, 90, 98, 139, 197
  minorities, 43–44
  women, 37
Communication processes, 28
Competency testing, 4, 187, 188, 192–200
  cutoff scores, 44, 46–48, 57, 99, 184, 189–190, 196, 198, 200, 204–205
  minorities, 44
  scales, 188–192, 203, 210
  see also Mastery testing
Comprehensive Occupational Data Analysis Program (CODAP), 78, 90–91
Computers and computer science
  expert systems, 28, 86
  JPM data base, 102
  personnel classification programs, 35, 38, 187
  sampling, 134, 138
  simulations, 67, 134, 140
  task inventories, 58, 78, 90
  testing assisted by, 158, 187, 140
Congress of the U.S.
  AFQT, 53, 160, 163
  demography and policy, 36, 37
  oversight role, 33, 34, 54–56, 160, 163
Conscription, military, 3, 47, 48
Construct validity, 59–60, 73, 74–75, 143, 147, 153, 155
Content validity, 75–76, 90–91, 94, 96, 128–140, 147, 164
  definition, 5–6, 128
  work samples, 59–60
  see also Tasks and task analysis

INDEX   253

Cost factors, 6–7, 31, 60–61, 62, 208
  AFQT, 186, 188, 189, 198–199, 201–
    202
  ASVAB, 184, 186, 196, 198, 201, 207
  cost-performance models, 12–13, 46,
    55, 56, 60, 91, 184–185, 188–189,
    193–203, 209–210
  hands-on testing, 6, 208, 209
  JPM Project, 71–72, 91, 184–185,
    209
  Rand model, 194, 196–200, 201–203
  recruitment and retention, 37, 54,
    184, 193–194, 197–199
  sampling, 105, 106, 128, 132, 138,
    139
  social, 29–30
  task analysis, 86, 91, 120, 128, 132,
    138, 139
  training failures, 141
  utility difference approach, 194–196,
    199–200, 201–204
  wages and salaries, 194–195
Criterion issues, 11–12, 26, 28–30, 68,
    73, 78, 91, 102
  fairness, 29, 171–183
  historical perspectives, 22–28, 142–
    143, 189
  job knowledge tests, 150–152, 153,
    155–156, 164–166, 168–169, 175
  job performance, general, 19, 26–29,
    30, 142–145, 152–153, 169–171,
    172–173, 177, 183
  minorities, 172–178
  reliability, 158–159
  sampling, 159–160
  scores and scoring, general, 144
  selection of personnel, general, 29–
    30, 141, 152, 159
  social factors, general, 29
  training outcomes, 141–143, 155–
    156, 170
  work samples, 59–60
Criterion-related validity, 26, 59–60,
    102, 141–183, 191, 196–197, 204,
    205
  AFQT, 160–164, 175–180
  ASVAB, 148–149, 156–158, 162–
    163, 165–170, 172–174, 179, 183,
    205

  graphs and tables illustrating, 145–
    146
  hands-on testing, 147–149, 153–155,
    160–163, 168–172, 179
  JPM project, 142–143, 147–183, 179,
    183
  predictive validity and, general, 26,
    59–60, 102, 144–147, 149, 152,
    156–171, 172, 174–178, 196–197,
    204, 205
Cutoff scores, 44, 46–48, 57, 99, 184,
    189–190, 196, 198, 200, 204–
    205

D

Data bases, JPM, 102
Delphi technique, 71, 192
Demography, 32, 36–38
  historical perspectives, 15–16, 18–19,
    32, 36, 39–44
  recruits, 36–38, 198, 210
  sampling, 106, 108
  see also Gender factors; Minorities
Department of Defense, 2, 4, 13, 32–33,
    37–38, 207, 209
  Congressional oversight role, general,
    33, 34, 54–56
  minorities, 39–43
  standards, recruitment, 46–49, 58
  see also Joint-Service Job
    Performance Measurement/
    Enlistment Standards Project;
    specific Services
Department of Labor, 16, 50
Deskilling, 45
Differential validity/prediction, 169–
    171, 177, 201
Draft, *see* Conscription, military

E

Econometrics, 185
  Rand model, 194, 196–200, 201–
    203
  utility difference approach, 194–196,
    199–200, 201–204
Economic factors, 32, 198
  military budgets, 33, 34

minority participation in military, 38, 43
recruitment incentives, 37
see also Cost factors
Educational testing, general, 15, 18, 22, 34, 49
Elementary and secondary education, 15, 18
ASVAB, use by high schools, 34, 49
Enlisted Personnel Assignment System (EPAS), 188, 202
Enlistment standards
cutoff scores, 44, 46–48, 99, 184, 189–190, 196, 198, 200, 204–205
enlistment, 12–13, 32, 44, 46–49, 52–55, 58, 61–62, 104, 184–188, 197–198, 208–209
jobs, general, 109–110, 128–140, 183, 184–206, 208
jobs, minimum, 35, 44, 49, 53–55, 57, 61–62, 77–78, 104, 187, 188, 192–200
jobs, minimum entry-level, 190, 192, 197–198, 201, 204–206, 210
jobs, multiple, 188, 200–205, 209
predictive validity, 108–109
Entry-level jobs, 5, 33–36, 57, 207, 208
minimum standards, 190, 192, 197–198, 201, 204–206, 210
Equal opportunity, *see* Fairness analysis
Error of measurement, 3, 26–27
generalizability theory, 11, 122–127
item heterogeneity, 119
multiple sources, 121–127
purposive sampling, 132–133, 136
random *vs.* systematic errors, 123
range restriction, 160
rater error, 10–11, 113–115, 118, 126
sampling, 105, 106, 123, 132–133, 136
scoring, task performance, 98–99
standard deviation, 117–118, 135, 136, 175–176, 181–182, 195, 204
test administration factors, 111–114, 208
type II errors, 176–177
Experience, on job, 163–164, 196–200, 201, 202
Expert systems, 28, 86

F

Factor structure, 21
Fairness analysis, 12, 29
ASVAB, 44, 50, 52, 172–174, 179
criterion values, 171–183
job performance, general, 12, 172–173
predictive validity, 172, 174–178, 182
recruiting, 38–44
Fairness in Employment Testing, 179
Fidelity, 139–140
see also Simulations; Surrogates

G

Gender factors, 47, 172–173, 175, 181–183
computer-aided classification, 35
see also Women
General Aptitude Test Battery (GATB), 16
Generalizability theory, 10–11, 122–127, 151, 204–205
Grade-point average, 57
Group mean, 17–18
Group testing, 18, 19–20

H

Halo effect, 26, 27
Hands-on testing, 7, 11–12, 30, 60, 65–67, 68–69, 75, 101, 103, 208, 209
as benchmark, 60–61, 126, 147
content representativeness, 129–138
cost factors, 6, 208, 209
fidelity, 139–140
reliability, 11, 119–120
scoring, 98–100
standardization, 110–115, 139–140
validity, 147–149, 153–155, 160–163, 168–172, 179
walk-through performance tests, 66–67, 94–95, 140, 152–153
Hispanics, 43
Historical perspectives, 1–2, 15–30, 78
armed services organizational structure, 32–33

Black Americans participation in
Services, 39–43
classical test theory, 17–18, 19
classification, personnel, 19, 22–23,
29, 46
criterion problem, 22–28, 142–143, 189
fairness analysis, 12
intelligence testing, 18, 19–22
JPM project, 3–5, 8, 56–72
military demographics, 15–16, 18–19,
32, 36, 39–44
multiple-choice tests, 18, 19, 20, 21
psychometrics, 17–18
recruitment, general, 46–49, 53, 54,
55, 186
selection of personnel, 19, 22–23
statistical analyses, 17–18, 21, 22
work samples, 59
Human engineering design, 45
Human resource management, 184–210
Human-technology interface, *see*
Technological innovation

I

Individual Training Standards, 58, 77–78, 95–96
Intelligence tests, history, 18, 19–22
Internal consistency reliability, 119,
120–121
Interrater reliability, 118, 119–120, 121,
123, 126
Interviewing, 7, 61, 152–153
historical perspectives, 23–25
walk-through performance tests, 66–
67, 94–95, 140, 152–153
Item analysis, 119, 205

J

Job Orientation Bank, 158
Job analysis, 74–91
Job knowledge tests, 67
criterion-related validity, 150–152,
153, 155–156, 164–166, 168–169,
175
paper-and-pencil tests, 61, 67, 121,
139–140, 142, 150–151, 153, 155–
156, 164–166, 175, 196

Job performance, 25, 208–209
as a construct, 74–75
definitional issues, 58, 75, 93, 101;
see also Tasks and task analysis
enlistment standards and, 12–13,
55, 61–62, 104, 184–188, 208–
209
experience and, 163–164, 196–200,
201, 202
salary-based, 194–195
standards, general, 109–110
Job performance measures
benchmarks, 60–61, 126, 147
competency scales, 188–192, 203
content representativeness, 128–140
development, 68–71, 73–102
differential validity/prediction, 169–
171, 177, 201
fairness analysis and, 12, 172–173
peer ratings, 7, 23–25, 67, 167
scoring, general 144
supervisor ratings, 26–27, 67, 93–94,
104, 139, 153–155, 195, 196
walk-through performance tests, 66–
67, 94–95, 140, 152–153
see also criterion-related validity
Joint-Service Job Performance
Measurement/Enlistment Standards
Project (JPM), 2–11 (passim), 13,
30, 55, 56, 57–72, 103, 140, 184,
210
classical test theory, 58
cost-performance models, 71–72, 91,
184–185, 209
history, 3–5, 8, 56–72
Judges, *see* Raters and ratings

K

Korean War, 39, 47

L

Labor unions, 16
Language skills, 20, 46, 150
Laws, specific federal
Age Discrimination Act, 16
Civil Rights Act, 171–172
Selective Service Act, 47

Universal Military Training and
Service Act, 47
Leniency effects, 26, 27
Likert scales, 26–27
Linear regression, 146, 174

M

Manpower management, 7, 32–33, 45–46, 184–210
 historical perspectives, 19, 26, 28
Manuals, *see Soldier's Manuals*
Marine Corps, 64–65, 67, 95, 68, 72, 91, 114, 165–166, 168–168, 188
 Black Americans in, 40
 occupations studied, 64–65
 reliability assessments, 124–126, 127
 sampling, 107, 130, 133
 task analysis, 77–78, 94, 95–98, 130, 147–149
Mastery testing, 8, 189
Military Entrance Processing Stations, 35, 187
Minorities, 12, 71, 172–180
 ASVAB, 44, 50, 52, 172–174
 Black Americans, 12, 39–43, 173–174, 175–181
 classification, general, 41–44
 combat participation, 43–44
 computer-aided classification, 35, 38
 differential validity/prediction, 172–178
 fairness, 172–181
 racial bias, 19, 38–39
 recruitment, 38–44
 sampling, 106
Models
 cost-performance, 12–13, 46, 55, 56, 60, 91, 184–185, 188–189, 193–203, 209–210
 econometrics, 185, 194, 196–199, 200, 201–203
Motivation
 proficiency *vs.*, 59
 under testing conditions, 139
Multiple-choice tests, 1, 7
 history, 18, 19, 20, 21
 minorities, 44
Multistage sampling, 106

Multivariate analysis, 21, 134–135

N

National Intelligence Test, 20
National Research Council, 19, 25, 39–40
Naval Aviation Program, 22
Navy, 22, 47, 63–64, 66, 67, 69, 72, 188, 192
 Black Americans in, 40
 classification of personnel, general, 188, 192
 occupations studied, 63–64
 recruitment strategies, 37
 reliability assessments, 119–120, 121, 124–126, 127
 sampling, 106–108, 129–130, 135–137
 task analysis, 92–93, 120, 129–130, 135–136
Norms and norming, 3–4, 50–51, 56, 91, 109–110, 208–209

O

Observation techniques, 28, 74, 81
 test administration, 119–120
Organizational factors, 6
 armed services organizational structure, 32–33
 see also Human resource management

P

Paper-and-pencil tests, 61, 67, 121, 139–140, 142, 150–151, 153, 155–156, 164–166, 175, 196
 see also Armed Services Vocational Aptitude Battery
Pearson's product-moment correlation, 18
Peer evaluation, 7, 23–25, 67, 167
Persian Gulf War, 37, 41
Personality traits, 25, 78, 81, 84, 88–91, 95, 102, 167, 209
 interviewing, 152
Personnel Research Bureau, 22

INDEX   257

Personnel selection, *see* Selection
Placement, *see* Classification, personnel
Position Analysis Questionnaire, 204–205
Predictive validity, 25–26, 61–62, 68, 72, 104
  differential validity/prediction, 169–171, 177, 201
  fairness, 172, 174–178, 182
  standardization and, 108–109
  work samples, 59–60
  see also criterion-related validity
Problem-solving skills, 142
Processing and Classification of Enlistees (PACE), 187–188
Procurement Management System (PROMIS), 187, 188
Profile of American Youth, 4, 50
Project 100,000, 48–49
Psychometrics, general, 10
  defined, 1–2
  history, 17–18
  see also Fairness analysis; Reliability; Validity
Psychomotor skills, 142, 157, 158
Purposive sampling, 131–132, 133–138

Q

Qualified Man Month (QMM), 196–200, 201, 202

R

Rand model, 194, 196–200, 201–203
Random sampling, 105–106, 123, 132–134, 159
  purposive *vs.,* 133–134, 133–138
  stratified, 106, 133, 138
Raters and ratings, 10, 11, 67–68, 153, 155
  cognitive processes of, 28
  effects on examinees, 139, 152
  expertise, 9, 28, 69, 71
  interrater reliability, 118, 119–120, 121, 123, 126
  peer, 7, 23–25, 67, 167
  supervisor, 26–27, 67, 93–94, 104, 139, 153–155, 195, 196

Reading ability, 46
  Army Beta, 20
Recruit Distribution Model, 188
Recruit quality, 4, 52–55, 184–186, 207
Recruitment and retention, 32, 33–44, 46, 52
  ASVAB, 57
  conscription, military, 3, 47, 48
  cost factors, 37, 54, 184, 193–194, 197–199
  demography, 36–38, 198, 210
  enlistment standards, 12–13, 32, 44, 46–49, 52–55, 58, 61–62, 104, 184–188, 197–198, 208–209
  fairness, 38–44
  historical perspectives, 46–49, 53, 54, 55, 186
  incentives, 37
  minorities, 38–44
  quality control, general, 4, 52–56
  specialization, 33, 34–35, 36, 53
  technical schools, role, 36, 53–54, 57
  volunteer army, 3–4, 33–36, 47, 49, 56, 57–58
Reliability, 10–11, 21, 26, 27, 116–127, 147
  analysis of variance, 122, 123, 124–126, 135
  classical test theory, 117–118, 121–122
  criterion reliability, 158–159
  generalizability theory, 10–11, 122–127, 151, 204–205
  hands-on testing, 11, 119–120
  internal consistency reliability, 119, 120–121
  interrater reliability, 118, 119–120, 121, 123, 126
  JPM project, 119–121, 124–127
  Marine Corps, 124–126, 127
  Navy, 119–120, 121, 124–126, 127
  paper-and-pencil tests, 150–151, 153, 155–156, 164–166, 175
  test-retest reliability, 148
Reservists, 38
Restriction of range, 26, 159–160

S

Salaries, *see* Wages and salaries

Sampling issues
  Army techniques, 107
  availability, 107
  content representativeness, 129–138
  cost factors, 105, 106, 128, 132, 138, 139
  demography, 106, 108
  errors, 105, 106, 123, 132–133, 136
  JPM project, 104–105
  Marine Corps, 107, 130, 133
  multistage, 106
  Navy, 106–108, 129–130, 135–137
  personnel, 8–9, 71–72, 103, 104–108
  purposive, 131–132, 133–138
  size, 136, 137, 173, 175, 176
  specialties, 8, 63–66
  tasks, 9, 59–60, 62–66, 68–69, 74–75, 93, 96–97, 101, 126–127, 128–130, 131–138
  see also Random sampling
Scholastic Aptitude Test, 20–21
Scores and scoring, 2, 3–4, 11, 98–100, 108, 109–111
  computation of, 99–100, 114–115
  cutoff, 44, 46–48, 57, 99, 184, 189–190, 196, 198, 200, 204–205
  errors and error analysis, general, 98–99
  hands-on testing, 98–100
  job performance criteria, 144
  JPM project, 99–100
  weighting, 147–149
  see also Raters and rating
Selection, personnel, general, 1, 3, 5, 32–33, 46, 141, 207
  aviators, 22–23
  conscription, military, 3, 47, 48
  historical perspectives, 19, 22–23
  minorities, 44
  performance criteria, 13, 56–72
  validity, 11–12, 141
  see also Recruitment and retention
Selective Service Act, 47
Simulations, 7, 9, 67, 138–140
  benchmarks and surrogates, 60–61, 126, 147
  computer, 67, 134, 140
  fidelity, 139–140
  see also Surrogates

Skill level, classification
  deskilling, 45
  minorities and women, 41–43
  see also Specialization
Skill Qualification Test (SQT), 196, 197, 199–200
Soldier's Manuals, 58, 69, 76, 77–78
Spatial ability, 157–158
Standardized testing, general, 103, 108–115, 139
  elementary/secondary education, 15
  hands-on tests, 110–115, 139–140
  norms and norming, 3–4, 50–51, 56, 91, 109–110
  work samples, 59–60
  see also Criterion issues; Multiple-choice tests
Standards, see Enlistment standards
Statistical analyses, 116
  ANOVA, 122, 123, 124–126, 135
  Bayesian, 105
  criterion-related validity, 29, 145–146, 158–159
  factor structure, 21
  graphs and tables, 145–146
  historical perspectives, 17–18, 21, 22
  linear regression, general, 146, 174
  multivariate analysis, 21, 134–135
  random sampling, 105–106, 132–133
  sampling, other, 104, 105
  see also Analysis of variance; Construct validity; Predictive validity
Student Testing Program, 49
Subgroups
  sampling, 106
  see also Fairness analysis; Minorities; Women
Subjectivity
  raters, 11, 153
  supervisor ratings, 26
Superior Evaluation Technique, 195
Supervisors, see Raters and ratings
Surrogates, 60–61
  benchmarks and, 60–61, 126, 147
  computer simulations, 67, 134, 140
  paper-and-pencil tests, 61, 67, 121, 139–140, 142, 150–151, 153, 155–156, 164–166, 175, 196

T

Tasks and task analysis, 58–59, 62–66, 74, 76–98, 95–98, 164, 208
  cognitive task analysis, 84, 85–88
  computer inventories, 58, 78, 90
  cost factors, 86, 91, 120, 128, 132, 138, 139
  Delphi technique, 71, 192
  difficulty level, 8, 89, 134, 136, 137, 188, 204
  editing, 94–95, 96
  errors and error analysis, 134, 135, 136
  expertise, general, 9, 28, 69, 71
  frequency, 88–89, 134, 136, 137–138
  inventories, 6, 58, 78, 80
  JPM project, 90–91, 93, 99–102, 130–131
  Marine Corps, 77–78, 94, 95–98, 130, 147–149
  modifiability, 89
  Navy, 92–93, 120, 129–130, 135–136
  personality traits in, 78, 81, 84, 88–91, 95, 209
  relative vs. absolute measures, 8, 189
  sampling, 9, 59–60, 62–66, 68–69, 74–75, 93, 96–97, 101, 126–127, 128–130, 131–138
  sequencing, 98, 139
  specialists, 63–69, 78, 130, 167, 203, 204
  task importance, 88, 89, 98, 101, 129, 130–131, 132–133, 138
  variability, 89
  weighting, 147–149
  see also Content validity
Technical schools, military, 36, 53–54, 57
Technological innovation, 44–45, 90
Test administration, 9–10, 110–115
  computer-aided, 158, 187, 140
  error of measurement due to, 111–114, 208
  history, 20
  JPM project, 112–113, 114–115
  location, 35, 111–113
  observational techniques, 119–120
  repeat, 118–119
  time factors, 104–105, 111–112, 122
  training for, 113–114, 119
Test construction, 21, 94–98, 100, 101
  see also Tasks and task analysis
Test-retest reliability, 148
  see also Reliability
Training criteria, 45, 141–142, 143, 155–156, 170, 197–198
  cost factors, 141
  expertise and, 188
  manuals, 58. 69, 76, 77–78
  technical schools, 36, 53–54, 57
  test administrators, 113–114, 119
Trait analysis, 25, 78, 81, 84, 88–91, 95, 102
Type II errors, 176–177

U

Universal Military Training and Service Act, 47
Utility difference approach, 194–196, 199–200, 201–204

V

Validity, 2, 11–12
  classification and, 11–12, 141, 152
  construct validity, 59–60, 73, 74–75, 143, 147, 153, 155
  content validity/representativeness, 59–60, 75–76, 90–91, 94, 96, 128–140, 147, 164
  differential, 169–171
  historical perspectives, 18, 21, 22–30
  Pearson's product-moment correlation, 18
  selection, general, 11–12, 141
  see also Criterion-related validity; Predictive validity
Variability, tasks, 89
Vietnam War, 40, 48
Volunteer Armed Forces, 3–4, 33–36, 47, 49, 56, 57–58

W

Wages and salaries, 194–195
Walk-through performance tests, 66–67, 94–95, 140, 152–153

Wars, *see* Combat situations; Korean War; Vietnam War; World War I; World War II
Women, 36, 37, 41–43, 44, 71, 181–183
computer-aided classification, 35
sampling, 106, 108
World War I, 18, 19–20
World War II, 22–25, 38, 46–47
Written tests, *see* Paper-and-pencil tests